An Introduction to

Repairing & Restoring

An Introduction to Repairing & Restoring

Books, Clocks, Furniture,

Pottery, Porcelain, Prints, Paintings,

Frames, Silver, Pewter, Brass

ARCO PUBLISHING, INC.
New York

Library of Congress Cataloguing in Publication Data
An Introduction to repairing and restoring.
Includes bibliographies.
1. Repairing — Amateurs' manuals.
TT151.I57 702'.8'8 80–22357
ISBN 0–668–05147–7

Published by Arco Publishing, Inc.
219 Park Avenue South, New York, N.Y. 10003

Printed in Great Britain

Contents

Introduction

Any market browser, antique hunter or collector of personal treasures may find pieces in need of renovation or repair. Often a desirable article can be acquired fairly cheaply if damaged, and the buyer can have the added personal satisfaction of restoring it. With this manual, the absolute novice can tackle minor repairs with confidence, but equally it is made quite clear when professional help should be sought and, indeed, those times when a certain amount of wear and tear positively enhances the object's appeal and it is best left well alone.

The six most popular subject areas are covered in detail and each is illustrated throughout with line drawings giving clear instructions on the methods to use. The authors, each specialists in their own field, pass on their invaluable first-hand experience to make this manual of lasting reference value to the amateur renovator or restorer.

You need little or no experience in bookbinding and repairing to follow the basic techniques outlined. Much satisfaction can be gained from prolonging the life of a treasured book and here guidance is given on the repair of hardbacks, paperbacks and pamphlets, and simple and elaborate styles of binding are described.

Although the repair and renovation of clocks is a skilled and intricate craft, the amateur can successfully complete minor repairs, so saving a considerable amount of money, by following the instructions set out. The book outlines the tools and materials required, describes the workings of the commonest types of movement, summarizes the processes of dismantling and cleaning, and also features some of the more common types of old clock.

Eventually everyone has furniture which needs repair since damage and deterioration are inevitable, or stripping a heavily-painted chair or chest of drawers may be desirable. The cost of new furniture has risen considerably over the years but, with the aid of a few pieces of equipment and an elementary knowledge of woodworking techniques, old furniture can be given a new lease of life cheaply and effectively.

Collecting old pottery and porcelain can be an expensive pursuit if you buy perfect pieces, but this book shows how to repair damaged items and sentimental pieces at low cost, and guides you through the various stages of renovation from cleaning and mending cracks and chips to repainting and regilding repaired items.

Many minor repairs and improvements to prints and paintings can be tackled by the amateur once he or she is familiar with the techniques involved. Detailed information is given on how to deal with flaking paint, torn canvas and surface grime, and shows how reframing and remounting can improve the appearance of a print or painting, and how a renovated frame can enhance a new acquisition.

Expert guidance is given on the types of repairs which can safely be attempted by the amateur to silver, pewter and brass, and there is information on how to identify different kinds of metal before attempting renovation. All kinds of repair techniques are discussed including the removal of dents, cleaning and polishing, soldering, making new knobs and handles and casting new parts.

You may well be surprised when you look through your discarded or rejected treasures to find how comparatively easy it will be—with the aid of this manual—to give them a new lease of life.

Books

Alison Harding

Illustrated by Evelyn Bartlett

Equipment and Materials

The craft of book repair is both useful and creative. There are ways in which damaged or unprepossessing books can be improved, as well as different forms of cover to be tried. A new spine requires material of your own choice to be fitted to that originally used whilst a book which has come apart offers a challenge to its owner. Labels or paper wrappers give scope for the imaginative use of familiar materials—as well as having a sound practical function. The temptation to over-restore has to be resisted sometimes, and in all work connected with book repair, the character and purpose of the volume have to be considered.

Patience and accuracy—the characteristics of the traditional craft-binder—will be needed when you start. But the help of others who work with books is usually offered willingly to the beginner, and their advice can often save time and materials. You will find that bookbinding is an ideal home occupation and, provided you are willing to make mistakes as well as to learn, a most rewarding one.

What you Need
Materials and tools for some repairs can be found in the average home or easily purchased. But if a wide variety of jobs is contemplated, it is as well to obtain some of the special bookbinding items from reputable suppliers. Better quality materials help to produce a sound result, whilst ingenuity and improvisation can often increase the scope of the amateur without great expense. It is wise to practise measuring or cutting operations before using the material proposed for the actual job, especially when working with leather or expensive papers.

Before beginning any repair or binding work, assemble the necessary tools and materials. Basic items include: press, pressing boards, knife, scissors/shears, metal rule, needles, linen thread, tape, paper, board, cover fabrics, mull, adhesive and brushes, folder.

Pressing
The largest essential item is a press, necessary for all but the most minor repairs. Traditionally the bookbinder uses a 'plough and press'. Constructed of wood and standing on its own 'tub' or base designed to catch shavings when a book is being trimmed by the cutting edge of the plough, this 'lying press' is where the book is trimmed, shaped and dried during the processes known as 'forwarding'. The binder also uses a 'standing press', which takes several books at a time, and a small 'nipping press' for pressing the newly bound books, as well as a 'finishing press' to hold a book for gold-tooling or other parts of the finishing process.

A small, all-purpose press which is designed for the amateur, usually working on one book at a time, can be obtained from suppliers; alternatively, an improvised form of press is feasible. Two smooth rectangular pieces of tight-grained board (such as 'marine' plyboard) which are larger than

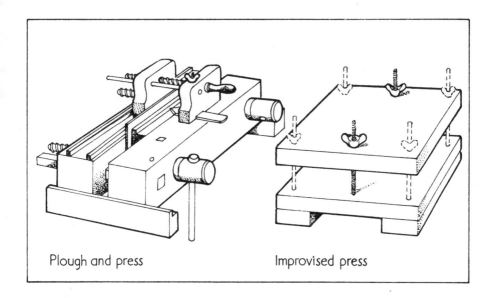

Plough and press

Improvised press

the books to be pressed—about 300 × 225mm (12 × 9in) and 12mm ($\frac{1}{2}$in) thick would suit most purposes—are joined together by two 130–150mm (5–6in) bolts with wing nuts, or by two clamps. Use four bolts, one at each corner, if preferred; the bolts need to be countersunk into the lower board. Two supporting pieces of wood may be glued or screwed to the lower board as shown in the diagram. A flower-press gives an example of what could be used, although the boards of this are rather narrow when you need to stand the press on its side, and the bolts too short to accommodate a thick book.

A bench or table vice could serve as a press, the book being held upright between two pressing boards. These boards are about 6mm ($\frac{1}{4}$in) thick smooth laminated wood or plyboard and are used, in different sizes, to separate books when the binder is pressing several together. They are also needed during gluing operations and when 'knocking up' or shaping, and for other work on the spine of a book. Always use a size larger than the book. Thick Perspex boards are also suitable for pressing purposes. Special boards are needed for 'backing' or cutting, and thin tin sheets for some purposes. Whilst a vice can be used for operations when the book is held upright, it cannot be used for horizontal pressing, for nipping done after gluing or pasting, or for rounding the spine.

If only a short pressing time is needed—for example, after mending leaves or gluing minor cover tears—the book may be laid between boards with a weight, such as bricks or heavy books, on top. Make sure that the weight is evenly distributed, and that the boards are absolutely smooth to avoid damaging the book.

Equipment and Materials

Cutting and Trimming

Whilst it may be possible to use a guillotine or board cutter during bookbinding classes or by visiting a nearby binder or printer, boards for covers, paper for lining and endpapers, etc, will probably have to be cut at home. Large cutting shears may be used for heavy materials, sewing scissors for lighter ones, but the final shape of cover boards and the fabric or leather which is to go over them must be cut with all possible accuracy. For this, a cobbler's knife bevelled on one side only, or a similar Stanley knife, is used in conjunction with a metal straightedge rule or T-square. A small sharp kitchen knife could be substituted, or a scalpel with interchangeable blades for different purposes. A paring knife is essential for leather, and a carpenter's spokeshave useful. Some kind of sharpening stone is necessary, and a leather strop for maintaining the 'edge'. If a plough is available, the beginner should practise on unimportant books or waste magazines. Whatever cutting tools are used should always be perfectly sharp and free from oil or grease.

Dividers and compasses are also useful when measuring for accurate cutting.

Sewing

The traditional *sewing frame,* on which the sections of a book are sewn together with tapes or cords, can be obtained from craft or binding suppliers. A frame is not essential since sewing can be done at

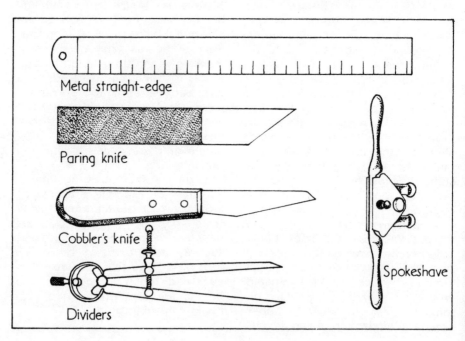

Metal straight-edge

Paring knife

Cobbler's knife

Dividers

Spokeshave

the edge of the working surface, but one can be simply constructed with wood or made from the open end of a box; even the ladder back or base of a chair can be used to support the sewing. Sewing keys hold the tapes or cords in the frame.

Needles: straight, bookbinder's needles, with small eyes, can be obtained from suppliers; milliner's needles could be used. If ordinary sewing needles are used, these should not have a bulge at the eye; this makes too large a hole, resulting in loose sewing or damage to the leaves of the book.

Thread: linen thread is best for most sewing jobs, although silk or embroidery thread is needed for finer work. Bookbinding threads come in different weights; two- or three-cord for general purposes and four- or five-cord for extra heavy work. Skeins are of a convenient length for sewing.

Tape: bleached cotton or linen tape, 12mm ($\frac{1}{2}$in) in width, is satisfactory for most sewing. Ordinary household tape may be used provided it has a selvedge, although a heavy wider binding tape is best for large books or heavy magazines. Narrow webbing is also suitable.

Cord: if you wish to attempt sewing on cords or try making a headband for a special book, hemp cord will be needed; a strong, medium-weight string could be used. For headbands, embroidery or binding silk will be necessary.

Scissors: small, pointed embroidery scissors are used for delicate work, larger ones for cutting out lining or covering materials.

Drawing pins: these are necessary for fixing tapes.

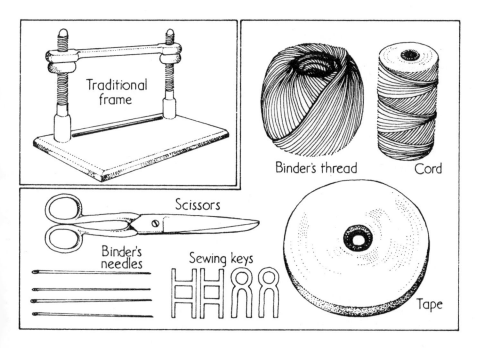

Traditional frame

Binder's thread

Cord

Scissors

Binder's needles

Sewing keys

Tape

Equipment and Materials

Paper, Boards and Fabrics

For repair to pages, a large sheet of binder's 'Japanese' tissue will be needed. Strong brown 'Kraft' paper (obtainable at newsagents) is necessary for mending the spine, and bond, cartridge or decorated papers for making endpapers. Japanese tissue, bank and bond papers are also used for making 'guards'.

Cover boards are made from millboard, strawboard, heavy card, or even thin plywood. For board fabric, the binder may choose from a wide variety of materials: traditional leathers, including calf and morocco; bookcloth in different weights; heavy cotton; linen; and silk.

Clean newsprint is best for gluing and pasting upon; waxed or greaseproof paper will be needed to protect the inside of the book during these operations.

Sandpaper, fine or medium, can be useful in repair or cleaning work.

Mull, stiffened muslin, is used for reinforcing the spine of a book—holland, calico, cambric or dressmaker's muslin will serve adequately. Winemaking cloth, sized, would also be suitable.

Gelatine size can be used for extra stiffening of backing material where necessary.

Adhesives and Brushes

A variety of *PVA adhesives* are available and used by binders, except for work with leather. PVA can be diluted according to the strength needed, but must always be used with great care since its permanence means that a book might be damaged if it is used incorrectly. Brushes must be washed quickly and thoroughly before the adhesive hardens.

Animal glue: this is still preferred by many binders and can be obtained in small quantities ready for use, or as slabs or 'pearls' which need to be prepared. 'Hot glue' is better for the spines for flexibility; 'cold glue' for covers and cases. A gluepot and hot plate are used for heating glue.

Flour paste: starch pastes are widely used for work with paper and leather, but are not suitable for bookcloth, except buckram. Paste is also used with mull for stiffening. To make it, use one part flour (wheat, corn or rice) to six parts water, although amounts can be varied according to the consistency required. Mix the flour to a paste with a little water. Boil the remainder of the water and stir it into the paste, blending in any lumps with a wooden spoon. Put the mixture back in the pan and bring it to the boil, stirring gently until the paste thickens. Remove from the heat and cool before storing in a jar. Do not use after two or three days unless refrigerated as acidity spoils paper. A very small amount of thymol crystal can be added as a preservative if required, but this can cause deterioration of paper.

Brushes: separate ones are needed for different adhesives; a 12mm ($\frac{1}{2}$in) brush, preferably rounded, is a useful size. A fine paintbrush is useful for delicate repair work.

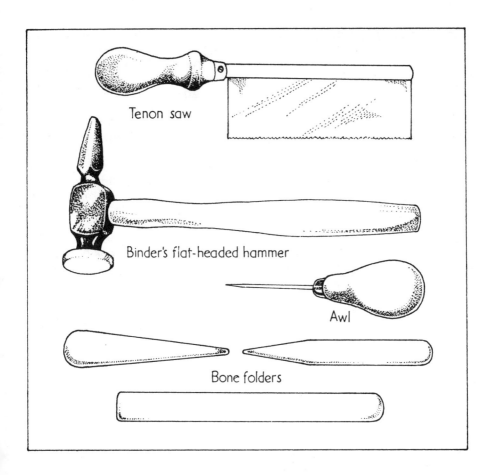

Tenon saw

Binder's flat-headed hammer

Awl

Bone folders

Small Tools
A fine pointed awl for making holes in paper and a heavier bodkin for holes in boards (a needle fixed in a cork at its eye end would make a substitute); a hammer with a round flat head; a small (tenon) saw; a bone or plastic folder—used wherever paper needs to be flattened and smoothed—should be obtained from suppliers.

Where to Work
If possible, try to find somewhere where materials and work may be left undisturbed. Binding and even minor repairs can be time-consuming; the work involves gluing or pasting with subsequent lengthy pressing, so it helps to have everything to hand in one place. The surface used should be perfectly flat—a marble or Formica slab, or an old pastry-board, could be used, laid on a larger table or bench in a well lit part of the room. A warm, dry, clean atmosphere is best, since paper, paste and other materials can be affected by damp, and good work easily spoiled by dust or dirt.

Structure of a Book

When a book has fallen apart, understanding of the way in which it was originally constructed is necessary if it is to be put together again. Similarly, if you wish to bind together old magazines, or to make a case for a collection of personal notes, it helps to know which parts of your volume will need strengthening to take the strain of constant use. If some thought is given before starting work on a favourite or much-used volume, you may avoid spoiling it during repair, and may even improve on the way in which it was originally bound.

Inside the Book
Sections

The contents of a book are made up of sections (also called signatures), each consisting of a number of leaves folded and assembled one inside the other. The traditional method is to sew the sections together by hand or machine, but more recent developments in mass book production mean that they are often glued together. Sometimes the backs of the sections are guillotined before being glued, with the result that when the book falls apart, it is a mass of unconnected sheets. Where such an 'unsewn binding' occurs in a textbook or other volume in daily use, you may wish to make it last longer by restoring the sections, perhaps giving it a strong case to replace its original cover—usually paper or light card which is unequal to constant wear and tear. The number of leaves in a section depends on the type of paper and the size of the book.

(left) *A sixteen-page section;* (right) *Folding of leaves*

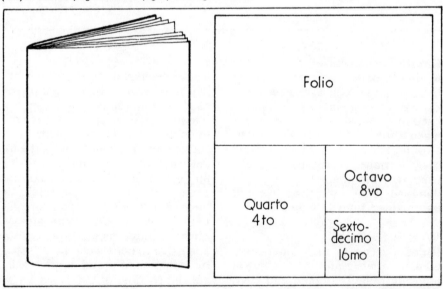

Folio

Quarto
4to

Octavo
8vo

Sexto-
decimo
16mo

Leaves

The leaves or pages of a book are printed on a larger sheet which is then folded—once for folio size, twice for quarto, three for octavo and four times for sextodecimo. The leaves are numbered during printing, and often an older book will also have letters to denote sections. These 'signatures', which come in alphabetical order, are useful when 'collating' or checking the contents; the first section containing the 'preliminary' pages—title page, chapter headings, etc—may be unnumbered. Sometimes sections will run into double letters (Aa, Bb, etc), or may have a volume number as well as a letter.

Modern books are machine trimmed, but older ones, or hand-printed books, may keep the original rough or deckle edge of the paper; if you are repairing such a book, it is better not to spoil its character by trimming the edges. Sometimes the edges of a book have been coloured or gilded to preserve the contents, or there may be a painted design on the 'fore-edge', or front, of the book.

Plates, maps These are nearly always 'tipped in', that is, joined to the page to which they relate by a thin line of adhesive; occasionally they are folded round the back. Illustrations, or 'plates', are often on a different kind of paper from the text—shiny art paper—which can present problems to the restorer. When a plate is loose it may damage the adjacent leaves, necessitating 'guarding' or resewing of a whole section.

Maps or plans are sometimes set in the text and sometimes folded in at either end of the book; often they will need strengthening or repair.

Parts of a book

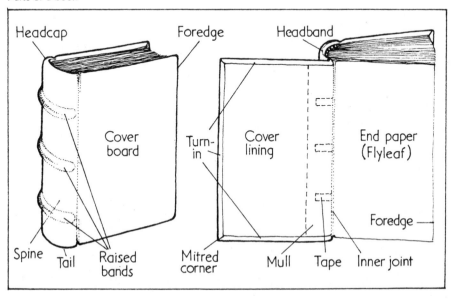

Headcap   Foredge   Headband

Cover board   Turn-in   Cover lining   End paper (Flyleaf)

Foredge

Spine   Tail   Raised bands   Mitred corner   Mull   Tape   Inner joint

Structure of a Book

Endpapers

These include the flyleaf, and technically provide a link between the contents and the cover of a book. Stronger volumes have sewn-in endpapers, perhaps ·specially folded to make a strong hinge; simpler endpapers are pasted, or tipped, to the covers and first and last sections; whilst in paperbacks or pamphlets there may be no connection apart from the glue or staples holding the contents within their covers. But as well as serving a valuable primary strengthening purpose, endpapers can give scope to the home binder for improving the appearance of a book by the use of coloured or decorated papers.

Spine and Joints

The spine, or back of the sections, is the least visible but most important part of the book, affecting its durability and its capacity to open and shut easily. Early books were held together by strips of leather sewn across the spine and fastened on to the cover boards. Tapes and cords are still used in this way, but many spines are now held together only by glue.

Reinforcement of the spine is effected by attaching linings of mull or similar material, and strong paper. Sometimes a 'hollow' is made by paper folded and glued to

(above) *The spine;* (below) *Binding styles*

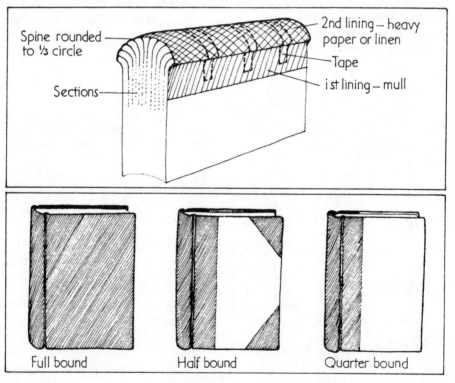

both the lining and the inside of the cover. Heavy paper, without mull, is used when sewing on cords.

The joints are where the spine meets the cover boards, and a hinge is formed by the extension of the mull lining to join the cover. Tapes or cords, if used, also extend under the cover lining to reinforce the joints. When the book is 'rounded and backed', a groove is formed which is known as the joint, where the board fits against the spine.

In some cased books the hinge is formed by pasting only an end-paper on to the board, but this can be unsuitable for a book in constant use.

Headbands
These are made of silk worked over a gut or cord core and often appear at the top and bottom (head and tail) of the back of a book. Like the 'raised' bands (cords) which are sometimes seen on the outside of the spine as ridges in the covering material, usually leather, headbands were originally devised to add strength to the binding. Now they are usually decorative only and false bands are often added to make a book look expensive. Sometimes, 'headcaps' appear at the head and tail, these are made by moulding leather over a cord core.

Case or Binding
In describing the methods of attaching boards, bookbinders distinguish between 'bound' books, which have the outer covering material added after the boards are joined on, and 'cased' books, where the whole cover is made before being put on to the book. While the former traditional method has the advantage of strength and is essential for a craftsman-made leatherbound volume, a new case can be attractive and durable, especially if it incorporates the strong sewing necessary for a well bound book.

Cover boards
Originally made of wood in massive early books, these now range from traditional heavy board or 'split boards' (which are two kinds of board joined together to make a strong cover), to lighter card which needs only a plastic coating. For sewing on cords boards are specially prepared as described later (page 40).

Cover materials
The binding or case may be covered in a variety of ways. Where one material only is used, a book is 'full-bound'; or it may be 'half' or 'quarter-bound', using two materials, which can look very attractive and be more economical than, say, full-bound calf.

Labels and decoration The final stage of book production, finishing, may include the addition of a plain or gold-tooled label on the front cover and spine and the traditional use of tooling to decorate the edges or panels of a leather cover. Modern binders use onlays or inlays of different materials to achieve special effects, and the amateur binder may also enjoy the production of a well finished binding.

Planning and Preparation

Assessing the book
Before carrying out any work it is wise to consider a number of points.

Completeness
If any plates or pages of text are missing, you may decide against repair; lost endpapers, however, can be replaced. Missing title pages can sometimes be photocopied from a library or other source; this is common practice with an old or rare book. An out-of-print book may be difficult to trace, but with a newer book it may be possible to obtain copies of a piece of text. To collate a book, check the page numbers or signature letters, and check the number of plates against the list given in the preliminary pages.

Rarity
If you think you may have a rare book, perhaps the first or unusual edition of a famous author, perhaps a fine imprint from a private press, it is worth checking with libraries, booksellers or specialists before doing your own repairs. An old or leatherbound book is not necessarily scarce or sought after, but often even an incomplete old book on a special subject, such as gardening or cookery, may have its value reduced if you try to repair it. A book's replaceability and sentimental value should also be taken into account—if you wish to repair it, it is sensible to practise on something of little worth.

Interesting features
These may include bookplates or other marks of ownership; binder's or publisher's labels; and marginal notes by an earlier reader. Particular kinds of decorative binding, or the work of an individual binder or printer are often sought after. Sometimes plates are more valuable than the book from which they have become detached, and in this case it is better not to try to put them back. Almost always, an original binding adds to an old book's value, so the time and effort of careful restoration are well spent.

Future use
The use that a book will be put to after repair needs to be taken into account when deciding what work to do. Textbooks or paperbacks will need a durable rather than a decorative cover; a book that is part of a set will need to be restored as nearly as possible to the condition of its fellows; whilst a personal notebook or handmade volume offers scope for more creative binding.

If you are undecided, consultation with a local binder, librarian or bookseller may help, and if a particular operation seems too delicate or complex, it may be worth watching a bookbinder at work, or attending a course. Whilst there is much that can be done at home by the amateur, and much pleasure to be gained from the end result, some aspects of the work such as washing of pages, or removal of 'foxing', are better left to the expert in book restoration.

Preparation for Repair

Check completeness of contents before starting work. Note down where internal repairs are needed, and the position of any loose leaves or plates. Some leaves may only need cleaning, others may be torn or 'dog-eared'. It is useful to work out the order in which to deal with repairs, and have the correct tools and materials available. Examine the inside of the cover to see whether the endpapers are coming away; if the cover is already detached, look at the spine to see if the sections are still firmly stitched or glued. It is possible that you may not need to resew the contents, but if the sections are split, major repair may be necessary.

If the cover material is coming away from the boards, decide whether you wish to re-cover them in a new material, or whether cleaning and gluing back the old material will be adequate. A new cover can be made for the spine alone, possibly incorporating the old label; a skilled binder can even lift the old leather from a spine and replace it on a new one.

Alternatives for Covering

Strengthen and renovate the old cover, using new endpapers.

Re-cover the existing boards, adding a new spine and possibly a paper hollow; one or two materials may be used.

Reback the cover, adding new spine material, and using original boards and fabric.

Renew the glue in an unsewn binding; glue back the old case if it is not badly damaged and sections are intact.

Replace a glued spine by a new one sewn in sections; put the book back into a strengthened case.

Recase or *rebind* the entire book. This involves 'pulling', or taking apart, the book as described overleaf.

Sequence of Operations

It is useful to have in mind the order in which you intend to carry out repairs. Whilst these will, of course, vary according to the scale of the work to be done, in general you would expect to do them as follows:

Collation
Pulling (if sewing or regluing)
Internal cleaning and repairs (including guarding of sections)
Replacing the endpapers
Sewing (comes before the endpapers for some procedures)
Rounding and backing the spine
Replacing the spine linings
Making the case, or preparing the boards for leather binding
Covering the book
Finishing (adding labels, decoration by tooling, etc)

Pulling a Book

If internal repairs do not involve the sections, there will be no need to pull the book; this also applies when only the cover is damaged and you do not need to do any sewing work.

Having checked for completeness, note down the position of plates and of preliminary pages to ensure that you put them back in the correct order.

To remove the cover, cut through the endpaper at the front joint with a sharp knife, taking care not to damage the opening section. Repeat at the back joint, then ease the cover away from the spine. Gently scrape off any remaining lining material or glue, then cut the threads of each section from the inside of the centre sheets as shown in the diagram. Take care not to enlarge the sewing holes as you pull out the thread; use a folder to flatten the pages and scissor ends to lift the thread. If bits of glue or paper cannot be removed from the spine by gentle scraping, it may be covered with a thin layer of paste, preferably whilst held in a press or vice. This 'wet pulling' is a last resort as it can damage the sections—these must be scraped clean after about ten minutes, then allowed to dry completely before the sewing threads are cut and pulled out. The sharp point of a knife is best for prising off bits of old glue; if you cut along the spine you may harm the section folds.

Pulling a book: (left) *cutting at joints* (right) *lifting threads, cutting at section centre*

The grooves left by the former binding need to be flattened; you can do this with finger and thumb, or, if the groove is very stubborn, by careful hammering with the section laid groove downwards on a hard surface. It is wise to protect the sections from dirt and possible careless blows by putting waste paper underneath and on top. Flattening in a press, with the sections laid in twos between boards head and tail alternating, will remove the grooves in most cases.

Staples or the wire stitches of magazines are removed with a screwdriver or other flat-ended tool, after the turned ends have been opened with a blunt knife. If a coin or other flat piece of metal is laid on the book, the wire can be levered out and then pulled away with pliers. If the wire is rusted in, the resulting marks may need to be cut out; the backs of magazines can be recut entirely if there is enough inside margin to allow for binding. Some of the rust can be removed by brushing; the

sections are then 'guarded' and sewn.

Nipping and Pressing
After any internal repair work has been carried out, a book that has been pulled will need to be thoroughly pressed. Make sure that all glue or paste is absolutely dry, and that any surplus has been scraped or rubbed away; place waxed or greaseproof paper to protect the leaves next to any that have been repaired with adhesive. Put the book between boards and press, remembering that hand-printed or hand-coloured books should only be lightly pressed, as should books with any kind of raised or gilded covers. If the book has been pulled, sections should be pressed in layers of three, with a pressing-board between each layer. Sometimes a book needs to be nipped in the press to give a firm join after pasting etc; this is a quick (up to ten seconds) pressing, under heavier pressure than that needed for the more lengthy final pressing of the book.

Removing a staple or wire stitch

Internal Repairs

These are carried out before any attempt is made at re-covering a book, or before cleaning a cover which is being retained. If the book has been pulled, you can deal with each section in turn, or with one problem—such as torn pages—throughout, but care must be taken to keep the sections in order. Have to hand clean waste paper for protection of leaves (typing or copy paper, or blotting paper), and keep the tools and work surface clean.

Creases and Folded Corners

These can be smoothed with a bone folder, sponged flat with a lightly dampened sponge or ironed with a warm to medium-hot iron through clean paper. Protect the underlying sheets, and take care with coated or treated papers which should not be dampened. If the page is dirty, cleaning should come before applying heat or moisture.

Cleaning Leaves

Surface dirt or dust can be removed by the use of a small soft brush (such as a 12mm ($\frac{1}{2}$in) paintbrush); a soft india-rubber; or day-old bread. Clean the paper gently, using the brush to remove dirt particles or bread-crumbs, moving from the spine across to the fore-edge. Powdered rubber can be obtained, and this should be gently rubbed on with cotton-wool or fingers. For more persistent marks try a harder brush or rubber, fine sandpaper or good quality cuttlefish, remembering that these are abrasive and can easily damage the surface of the paper.

Art paper or other paper used for illustrations is difficult, if not impossible, to clean without causing further damage, although pencil marks can sometimes be removed with a soft rubber.

Grease marks can be removed by dabbing the stain with carbon tetrachloride; *oil* marks with petrol; and some *ink* stains with citric acid (try lemon juice). But such toxic or inflammable agents must be used with great care.

Marginal notes and library stamps can detract from the appearance of a book, but indelible inks can only be hidden not removed. Typewriter erasing fluids may be used but will probably look much whiter than the surrounding paper. A strip of paper carefully pasted in over the defacement usually looks better on an older book, and may be stained to match the page, as for a torn leaf. Use a starch or flour paste, and protect the page beneath while working.

Washing or resizing of leaves may be advisable for a valuable book but should be left to an expert. Similarly, the removal of stains caused by damp or ageing, is better not attempted.

The edges of leaves—the fore-edges and head or tail edges—are often very dusty; surface dirt can be brushed away with the book held shut. More ingrained dirt can be reduced by carefully cleaning each leaf at the edges with a soft rubber or brush, flicking the particles away and using clean paper to protect the leaves from your own finger pressure. Gilded or coloured edges can be brightened by gentle rubbing with cottonwool, but avoid wetting them—this removes the colour, and moisture can seep in between the leaves.

Adhesive tapes—such as sellotape or sticking plaster strips—can be difficult to remove, especially if they are on shiny surfaces or over print. They should not be used for book repair work because of the damage they cause. Transparent tape can be removed by carefully touching it with the tip of a hot iron; any adhesive left should be gently rubbed off with cottonwool and carbon tetrachloride. If this method does not work with heavier tapes, a knife point can be tried, but you may need to cut away and patch the leaf.

Mending Tears

A fine paintbrush, some starch or rice flour paste and some bookbinder's Japanese mending tissue are needed. A piece of glass or other easily wiped, flat surface is best to work on. The fibres of the

tear are rejoined by pasting each edge lightly, then laying one piece of tissue below the join and another on top. Place clean paper over the leaf and tissue rub gently with a finger or folder, then place a weight on top and leave until well dried. Gently remove the pieces of tissue and smooth the join with your fingers or folder; the tissue fibres blend with those of the leaf to effect the join.

If a corner or other part of the leaf is missing, try to find paper similar in weight and colour. A piece that is too light can be stained to match a page in an old book—dab tea, coffee or a weak permanganate of potash solution on to the paper with cottonwool. First make sure that the grain of the added paper runs with that of the leaf, then draw the shape of the tear on the paper and join as above.

Small holes can be filled with paper pulp, made by mixing blotting paper with gelatine size. Stain it to match and rub it into the holes with a finger or folder.

(left) *Mending a torn leaf;* (right) *Repairing a damaged corner*

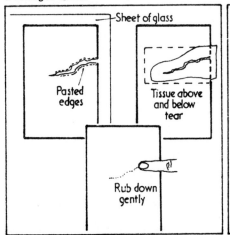

Sheet of glass

Pasted edges

Tissue above and below tear

Rub down gently

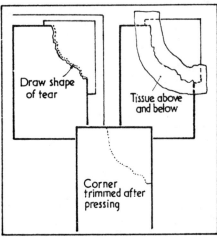

Draw shape of tear

Tissue above and below

Corner trimmed after pressing

Internal Repairs

Guarding and Tipping

If a book has been pulled, damaged section folds may be opened out flat. Smaller tears can then be mended with tissue as above but often the back of a pair of leaves should be provided with a paper guard. If badly torn, a whole section may be guarded at its back fold, then replaced for sewing. When a book is not taken apart, a single leaf or plate can be given a guard which is carefully pasted as far as possible into the margin of the next sheet (see Fig. below). An alternative but lengthy treatment, where there are many torn folds, is to recut the leaves, and make new sections by 'over-sewing'. This is sometimes necess-ary with a glued paperback book which has come apart at the spine (see Sewing Procedures, page 37).

When cutting guards—from thin but strong paper such as bank, bond or Japanese tissue—the grain of the paper must run along the length of the guard to avoid any buckling which would distort the leaf and make sewing difficult. To test the grain, or 'machine direction', of paper, either fold or bend a sheet along two sides; the one which folds or 'bends' more easily runs 'with the grain'. For special books, and a less obtrusive join, tear rather than cut the edge of the strip. Guards may be cut singly, or in a number together when mending several books of the same size.

To guard a whole section

Measure and then cut with a knife and straightedge, a slip of paper which is a little longer than the page size and about 12mm ($\frac{1}{2}$in) wide—more or less according to the width of the book's inner mar-gin. Paste it almost to the ends, then lay it on to a second, larger strip of waste paper, paste side up. Lay the section to halfway across the pasted strip, and then use the waste sheet to lift the second half

(left) *Guarding a single leaf;* (right) *Guarding a pair of leaves*

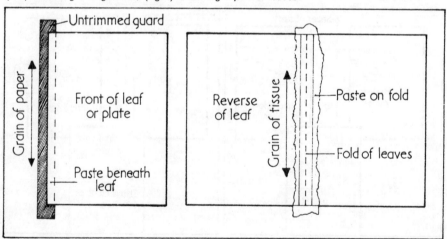

of the strip over the fold. Press down firmly all along the fold, and trim away the excess strip. Always remember to use protective waste paper whilst pasting, and waxed or greaseproof sheets during drying and pressing.

Loose leaves

Leaves or plates which have been separated from the text can be either tipped in, or guarded, as in the diagram. If the leaf next to a loose illustration is coming away, it will need to be put back at the same time. To insert by tipping, apply a thin strip—3mm ($\frac{1}{8}$in)—of paste to the edge of the plate or leaf and replace it on the next sheet in the text, taking care to protect the adjacent pages with clean paper. Recut the inside edge before pasting if necessary, and square up the outside corners before pressing down the pasted edge. A knife or folder may be used to press the pasted edge right into the section.

When guarding a single leaf,

paste the guard to the reverse side, after carefully trimming away any ragged edge. Fold the guard round the edge and tip it to the preceding leaf, which takes the strain.

Guarding plates

When making guards for illustrations, you must take into account the type of paper on which they are printed. A thin guard, made and attached to the plate as for a leaf, folded once and fixed to the one preceding, may be all that is necessary. But if a plate is printed on card or very heavy paper, it will need a hinge of card mounted on to a guard of linen. The width of the card hinge depends on the size and weight of the plate, and the amount of margin to spare at the inside edge when trimmed. The linen guard needs to be wide enough to allow about one-third to be attached to the plate, one-third to the hinge, and one-third to be fixed into the section.

(left) *Section guarded at folds;* (right) *Plate guarded with card and linen*

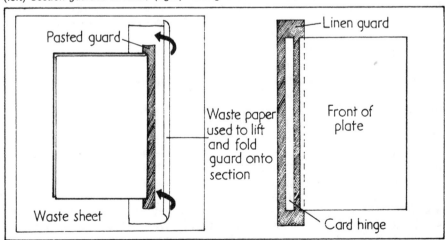

Endpapers

If the cover boards are loose or damaged, new endpapers are generally needed, but you may wish to keep specially decorative or interesting ones.

If dirty or torn at their edges but sound at the joints, you can restore endpapers as for other leaves, but be careful with special surfaces or unusual materials. Silk, embossed or coloured endpapers should not be treated with chemicals; use a slightly damp sponge or bread for reducing stains. Where the endpaper acting as a lining for the inside of the cover is defaced or badly stained, a piece of matching paper can be cut to size and pasted over it; it should be pressed into the joint with a folder. Extending the paper 6mm ($\frac{1}{4}$in) on to the flyleaf will strengthen the joint.

A detached endpaper, or one that is torn at the joint, can be replaced and guarded as follows. Remove the leaf, trim the edge, then square it up with the edges of the section and tip it back on to a 3mm ($\frac{1}{8}$in) strip of paste, rubbing carefully along the join. Make a matching guard, wide enough to extend 6mm ($\frac{1}{4}$in) on to the cover board, over the joint, and 6mm ($\frac{1}{4}$in) on to the endpaper. Paste into place, pressing it firmly in to the joint with a folder. Trim and leave to dry with the cover open, and if necessary (for a large or heavy cover), place a support under the cover during drying. When dry, put in a protective sheet and press the book lightly. A new single endpaper can be similarly tipped or guarded in.

Sometimes, especially in a paperback or weak binding, the joint is damaged and the cover itself begins to fall away. Strengthen the first or last section with paste at the back and tip in a new folded endpaper. This will postpone the recasing that may eventually be needed.

Simple Folded Endpaper

Remove the old endpaper. Choose suitable strong paper (bond, cartridge, coloured, patterned), making sure the grain runs from head to tail for clean cutting. Use a straightedge, with the flat edge of the knife held tight against it and the bevel away from you. Do not press the knife too hard—any pressure should be on the rule—and cut on a thick board. Cut the paper 6mm ($\frac{1}{4}$in) bigger all round than the opened book. An exact fit is important so it is better to trim after the endpaper is fixed in, but if you prefer to get the measurement correct beforehand, hold the paper inside and mark it, allowing for the fold. Fold the paper in half exactly, 'good' side inward. Several endpapers can be prepared at once if you are likely to need them.

Open the book, fore-edge towards you, and paste a 3mm ($\frac{1}{8}$in) strip along the joint edge of the first (or last) section; use a piece of waste paper a little longer than the book to get an even line, holding this firmly down to prevent any paste from seeping under it. Remove the waste paper and press the endpaper into place upon the paste, its fold, head and tail exactly in line with the section below. Rub gently with a folder and leave to dry under a weight.

With the endpaper now in place, trim away any excess if not already removed. Lay a piece of board beneath the first or final section and cut the endpaper, with the straightedge held under the first or last section leaf, which is used to measure against. Then place a waste sheet between the two halves of the endpaper and apply paste, from the centre outwards, to the side which will be attached to the cover. Bring the cover board down on to the pasted side, pressing it firmly and quickly into place. Avoid opening more than necessary whilst laying a protective waxed sheet between the two halves. Nip in a press, for a few moments, then leave closed to dry under light pressure for twenty-four hours.

'Made' Endpaper

This is particularly suitable when using coloured or decorative papers, and provides an extra fly-leaf.

You will need a white endpaper cut as above, and a coloured one exactly the same size. Fold both, and apply paste to one half of the white piece, on the outside. Press the outside of the coloured sheet to it, so that their folds and edges match. Rub them smooth with a bone folder so that there are no wrinkles, then nip, dry, under a weight, and insert as for an ordinary endpaper. The coloured paper will be attached to the cover board, and the white one tipped in to the section. Remember to use several sheets of waxed paper to protect the book when drying.

These endpapers can be tipped in when a new case is fitted to a book, or when it is bound in leather. When tapes, and occasionally cords, are used, these and the mull on the spine are pasted on to the endpapers, giving the joint greater strength.

Whatever paper you use, and also if you try silk or other fabrics, perhaps screen printed, remember to test a small piece for possible shrinkage or staining when pasting. PVA is better for some fabrics.

(left) *Pasting section edge;* (right) *Trimming with knife and rule*

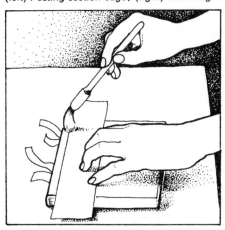
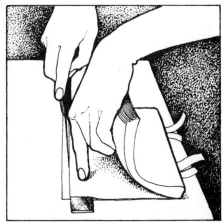

Repairs to Covers

Cleaning

This should be carried out with caution; as with any book renovation, it is easy to do further damage. Where possible, try your treatment in an unobtrusive area first, especially when using chemicals, any kind of coloured dye, or patent stain removers.

Paper or card covers

Where these have been treated and are smooth or shiny, a damp sponge can remove surface dirt; more absorbent surfaces should be cleaned with a soft rubber, or bread, as for inside leaves. For heavier marks, try a harder rubber or fine sandpaper, remembering that any abrasive will cut further into the surface.

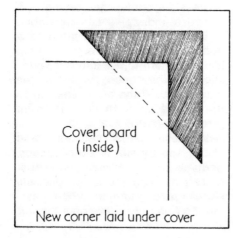

New corner laid under cover

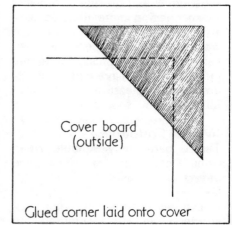

Glued corner laid onto cover

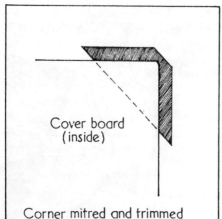

Corner mitred and trimmed

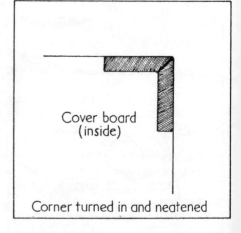

Corner turned in and neatened

Making new cloth corners

Bookcloth, buckram, linen

These are not usually waterproof, so if any chemical cleaner such as surgical spirit or petrol is used, it should be applied gently and sparingly with cottonwool, and only for heavy dirt or staining. The application of a thin paste and water solution after any other cleaning, can further improve and clean the surface. This should be sponged over the whole area of the cover, but care must be taken not to overdo it; avoid wetting any gold lettering. A patent bookcloth cleaner can also be used for surface restoration and will not harm gold.

Small tears or loose threads should be gently pressed back into place whilst applying the paste solution; any that seem too bad may be previously fixed with PVA or paste. Loose labels should be pasted back, or new ones fixed, after cleaning (see Decoration and Titling).

Leather

Hardened and dirty leather can be improved by rubbing in saddle cream, or neutral-coloured shoe cream, with a soft cloth. Libraries and binders use a formula containing anhydrous lanolin and neat's-foot oil; beeswax is also added to some dressings and gives a good polish. Stains are better not interfered with, but surface dirt can be brushed off before applying dressings. With stained or coloured leathers and any gold decoration, care must always be taken not to rub too hard. Weak paste solution, as suggested above for cloth bindings, can also be used for leather.

Vellum

Dirty vellum can be rubbed with cottonwool soaked in milk, which both softens and cleans; if any gold or colour is present, moisture may cause damage, so rub round rather than over these. Tears in vellum can be mended with silk thread, or PVA can be used to fix back any thin strips which have come away from the surface.

New Cloth Corners

Measure across the corner of the book, according to where you wish to place the new fabric; allow for the turn-in when mitring. Cut a triangle of material to match or tone with the cover. Lay it beneath the corner, with the cover open, deciding how far you wish it to extend on to the cover board. Trim the two short edges, which will be folded on to the inside of the cover. If you wish, two pencil marks can be made here to ensure that you glue the corner on correctly. Glue the triangle lightly on a waste sheet, then lay it on the outside of the cover and press it smooth with a folder. Turn the book over and mitre the corner by cutting across the triangle 3mm ($\frac{1}{8}$in) above the cover corner. Fold the edges on to the inside of the cover, again using a folder rather than fingers to lift and press down the material. Lay protective sheets inside and on top of the cover, and make sure that any excess paste has been wiped or scraped away before nipping the book in a press, or leaving it under a heavy weight.

Repairs to Covers

Corners and edges

Split or bumped boards can be repaired by inserting thinnish paste into the cracks with a fine brush. When dry and nipped flat, they can be recoloured using a matching shoe or leather cream or polish, rubbed in with a small piece of sponge. Water-soluble crayons are good for use on cloth and for filling in breaks in colour elsewhere on these covers after any cleaning has been done.

Badly damaged corners may be prised open with a knife tip, and paste can be either brushed in or injected with a plastic syringe. A small piece of millboard, pared to fit into the opening, is inserted and, when dry, cut with a knife to form the new corner.

The book must then be pressed, to ensure that new corners are uniform with the surface of the cover. If the corners and edges are carefully moulded with fingers or a folder while the paste is still soft, they can be left to dry in the required shape, then nipped and pressed.

Warped boards

Covers which have lost their original shape can be resized with paste solution, which should be rubbed lightly and evenly over the whole board just as for cleaning. Cover the inside and outside with protective sheets, and then press.

'Shaken' Books

Warped or partly detached covers often mean torn endpapers, strained joints and contents which have become 'shaken'—ie out of shape but with the sewing still

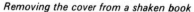

Removing the cover from a shaken book

intact. In this case, the cover must be removed entirely and may then be opened out and used again, or given new fabric if you wish (see Making a Case, page 44).

To remove the cover, use a sharp knife to cut about 37mm (1½in) away from the joints through the paper on the cover boards, to preserve the sewing tapes. Pull the boards away carefully and detach the endpapers; if necessary, cut through the mull as this can be replaced, but as far as possible avoid damage to the sections or glue. Knock up the contents, then place them between boards in a press, with the spine protruding and the boards supporting the book as far as the grooves of the joints. A rounded spine needs to be restored to its original curved shape of one-third of a circle; a flat spine should have no section folds protruding. The spine

is pasted, heavily enough for the adhesive to penetrate and allow any reshaping to be done by moulding with your fingers. Scrape away surplus paste with a folder and leave overnight to dry. If you do need to replace the mull, cut a new piece to size, using the original as a guide. Remove the old mull and fit the new piece on to the spine; glue it in place and leave to dry in the press.

Prepare new endpapers and tip them on to the first and last sections. Reattach the cover as if it were a new one (see Making a Case, page 44). First, make sure that the old cover material is soundly fixed to the boards; if necessary, a new piece of lining can be placed to reinforce the cloth at the spine, or a new hollow made. (See Rebacking a Cloth Cover, overleaf).

Board lining removed leaving tapes intact

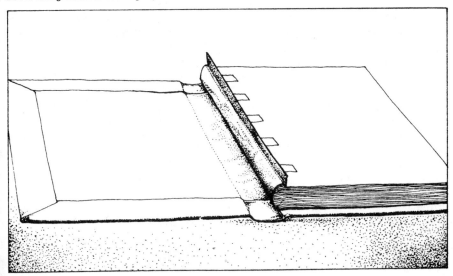

ITR&R - B

Rebacking a Cloth Cover

If the boards are sound and in place but the back is detached, rebacking can take place straight on to the book. The material should be either a neutral linen or toning bookcloth, as near as possible to the weight of the original. The old spine, if available, can be lifted from its lining and replaced on the new back, or used as a guide for new labels and lettering. Many cloth books are given a paper hollow at the spine, rather than a single sheet of brown paper, and this should be replaced with a new one when rebacking.

You need: Kraft paper, cloth, paste, and PVA/glue.

Remove the old paper lining by covering the spine with paste; leave for 20 minutes, then scrape it off with a folder. On each cover, score with a knife and straightedge 6–12mm ($\frac{1}{4}$–$\frac{1}{2}$in) from the joints; where there is a raised pattern on the cloth, score close to this so that the new join will be unobtrusive. Lift the cloth carefully along each score mark with the end of a knife or scalpel blade, separating the cloth from the board about 9mm ($\frac{3}{8}$in) in, to make a flap under which the new material will fit.

Replace the paper lining on the spine with the book held upright between boards in a press. An ordinary Kraft lining is cut with a knife along the grain—the lines on brown paper show the direction of the grain—a little more than the length of the spine and the same width. For a new hollow, cut Kraft paper 50mm (2in) longer than the spine and three times the width. Fix the ordinary lining in place on the spine with PVA/hot glue, or attach the hollow as follows.

Crease the paper into three equal sections; if the spine seems irregular, cut the paper a little wider and do not fold it too firmly, so that you can fit it to the shape of the spine. Glue the spine, press the central section of paper down well with a folder. Carefully glue the outside of the second section, without getting adhesive underneath, and press the third section down on to it, forming the hollow and matching the edges of the paper to the joints. Rub down well, and trim to the level of the boards at the head and tail. When dry, slit down each side of the hollow 25mm (1in) at both ends. Bend back the two upper layers of paper to trim the inside one to the level of the contents. If headbands are to be added, they are fixed to the inmost layer of Kraft paper (see page 51).

Cut the cloth for the spine with a knife and straightedge on a piece of board. It should measure 18mm ($\frac{3}{4}$in) longer than the book, and the width round the spine from beneath the lifted piece on each board. Make a pencil mark on the wrong side to help when gluing.

On a waste sheet, apply adhesive to the whole of the wrong side. Insert one long edge between the old cover fabric and board, pressing it in carefully with the tip of a folder and leaving an equal overlap at each end of the board. Press the cloth firmly down over the Kraft paper and ease it on to the second board; it may stretch, so rub to remove any air bubbles over the spine, and press along the joints. If no endpapers are present, press down the overlap inside the boards; otherwise lift the edges of the endpapers with a scalpel or knife and tuck the overlap inside. Working quickly but carefully, neaten inside the hollow with the folder tip and rub firmly down the joints. Use a little paste to replace the endpapers over the cloth, placing protective sheets between the covers and contents.

Lift the edge of the old cover fabric at the new join; apply adhesive beneath with a fine brush, then press down with the folder, scraping away any excess. Nip to make the join really firm, then press, with boards up to the joints of the book.

If rebacking with the whole cover detached, make sure your lining piece or hollow fits the book exactly by holding the spine of the book on it to measure against. New endpapers, if necessary, are tipped on to the book first, then pasted to the cover in the usual way.

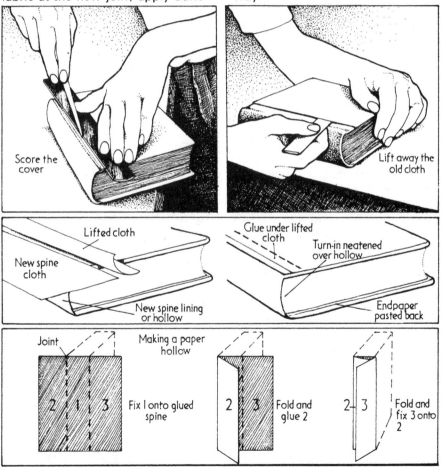

Score the cover

Lift away the old cloth

Lifted cloth

New spine cloth

New spine lining or hollow

Glue under lifted cloth

Turn-in neatened over hollow

Endpaper pasted back

Joint

Making a paper hollow

2 1 3 Fix 1 onto glued spine

2 3 Fold and glue 2

2 3 Fold and fix 3 onto 2

Sewing Procedures

All sewing should be practised first on old magazines or an unwanted book.

Apart from the needles, thread, etc, listed under Equipment and Materials, you will find helpful a board (an old pastryboard is ideal) on which to sew; a heavy weight (about 1.8kg/4lb), such as an old flatiron, wrapped in flannel or other material; and clothes-pegs (spring type).

Pamphlet Stitch

This is a good stitch to use when beginning sewing, to give practice in holding the book steady and controlling the needle. It is done with three, five or more holes, according to the size of the leaves and the type of paper, and can be used when putting a single section book into wrappers or binding, or for repairing leaflets or booklets.

Silk or fine but strong crochet thread may be used for delicate work, or where the stitch is decorative as well as functional, as in a hand-printed booklet; otherwise use a two-cord bookbinding thread.

Method

For a thick pamphlet, make holes from the inside of the section fold with a fine awl, holding the book firmly upright against a board with your left hand whilst doing so. There is always a central hole, with the upper and lower ones equidistant or, if preferred, the lower one marginally further from the tail than the upper one from the head. For thin paper, it is better to make the holes with the needle while sewing, to avoid tearing. Do not allow the leaves to slip after making the holes; a large paperclip or clothes-peg can be placed at the head and tail to prevent this, until you become proficient.

Sewing takes place at the edge of a board or table, with the section head at the right, the fold towards you and the section held open at the centre with your left hand. A large or heavy section can be held steady with the weight, but your hand should be sufficient for smaller leaflets.

The needle—use a lighter one for thin thread and paper—should be threaded with enough thread to make all the stitches and some extra for tying the final knot. To prevent the thread from slipping

(left) Securing thread; (right) Pamphlet stitching centre and side of a section

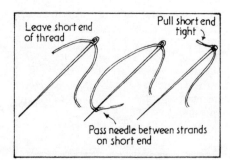

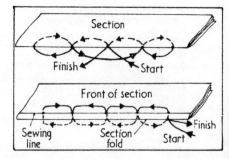

out at the eye, pass the needle point between the strands and pull the thread tight at the eye.

Insert the needle either at the inside or outside of the central hole, depending on where the final knot is to be. If you wish it hidden by the binding or glued wrapper, put it at the back; if sewing straight into a card or paper cover, put it in front. Leave 75–100mm (3–4in) of thread at the centre, sew in and out through the remaining holes, but bypass the centre one, leaving a larger loop; the final stitch takes the thread back through the centre so that a knot can be tied over the large loop.

A variation suitable for fastening together several single sheets is to place these stitches on the side of the book, about 9–12mm ($\frac{3}{8}$–$\frac{1}{2}$in) from the back edge with the knot either at the central or bottom hole. This looks attractive in coloured cord or thread on the outside of a card folder or limp cover, but does not open as easily as the more usual method.

Oversewing

This is used where single leaves need to be made into a section before a book is cased or bound; it is suitable for a single section book, or for one with many sections where too many guards would make binding difficult. If repairing a book with several plates which are on paper unsuitable for pasting, they can be oversewn together and put in as a section. When a paperback has fallen apart and you find that the back folds have been cut off, or if you need to cut away those of a magazine, you may wish to oversew rather than use glue alone to make the spine.

To make regular holes for oversewing first make a template. Mark and pierce some holes, using a thick awl at 6–12mm ($\frac{1}{4}$–$\frac{1}{2}$in) intervals along a piece of thin board, about 6mm ($\frac{1}{4}$in) from the edge; this can then be laid along the edge of each section as a guide. Depending on the amount of margin left on the inner edge of the pages, make the holes 6mm ($\frac{1}{4}$in) in, and the same distance from the head and tail as the position of the kettlestitches, which will need to be made when joining sections together. Oversew through the holes making a double stitch at each end; press or lightly hammer after sewing to get as smooth a surface as possible.

Sewing on Tapes

Even if you intend to try using a frame, it is a good idea to do some sewing at a table or board edge first, to get used to the stitches and the handling of sections. Where more than three or five tapes are used, a frame helps to control them, but just as good a job can be done without one.

Knocking up

All book or magazine sections are knocked up before sewing, ie made absolutely square at the head, tail and outside edges by holding them together and knocking each edge in turn on a flat hard surface. All old glue, staples, etc, should have been previously removed, and you should have checked that the sections are in the correct order.

Sewing Procedures

Marking up

You will need to mark the position of the tapes and sewing holes on the section folds. Three, five or more tapes are usual, but two wide 25mm (1in) ones could be used for magazines. Without disturbing the sections, place them upright in a press or between boards in a vice, with the spine protruding a little but held firmly. Use a straightedge and a hard pencil; dividers are useful if available. To mark for three tapes, divide the spine into four equal parts, making three marks on the central section fold. Make two more marks for the 'kettlestitches', which are sewn at each end of the section. One will be 12mm ($\frac{1}{2}$in) from the head, the other 15mm ($\frac{5}{8}$in) from the tail. (They can vary slightly according to the book, but these positions should suit most purposes.) For five tapes, divide the spine into six, and make seven marks in all. Two tapes are better placed a little nearer than halfway to the centre, since there is no central tape to take the strain. Mark the correct number of lines down over all the section folds, using your first marks as a guide. Then cut the required number of tapes to the width of the spine plus about 37mm (1$\frac{1}{2}$in) at each end. Centring a piece of tape over your lines as a guide, mark on the spine the position of the sewing holes to go on each side of the tapes.

With most books it is not necessary to make holes before sewing, but should you have to sew very heavy paper, for example in some magazines, you can make saw marks across the spine along your sewing lines after marking up. This is also necessary for some cord binding, and it is occasionally useful to saw for the kettlestitches only, when the sections are thick.

Sewing

Remove the book from the press, still keeping it square, and place it at the edge of the sewing board or table. Fix the tapes with drawing pins to the edge below the book, leaving about 37mm (1$\frac{1}{2}$in) of each tape spare below the pins, and lining up the remainder between the sewing marks. Place the book at one side of the sewing area face upwards; lift off the top section, find the centre, and place it face down on the board, so that the tapes and marks correspond. Use your weight, wrapped to protect the book, to hold the section steady and open at its centre while you are sewing.

Thread your needle—about 450mm (18in) of thread is a manageable length—using a two-cord thread for lighter books, and a three-cord for heavier ones and magazines. Pass the needle between the strands near the eye, and pull to secure the end. Starting at the head, sew through the first hole mark from the outside of the section; pull the thread through, leaving a tail of about 50mm (2in), and pass the needle along the centre of the section to emerge at the next sewing mark. Proceed over the tape and in at the third hole. Continue to sew in and out until all the tapes are secure and you emerge at the final mark. It helps to prevent the paper from tearing if you put the needle in at a right-angle, and always pull the thread in the direction you are sewing.

Place the second section face down on top of the first, and sew in and out, back from left to right, entering at the tail kettlestitch mark and emerging at the mark near the head of the section. Here, without cutting your thread, tie the tail from the first section to the thread in the needle, pulling it tight and making an ordinary reef knot. Next sew section three, repeating as for the first. If you need to join on a new piece of thread, use a 'weaver's knot' (see page 41), leaving the cut ends on the inside of the section. When you reach the final hole of section three, you will need to make a kettlestitch by passing your needle down between sections one and two, on the outside, making a loop through which your needle and thread are pulled to make a kind of chain-stitch (see diagram overleaf). Pull tight, upwards, and then enter

section four at the kettlestitch mark. Sew back to the end of the section and make a kettlestitch between sections two and three, catching in the loose end. Sew the remaining sections, making the kettlestitch at each end as you sew and finishing with a double stitch at the end of the top section.

Try to keep the tension reasonably firm but not too tight, and if the sections seem to bulge or 'swell', press them together as you sew. A thimble also helps.

Using a frame

Tapes (or cords) can be positioned with drawing pins as on a board; but the top ends are held in place with pins, and looped over the bar, instead of flapping loose. Sewing is done from the side of the frame, with one hand round the upright to hold the inside of the book steady. The bars of a chair make a good substitute. See diagrams overleaf.

(left) *Spine marked for tapes;* (right) *Sewing position, with weight holding section in place*

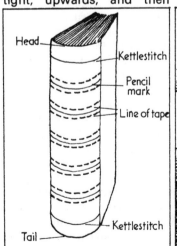

Head
Kettlestitch
Pencil mark
Line of tape
Kettlestitch
Tail

Sewing Procedures

Sewing on Cords

Cords are used rather than tapes for leather bindings. They are laced and hammered on to the boards, giving either a smooth spine (cords sunk into saw cuts) or one with traditional raised bands (cords held on the surface). A frame gives better support to cords, but they may be sewn without.

You will need: hemp cord: thin for recessed cords, thicker (or two thin ones) for bands; millboard for the covers; a light saw; pliers; paste; thin hot glue; tin sheets; waxed and white paper.

Marking up

Similar to marking up for tapes, but mark single lines only, one for each cord (usually three or five), and two for the kettlestitches. Cut the cord to the width of the spine plus 75mm (3in) at each end. Fix in place at a board edge, or cut them long enough to tie on to the bar of a frame and slot through keys at the bottom, if you wish. For raised bands, saw lightly, not too far into the sections, at the kettlestitch marks only. Saw the same for recessed cords at the kettlestitch marks, but at the cord marks gently saw at an angle to the depth of the cord. If endpapers are present, they should not be cut but removed, and replaced after sawing.

Sewing for raised bands

Place the sections as for tapes and prepare the thread. Enter the first section at the right hand kettle-stitch mark; pass the needle from inside behind the cord, slanting it to the left in the direction of the sewing and coming out to pass over the cord, re-entering from the right through the same hole. Continue to sew round all the cords, pulling the thread up at each; return along the second section, emerging from the right of each cord and re-entering from the left, with the needle slanted to the right. Make kettlestitches as usual from the third section on.

Sewing for recessed cords

Sew as for tapes, in and out, but using one hole only at each cord, securing the cord in the saw mark without making a loop.

When all the sections are sewn, cut the cords to 75mm (3in) if using a frame.

Gluing

Place the book in a press, then apply thin hot glue to the spine to sink into the saw marks and along the sections. Dry for an hour. Round and back as described below but avoid knocking raised cords with the hammer.

Preparing boards

Cut to size with a knife making them 3mm ($\frac{1}{8}$in) longer than the book at each end and 3mm ($\frac{1}{8}$in) wider at the fore-edge measuring from the joint. Sandpaper any roughness and blunt the corners slightly for a really smooth cover; line the boards with thin white paper—one sheet on the outside and two inside with paste between each layer. (Boards may be roughly cut, smoothed and lined, then cut to the exact size when dry.)

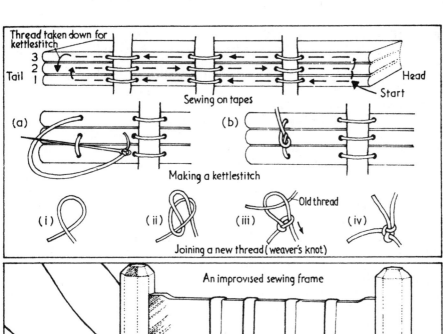

Thread taken down for kettlestitch
3
2
1
Tail
Head
Start

Sewing on tapes

(a)

(b)

Making a kettlestitch

(i)   (ii)   (iii) Old thread   (iv)

Joining a new thread (weaver's knot)

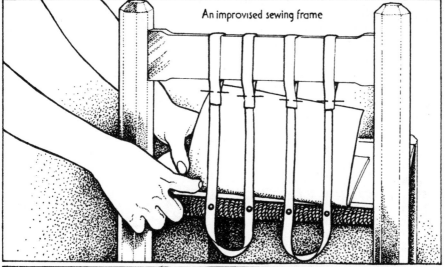

An improvised sewing frame

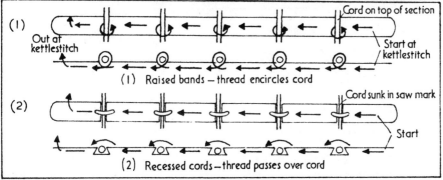

(1)
Out at kettlestitch
Cord on top of section
Start at kettlestitch

(1) Raised bands – thread encircles cord

(2)
Cord sunk in saw mark
Start

(2) Recessed cords – thread passes over cord

Sewing Procedures

Marking for cords

Draw a vertical pencil line 12mm ($\frac{1}{2}$in) from the inside edge of the first board. Place the board up to the book joint, then mark where the frayed cord ends reach (in the centre of the fraying). Remove the book and draw a right-angled line with a straightedge from each mark on to the vertical line. Make a mark for holes at each intersection and pierce with an awl. Draw a second vertical line 12mm ($\frac{1}{2}$in) away from the first, with a set of hole marks slightly higher than the first. Pierce these, and cut a shallow groove in the board between the hole marks and the edge, as shown in the diagram. Then tease

out the ends of the cords with a knife, thinning and tapering without cutting. Fit these 'slips' into the grooves to make sure they lie flush with the board.

Lacing cords

Stiffen the cord slips with thin paste and make points, then pull them through the first row of holes with pliers. Thread the slips through the second row, out to the top side of the board, pulling them through so that the board is in place at the joint of the book.

Repeat the marking for the second board, then prepare and insert the cord slips as for the first. Cut the slips flush with the boards and hammer them flat, with a hard surface underneath. Apply paste into the grooves, then sandwich each board between thin sheets of tin covered with waxed paper, and press the book firmly.

(above) *Cover marked for slips;* (below) *Rounding and backing the spine*

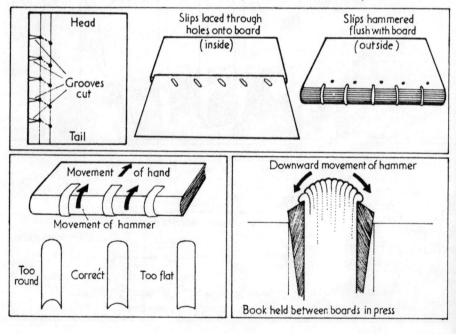

Rounding and backing the spine

So that the book will open properly, the spine must be shaped after sewing on tapes or cords (except for a light or thin book). Place the book spine up in a press or a vice, with protective boards. Stipple the back with hot glue, rub well into the sections, then dry for about an hour, until no longer tacky but still pliable. Take a cobbler's or binder's hammer and place the book on a bench with the fore-edge facing you. Holding the book very firmly in the centre, hammer gently from the centre of the spine along to the head, then from the centre along to the tail,

(left) *Book held between backing boards in press*; (right) *Movement of hammer for backing*

drawing the sections towards you and shaping them as you strike glancing blows with a circular motion of wrist and hammer. Turn the book over, keeping the new shape intact, and repeat on the second side until the book is shaped to one-third of a circle at the fore-edge.

Mark under the spine where the joint is to be (about the thickness of the cover board). Place a backing board against each mark and holding the book firmly between them, place it in the press, ensuring that the boards are held flush with the press edges (see diagram). Ease the joints over the edges of the boards with glancing blows of the hammer. The final shape of the spine should match that of the fore-edge.

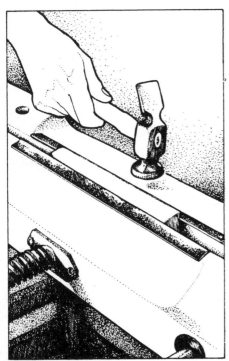

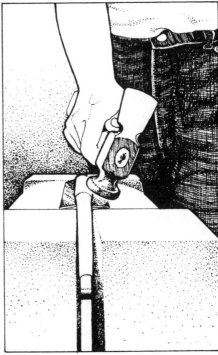

Making a Case

This is suitable for use with a book which has been resewn or has its old sewing intact, or for magazines which have been sewn up together. Paperbacks or unsewn bindings needing a more substantial cover can also be cased by this method. Before making the case, complete all other work, such as sewing, rounding and backing, replacing endpapers, and sinking cords for paperbacks or magazines. (see page 46).

Have ready: hot glue; PVA; mull; Kraft paper; new cover boards cut to size—about 3mm ($\frac{1}{8}$in) larger at the top, bottom and fore-edge—or the old boards if good; cover fabric; waste and protective sheets.

Place the book spine up in a press or vice with boards supporting up to the joints. Glue the spine. Lay on a piece of mull, cut to the width of the spine plus 18mm ($\frac{3}{4}$in) on each side. Glue on a Kraft paper lining, cut to the size of the spine (machine direction lengthways), and rub down well with a bone folder. Trim the mull to the edge of the tapes or cords, or to about 12mm ($\frac{1}{2}$in) on each side if there are none. Leave the book in the press to dry.

For the back cover lining, use a knife to cut a piece of heavy paper (card for heavier books) to the width of the spine and length of the cover boards. Then lay the cover boards and back lining piece in position on the wrong side of the cover fabric (a clean waste sheet should be placed beneath

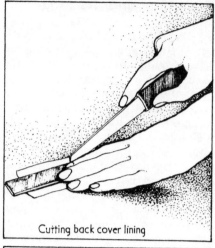

Cutting back cover lining

Book and lining piece
placed on fabric

fabric for protection). Allowing 12–18mm ($\frac{1}{2}$–$\frac{3}{4}$in) extra all round, and the thickness of the boards for the fabric at the joints, cut the cover fabric with a knife and straightedge to the required size. Remove the boards and lining.

Take the book from the press and lay the cover boards in place. Have scissors, glue/PVA and a bone folder to hand. Apply adhesive to the cover material, brushing firmly from the centre; do not allow the right side of the material to get sticky at the edges. With the boards held in position, lay the book on the righthand half of the glued fabric. Place the back lining piece against the spine, and bring the left half of the fabric over on to the book. Quickly lay the case open, removing the book, and adjust the lining piece to an exact central position.

Now take the scissors to mitre the corners. Cut across the fabric diagonally about 3mm ($\frac{1}{8}$in) away from each corner, without lifting the cover boards. Using the folder, press down the turn-in at the head and tail of the spine, then along the edges to the corners. Tuck the spare fabric in neatly at each corner, then fold over the side pieces and rub down firmly. The folder is used to make the edges sharp all round and to neaten the head, tail and corners. Work as quickly and carefully as possible, remembering that PVA dries fast; wipe your hands frequently to avoid marking the fabric.

Turn the case over, rubbing with the folder through the waste sheet to get the right side smooth; rub firmly along the joints. Turn over, trim any uneven edges with a knife and straightedge, then check the fit on the book; allow the case to dry.

Fitting the Case
Place the book in the case as you wish it to lie, making sure that the margins are correct. Then place a waste sheet between the front endpaper and contents, and paste down the tapes or cords and mull

Cover pieces in place on fabric

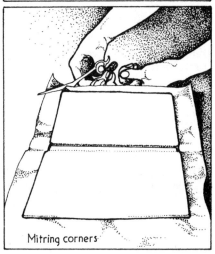
Mitring corners

on to the endpaper. Continue to paste all over the endpaper, then fit the cover board to it, pressing well at the joint and removing any surplus paste with the end of the folder. Turn over and repeat for the second cover board.

Insert waxed paper and nip, then leave under light pressure for twenty-four hours. (For labels and lettering see page 51.)

Paperbacks—Major Repair

Method I

This is suitable for heavier glued paperbacks which have come apart at the spine, and need not only regluing, but also more support. Magazines with flat spines and thick paper, which would be difficult to sew, can also be bound together in this way. You will need: binding cord (hemp string would do); hot glue/PVA; and a light saw.

Square up the book (or magazine sections) and place upright in a press with boards at each side. Saw carefully at an angle across the spine, to the depth of your cord; pencil marks may be made previously for guidance, dividing the spine roughly into three, five or seven, according to the size and weight of the book.

Sink pieces of cord, cut to the width of the book plus about 31mm (1½in) at each end. Stipple PVA well into the saw marks, then apply more PVA in several layers (four or five), allowing each to become tacky before putting on the next. Leave the book to dry in the press, then case.

A flat-spined book such as this will open less well than a rounded one; a hollow added to the spine can take some of the strain.

Method 2

A lighter, practical cover for thinner paperbacks, leaflets sewn together, music sheets forming several sections, or a thin old book. You will need: manilla or other light card for the covers; linen for the spine; PVA/glue and paste.

Assess the condition of the book; repair, if necessary, by regluing paperback sections, or by resewing as a pamphlet or with tapes, according to the weight and size of the book. Glue/PVA a new piece of mull on the spine; folded endpapers should be tipped in. Cut the cover pieces about 3mm (⅛in) larger than the book at the head, tail and fore-edge; cut a piece of

(above) *Glueing the spine;* (below) *Spine sawn for glued-in cords*

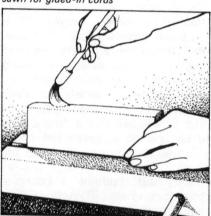

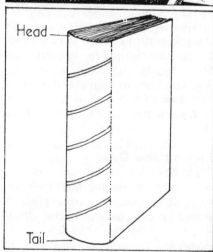

Head

Tail

linen for the spine, a little longer than the covers and the width of the spine plus about 12mm ($\frac{1}{2}$in) on each side.

Lay a waste sheet between endpaper and contents, then apply paste or PVA to the endpaper, laying in place and pasting down the mull and tapes as you do so. Lay the manilla cover on to the endpaper to within 3mm ($\frac{1}{8}$in) of the spine edge. Repeat for the second side, and nip the book in a press with protective sheets.

Make and fix a hollow on the spine (see Rebacking a Cloth Cover) and glue or PVA the linen cloth on to it. Instead of inserting the cloth as in a reback, it is laid over the edges of the manilla at the spine, glued well, then nipped and pressed. The original cover fabric from an old book could be laid down, ie fixed to the manilla cover, or the original spine fabric replaced on the new linen one.

Pamphlet Covers

When choosing a paper or card cover for a pamphlet, try to suit it to the type of paper used for the contents, and to its future use. Handmade or delicate marbled papers are better for hand-printed or valuable contents; plain grey, blue or brown manilla for library or everyday use; hand-decorated covers might suit a personal collection of cuttings or recipes.

Holes for sewing or for threading with ribbon or cord will need to be made with an awl against a board; a card template marked with the holes is useful for this and can also be used for making sewing holes for the contents. But a very light paper cover and contents that are not too thick, can be sewn all in one, using the sewing needle to make the holes.

Usually, covers for pamphlets, as for books, will be slightly larger than the page size of the contents—3mm ($\frac{1}{8}$in) top and bottom is usual, with the fore-edge margin slightly wider; however, these margins can be varied according to personal taste and the individual book.

A single section book sewn as a pamphlet may be tipped into wrappers, usually made of strong paper. For this, mark the centre of the inside of the cover, already cut to the required size, and crease with a folder. For a very light leaflet, it is enough to paste along the fold—previously guarded with a thin, but strong, strip of matching paper—and press this firmly into place along the inside of the cover fold. If preferred, the contents may be given endpapers, tipped in, or wrapped round the section and sewn with it. As usual when pasting, use protective papers during drying; nip, then press lightly for several hours.

For casing or binding a very thin book or a special pamphlet, the usual procedures are followed; but the spine needs to be more rigid than when covering larger books, and a heavier card would then be used for lining the spine.

Binding in Leather

The traditional binding material, leather, has become associated both with scholarship and luxury. A leather-bound book is certainly within the scope of the amateur, but like all bookwork it takes practice to do well. Try paring and cutting the poorer parts of the skin, until you are reasonably confident. If possible, tuition or professional demonstrations will be a great help.

Choice of Leather

A wide variety is available from suppliers, including vellum and calf. *Oasis* morocco (goatskin) comes in many colours and is fairly easy to work. *Skiver,* the cheaper parts of various animal skins, can be dyed or natural colour, but is not very durable. *'Library' calf,* coloured or natural, can be used for most purposes.

It is better to buy a whole skin, which can be ordered ready for use, but offcuts can also be obtained. The centre of the skin is best for a full binding; the sides can be used for new backs or half-bindings, and the scraps for labels.

Some skins need more paring than others—for example cheap calf; thick morocco needs paring all over with a spokeshave, before continuing as below.

You will need: skin; a very sharp paring knife and/or a carpenter's spokeshave; an oilstone; paste (creamy consistency); a folder; a smooth, flat, hard surface for paring (for example, a marble slab, heavy glass); waste sheets; a sponge; and protective tin sheets; waxed paper; and metal-edged pressing boards.

(above, left) *Paring with a knife;* (right) *Paring with a spokeshave;* (below) *Leather correctly pared for the cover*

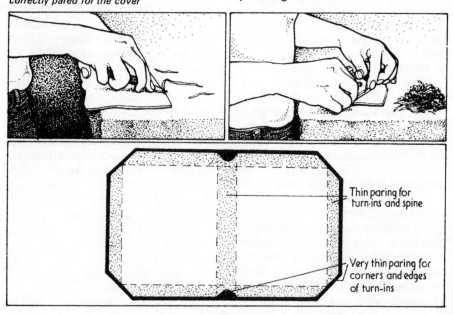

Thin paring for turn-ins and spine

Very thin paring for corners and edges of turn-ins

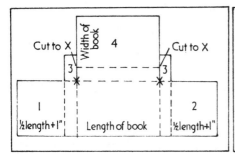
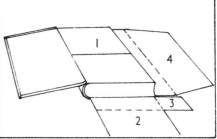

(left) *Paper cut to cap book; fold at dotted lines;* (right) *Capping up the edges of the book*

Paring the Skin

This is necessary on all but very thin leathers, and is done on the wrong side, round the edges of the piece cut for the book, so that it will turn, mitre and lie more easily, and fit better. First measure and then cut with a knife, a piece of skin the size of the open book plus 25 mm (1 in) all round; a paper template is a good idea since you can lay it down on different parts of the skin and choose the best place for the job. So that you will know where the exact edges are to be, use a ballpoint pen to draw round the book on the wrong side of the skin; mark for joints also, as a guide when fitting, and curve in slightly for shaping at the head and tail.

Place the leather face down on the paring surface, with the edge to be pared to the right, so that your left hand holds the skin steady. (Left-handed paring knives are obtainable and if used, the positions are reversed.)

Starting just inside the pen line, make small strokes at an angle into the flesh, which is to be shaved down to an even thinness all along the edge. Too sharp an angle makes holes, and it takes a number of correct strokes to pare even a small area. Keep the knife or spokeshave really sharp and remove the parings as they accumulate. You will also need to pare along the joint lines; the turn-ins at the head and tail, where the spine will be, are pared as thin as possible, shaving them away to almost nothing.

Preparation for Covering

The book is already prepared, with the cords laced in. The spine is rounded and backed with the paper lining on. A heavy paper is best under leather or a paper hollow can be made; the surface should be smoothed down well with sandpaper. If wished, headbands are either sewn or glued on. If headbands are not to be used, prepare two pieces of heavy cord (the same thickness as the cover board), cut to the same measurement as the distance across the spine between the boards, and stiffened with a little paste. These are used to form the head caps at head and tail of the spine.

Make a book-size 'cap' or cover from Kraft or bond paper and adhesive tape to fit over the entire book during covering; it should fit well but not too tightly over the corners of the leaves.

Covering and Finishing

Covering

Dampen the leather side of the skin with a sponge. Apply paste to the underside and fold it over so the paste is on the inside; allow the paste to soak in for about twenty minutes. Repeat once or twice more so that the skin is well soaked, then remove any excess paste. Remove and replace the waste sheets.

Paste the spine of the book, then hold it in place on the leather, lifting first one side then the other up on to the boards with the palms of your hands. Stand the book on its fore-edge and smooth down the leather very firmly over the spine and on to the boards, fitting it carefully in place. Lay the book on one side, rub the leather into the joint, turn it over and repeat for the second joint.

Stand it on the fore-edge again, and mould the spine, first over any raised bands, which are nipped with special 'nippers' so that they are really firm. Then stand the book at the edge of a bench and open it very gently to turn in the overlaps at the spine; if headbands are not used, the overlaps should be moulded over the prepared pieces of cord to make head and tail 'caps' as shown in the diagram. A little paste is needed to secure the cover at the headbands when you tuck the leather in behind them. Cut and mitre the corners, as with a case, then press the turnings down and mould the corners so they are not too sharp.

Tie bookbinding thread round the joints so that they keep their shape whilst drying. Place protective sheets (waxed paper wrapped round thin tin) inside each of the covers and lay the book in the press with metal-edged boards up to the joints.

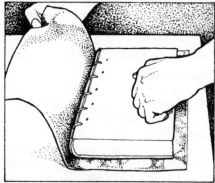

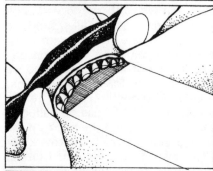

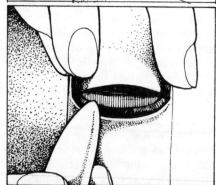

(top to bottom) *Lifting leather on to board; turning in behind headbands; moulding over headcaps*

Decoration and Titling

Restraint in decoration is always advisable, especially with older books, but finishing can be a creative and rewarding part of the work.

Colouring of edges This forms a protection for the contents and is usually done after the book has been sewn. The edges must be completely smooth and may need recutting with a guillotine or plough—a friendly printer or binder could help. Hold the book very tightly between boards in a press, the edge to be treated uppermost. Mix water-colour or dye with a small amount of glue as sizing, and sponge it on very quickly and lightly so that it does not penetrate between the leaves. Leave till dry.

Gilding is a highly specialized process best left to experts; gilt edges can be cleaned and brightened by brushing, or by wiping them with barely damp cotton-wool.

Headbands Old ones can be replaced or new ones added, using ready-made strips obtained from suppliers. But if they were originally sewn in or you wish to try making them, this is done after the main sewing and the rounding and backing of the spine. Choose colours to harmonize with the book.

To apply ready-made bands, cut them to the width of the spine at the head and tail. Fix them on to the sections with glue, holding the book in a press so that both hands are free. The linings of the spine are lifted back slightly so that the tape of the headband can be inserted to fit the head or tail just below the level of the cover and above the contents.

To make your own headbands, off the book, cover a length of gut, thin cord or nylon line with a similar length of light wide tape folded down the centre and glued together to encase the gut, leaving enough tape to fix to the spine. Thread a fine but strong needle with two different colours of embroidery silk and oversew the gut through the tape, using buttonhole stitches drawn close together so that the core is hidden. Fasten off at each end by leaving a tail which can be knotted.

Titling

Labels are the simplest form of titling; done well they can enhance the ugliest book. Old labels should, unless very firm, be removed during any cover cleaning. Paper, card or leather labels are pasted back after rebacking or making a new case or binding. Gently remove any old adhesive using a folder or possibly fine sandpaper; use a folder tip to remove any excess paste after replacing. A new label should harmonize with the texture and shade of the cover.

Always use a good quality paper or card which is not too absorbent; very shiny surfaces are better avoided. Use paste (not too thick) or PVA. Mark the positions of labels in faint pencil, using dividers and straightedge—inaccurate placing can be conspicuous. If placing a label on a spine, first open and close the book to make sure that it will not crease anything laid on it.

Covering and Finishing

Titling

Try to keep correct proportions between lines of lettering, using smaller letters for less important words; the space between individual letters is also important. It helps to make a pattern with lines measured up and letters placed; try this on the book first. If using a pen or fine brush with Indian ink, your own lettering style is likely to be more satisfactory than copying an old label.

To make a label that is individual in style, try small lino-cut, potato-cut or stencilled letters—they can look good in different coloured inks. For a patterned border, try a repeated design cut on the end of a piece of small-diameter dowel rod, or even on a cut-off eraser—these can also be used for letters.

If you want the traditional clear-cut letters of printer's type, you may be able to borrow some from a printer, or buy them from a printer's supplier who deals in small quantities. You should be able to order exactly the letters needed for the title and author, or complete alphabets. Small letters would need mounting on a cork or wood handle, but large ones could, with a steady hand, be inked and pressed straight on to the paper. The binder uses brass type which is set on to a handle or placed in a holder taking several letters at a time.

Leather labels

These are 'tooled' either on or off the book, using brass type, which is heated and applied in the same way as decorative lines and patterns. Smaller scraps of leather can be used, but make sure they are not pared too thin, or too stretched.

Lettering on covers

To letter directly on to paper or card covers presents no problem provided you make accurate templates, or fine pencil lines on the cover beforehand. To work directly on to cloth or leather, however, requires heated tools and gold or coloured strip foil through which an impression is made, sinking the

Titling with foil

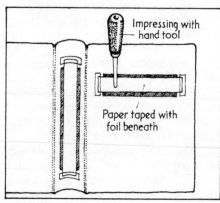

Impressing with hand tool

Paper taped with foil beneath

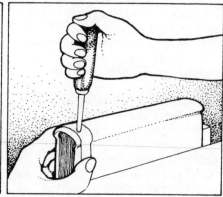

letters into the cover material. This is done either before putting the covers on, or with the spine of the covered book held in a press at the edge of a bench. If you wish, you can purchase lettering tools or brass type and a holder from binding suppliers, or improvise your own tools with printers' type as described above. The binder uses a special stove, but tools can be heated on any hotplate.

The title is first set out on thin hard paper such as bank typing paper. To make sure that the letters fit and look well, make either a 'blind' impression or lightly ink the lettering tools. Fix the paper in the required place on the spine or front cover with dabs of paste at the corners and slip foil, gold or colour uppermost, beneath. Heat the tools till they sizzle when damped, cool slightly, then press each in turn right through the paper into the cover. Remove the paper and foil and impress individual letters again if not clear. It is a good idea to practise so that you learn the exact moment for removing your tool from the heat, and how hard to press them; use scraps of leather or fabric for this.

Tooling designs: blind and gold

These are the traditional adornments for leather covers, and require heated brass tools similar to those used for lettering. Those most used to begin with would be one for straight lines—a pallet give a continuous line and a fillet is a brass disc which is rolled to make lines—and an ornamental one, such as a flower or star. Tools can be improvised by sawing and filing

marks to make a pattern on the head of a brass screw, held in a vice; or you can make a line using any fine, not too sharp point heated then held at an angle and drawn firmly along the foil, or without foil for a blind impression.

Blind tooling may be done either through paper as above or direct on to the leather; hotter tools make darker lines, effectively burning the leather.

Before any tooling, the leather is dampened, using paste solution. The surface should be firm but slightly porous; very thin or stretchy leather will not take tools. Simple patterns are most effective, but even these should be planned and drawn up first so that they are placed correctly. Some suppliers provide tooling instructions, as well as all the necessities for full-scale gilding.

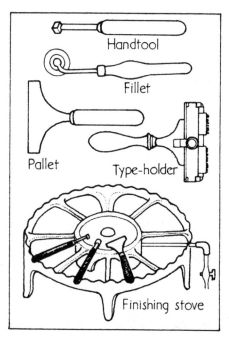

Handtool

Fillet

Pallet

Type-holder

Finishing stove

Glossary

Backing Forming the final shape of the spine of a book after sewing.

Collation The checking of pages, plates, and sections throughout the book.

Endpaper Blank sheet(s) at either end of the book; the first and last are pasted to the cover boards, the remainder protect the contents.

False bands Strips of leather, cord, etc, inserted under the spine cover. They replace the raised bands of the cord-sewn binding.

Finishing Final stage of bookbinding (labelling, decoration, etc).

Flyleaf Usually the first unpasted endpaper, used for inscriptions.

Fore-edge The front edge of the leaves.

Forwarding The process of making or rebinding a book, from 'gathering' the leaves to attaching covers.

Foxing Brownish mottling of leaves caused by damp which affects chemicals in the papers.

Full-binding Covering of one material only.

Grain The direction of the fibres in paper, formed by the wire used in papermaking.

Groove The shape formed at the spine edge of the sections during backing.

Guarding Repair of leaves using strips of paper, linen or tissue.

Half-binding Two materials used on the cover, one for the spine and corners, another for the boards.

Head The top of a leaf or binding.

Headband Silk worked on to the head or tail of the spine, originally as reinforcement but now chiefly decorative and often false; instead, moulded 'headcaps' are sometimes used on a leather binding.

Hollow A paper or light card lining sometimes placed on the spine for a smooth surface and easier opening.

Joint Formed at the spine by the backing process; also the hinge of material on the outside of the book. The cover boards fit into the grooves at the joints.

Kettlestitch A catch stitch made on the sections, joining them to each other when sewing the spine.

Knocking up Tapping the head, tail, and fore-edge of the book on a hard surface so they lie exactly even.

Lining First—the mull on the spine; second—the brown paper on the spine; board—white paper pasted to the cover boards to prevent warping.

Mitre To cut cover material diagonally across corners of a book.

Plate An illustration, often on shiny 'art' paper.

Preliminary matter 'Prelims', the first printed pages of the book, including the title page and all material not part of the main text.

Pulling Taking apart the sections of the book from their cover.

Quarter-binding The spine and part of the cover in one material, the remainder in another.

Setting the back Fixing the shape of the spine with glue.

Slips Cords or tapes fixed on to the cover boards.

Swell The thickness at the spine edge caused by the sewing of sections or sometimes by the use of guards.

Tail The bottom of a leaf or binding.

Tipped in When a narrow strip of paste holds in a leaf or plate.

Tooling Decorative impressions made by special tools on covers: either *blind* without any colour or *gold,* using gold leaf or foil.

Clocks

Eric Smith

Illustrated by Roger Day

Introduction

This book is an introduction to the repair and restoration of clocks. 'Repair' means bringing back to working condition; 'restoration', or 'renovation', means rather more—perhaps even restoring the article to new condition. This raises contentious questions. Do we *want* an antique clock to look like new? Do we know just how it would have looked when new? Can we fairly introduce modern or replacement material, perhaps invisible from the outside? Is the untouched 'original' more valuable even if it does not

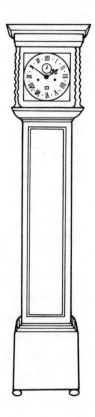

go or keeps bad time? How good should the time-keeping of a clock of a certain type be? Moreover, 'repair' and 'renovation' obviously overlap.

We cannot go into all this here, but the reader should always be aware of it. And be wary—both as a buyer and as a workman. You need to gather experience of old clocks, from museums, from books and journals, from sale-rooms. Only then can you distinguish between botching (which is vandalism), repair done by a craftsman which is not and does not pretend to be original, skilled restoration which may be acknowledged, and skilled faking to deceive—the difference between the last two can be difficult indeed to recognize.

In your own work, much depends on the date and value of the piece. You may have overriding grounds for making changes. More often the problem is how far to imitate what is there, or how much to brighten what is dull. Always have doubts when you can detect deception as a motive. The motive for repair is to keep as much as possible of the original clock as a going concern, not to deceive anyone that the clock is pristine when it is not so. You are not preserving fossils, but your aim is not to make a clock more valuable, or to look older, or of better appearance, than it could ever have been or looked. It is to restore the true spirit, mechanical and visual, so far as they can be known, of a particular clock. It may involve some research; it will certainly involve compromise, careful workmanship and caution in the use of modern materials.

You might have to consider whether to use genuine silk (if you have identified the original as such) or a synthetic substitute as the coloured backing to a fret in a case; whether to strip, polish or paint a battered simple 'grandfather' case; whether to clean up a lacquered carriage-clock case or to strip and relacquer it; whether to replace a pair of steel hands because the only original hand cannot be matched in style. Such are everyday questions to which there is no stock answer—much depends on the value and condition of the original, on the owner's feelings if you are not the owner, and on the replacements available. On the other hand, you might consider putting glazed panels in place of the silk-backed frets; adding some imposing brass finials to the long-case; having the carriage clock gilded; fitting elaborate brass hands because they come in the right size and look well. These would be deliberate alterations of the original and with some element of deception—unless, of course, the frets seemed to be replacements, there were already holes for finials and the carriage-clock case showed traces of gilding on it!

Even the humblest repair can be well or badly done, and in fact repairs seldom come singly. You must know the clock, which means completely dismantling and cleaning it, however slight the damage may seem to be. Then you must keep in mind the cardinal principle that work which (after assembly) is invisible must be as well finished and receive the same detailed attention as, for example,

work on the dial. You have to come to enjoy the work, the feel of the parts and the tools, the satisfaction of a detail successfully wrought. Try not to be so swamped with the anticipation of getting the whole job finished that you rush through and end up with a particular repair carried out but some uncertainty as to whether the clock will go for long. You want the satisfying reliability of a movement with wear taken up and parts appropriately polished, oiled and secured. It is better to think in terms of reconditioning than of an isolated repair.

This book explains first the workings of the commonest types of movement and their main parts; there are notes on the repair of some of these parts at the ends of their sections. The middle of the book summarizes the tools and materials likely to be needed, the processes of dismantling and cleaning, and some important repairs generally done at this stage. Finally, there are pages focusing on some of the more readily available types of old clock.

There is an extensive literature on both the historical and practical sides of horology, and the list of books and journals at the end of the book may form an introduction. To subscribe to or obtain regularly one or two of the journals is a stimulating way of keeping in touch, and will also bring to your notice many of the suppliers of tools, materials and reproduction parts, as well as skilled services, which are now available to the amateur with a practical interest in clocks.

Gear Trains

The gear train reduces the power against which the governor has to operate, and is so designed that proportionately fewer revolutions are made by each driving than driven wheel in a given time. A train comprises wheels and pinions, a wheel normally driving a pinion on the adjacent arbor. Pinions are small wheels, as a rule of no more than 12 teeth, and either of steel solid with their arbors or of steel wire mounted in brass discs ('lantern pinions'). The whole motor has the function, besides turning the hands, of keeping the oscillating governor in motion. Save in many electric clocks, the oscillator is not the power which turns the wheels.

Going Trains

Time trains vary, principally according to how long the clock is to run between windings, but also according to the nature of the os-cillator and whether some refine-ments—for example, a centre seconds hand or calendar indica-tion—are incorporated. Generally, however, the minute hand is attached to the centre wheel and this is directly driven through a pinion (small steel wheel) on its axle (arbor) by the great wheel and power-supply in a 30-hour (ie 1 day) clock; in an 8-day (ie 1 week) clock (spring driven) there is an intermediate wheel between the great and centre wheels, and in clocks of longer duration there may be more than one such wheel. The central (minute) arbor revolves

once in an hour. Reducing this (for the hour hand) to one revolution in 12 hours is accomplished by two wheels (motion wheels) out-side the main gear train—one wheel would suffice, but two are needed for both hands to be con-centric. In a striking clock the motion wheels normally let off striking and chiming through levers and may operate a calendar. They are often, but not always, the siting of the frictional arrangement whereby the minute hand can be turned independently of the move-ment for setting the clock to time.

Sounding Trains

The time between blows when the train is running is controlled by the mass and friction of the train and by a revolving fan (fly). The number of blows is controlled by one of two basic systems which will be outlined later. The wheels

Motion work

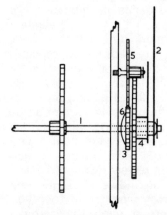

1 Centre wheel and arbor going to minute hand 2
3 Cannon pinion carrying minute hand against friction washer 6
4 Hour pipe with hand round cannon pinion pipe
5 Minute wheel
6 Domed friction washer between centre arbor and cannon pinion

of sounding trains (including the fly) are one more in number than those of going trains, with a similar additional wheel for 8-day running if spring driven.

Repairs

Broken wheel teeth can be replaced by filing out a section of the wheel and soldering in a shaped replacement. Cutting a new wheel or pinion requires special equipment and skill. Pinions solid with their arbors must be replaced if badly worn. The wire trunnions of lantern pinions can, however, be replaced with wire of identical size. Sometimes a wheel can be moved on its arbor to engage with an unworn part of the pinion and sometimes it can be reversed (see page 89). In general, damaged wheels and pinions require replacement and you will need to have the work done for you.

A standard book will supply examples if you have trouble in calculating the sizes of missing wheels and pinions. The rule is that the total number of wheel teeth divided by the total of pinion teeth gives you the reduction ratio from fastest to slowest wheel. Establish the ratio needed, say from scape wheel to centre wheel, and then see how many more wheel/pinion teeth are needed on the missing part to complete this ratio. It is no less essential to have correct ratios in striking (and chiming) trains and you should consult a fuller manual if you have a problem in this area.

If, as is most likely, you have to have a new wheel cut, take no chances; send it, its neighbour and the plates to the firm who are to do the work. To send the wheel alone is to invite the making of an ill-fitting wheel.

Layout of gear trains

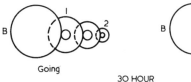

Going

30 HOUR

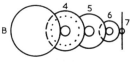

Striking

I	Centre wheel
2	Scapewheel
3	Intermediate wheel
4	Pinwheel
5	Locking wheel
6	Warning wheel
7	Fly
B	Barrel/pulley for weight/mainspring

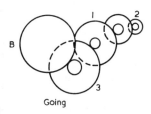

Going

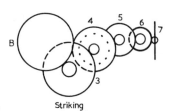

Striking

EIGHT DAY (spring driven)

Weights

Most clocks are driven by falling weights, coiled springs or electricity. Weights and springs may be rewound manually, by an electric motor or by an electromagnetic device actuated by the clock. In almost all mechanical clocks, the power is applied at one end of the train to keep the oscillator in motion at the other end. In many electric clocks, however, the oscillator (or oscillating current) itself drives the train from the 'fast' end.

Weight drive exists in two principal forms. In one, the line to which the weight is attached is coiled round a cylinder (barrel) on the driven arbor. In the other, it merely passes over a spiked pulley on this arbor, the spikes preventing it from slipping. Eight-day clocks use the first form and 30-hour clocks usually use the second, their rope or chain also driving the sounding train, whereas the 8-day clock employs additional weights and lines for this purpose.

The clock is wound by raising the weight and the barrel rotates as it is wound. This would be impossible if the barrel were fixed to the great wheel and thus tried to turn the train. The barrel is therefore fitted with some form of ratchet (click) mechanism which allows drive in one direction only. This device takes the full power of the weight and must be strong and well riveted. Thus the barrel and arbor are fixed to each other but they can turn independently of the train during winding. The arbor ends in the winding square for the key.

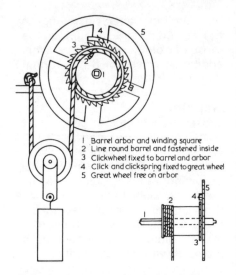

1 Barrel arbor and winding square
2 Line round barrel and fastened inside
3 Clickwheel fixed to barrel and arbor
4 Click and clickspring fixed to great wheel
5 Great wheel free on arbor

Eight-day long-case power and winding

The old 30-hour clock employs an endless loop of rope or chain in such a way that one side is pulled down to wind the clock. This is simple and also has the advantage that power remains on the train meanwhile. It is important to have the chain so that it turns the wheels in the right direction, and also to have a good fit between the chain and the spiked pulley. These movements may have full plates to take the wheel pivots or may have a top and bottom suspended by vertical iron posts, with the pivots running in strips of brass wedged to the top and bottom (see page 93). In the old posted movement the two trains are arranged from front to back (rather than side by side as in full plate chain and most other striking movements). The chain then does not enter the pulleys vertically and will slip if it is not a good fit and does not have sufficient counter-weight. In either type of 30-hour movement, the

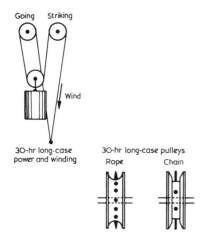

Going   Striking

Wind

30-hr long-case
power and winding

30-hr long-case pulleys
Rope   Chain

going train pulley is fixed to its arbor, whilst the striking pulley is loose and connected to its great wheel by some form of click so that winding does not take the power off the going train. If the striking is immobilized, such a clock will run for some 5 days.

Repairs

Weights, lines and chains are available through suppliers. Frayed lines of 8-day clocks must be replaced, but whether with oiled gut, perlon line, steel or phosphor-bronze cable is rather a matter of taste. On a good movement I feel that anything but gut is incongruous; wires are stronger but tend to mark the barrels. Pass the replacements through the seatboard holes and fasten them with large looped knots or else make them secure to thick pins which cannot pass through the holes. Pressing the ends of gut and synthetic lines to which heat has been applied,

will form knops which cannot slip through the knots.

30-hour clock chains are difficult to measure against pulleys. For replacement, it is safer to send the pulley with the chain or to buy a new pulley with a matched chain. The hole of the new pulley usually needs enlarging, and even then the arbor may need reducing. It is much better to have this done on a lathe—though the less that can be done to original pulleys and arbors the better. If you have to replace an endless rope (rather than chain), you must obtain the proper soft rope from a supplier. The rope can be joined by splicing and the use of an elastic glue, if necessary. Separate the strands and tie a central group into a reef knot. Then splice and darn in the outer strands and trim them off.

The best weight is the least which will drive the train reliably—there is no rule, and you can experiment (for example, with tins of scrap metal) before committing ourself to a new weight. In the long term it is folly to put a heavier weight on a worn movement to make it go; the answer is to attend to the pivots and holes (as described later) and, if necessary, to have worn pinions replaced or their wheels moved. Generally, a 30-hour long-case clock's weight is in the region of 2.7–3.7kg (6–8lb), whilst the weights of 8-day clocks are nearer 5.5kg (12lb), the striking weight being the heavier of the two. The weights of Vienna and similar wall clocks (8 day) may be as little as 1–2kg (2–4lb). Longer durations call, of course, for heavier weights.

Springs

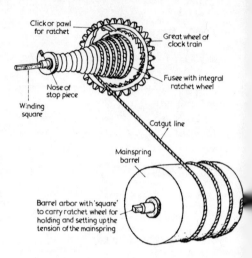

Labels on diagram:
- Click or pawl for ratchet
- Great wheel of clock train
- Fusee with integral ratchet wheel
- Nose of stop piece
- Winding square
- Catgut line
- Mainspring barrel
- Barrel arbor with 'square' to carry ratchet wheel for holding and setting up the tension of the mainspring

Fusee

A spring poses a problem because its power declines as it runs down. The fusee (from the French and Latin words meaning 'spindle') is the first solution. It is a sort of variable gear, tapered in profile from base to top. The base of the fusee is in effect the great wheel, driving the train, whilst the fusee itself is connected to this wheel by clickwork and to the barrel containing the mainspring by a wire, line or chain.

The ideal theoretical shape for a fusee has been much discussed and must depend in part on the particular characteristics of an individual spring, but the principle is that the spring pulls on the smaller top part when fully wound, and on the broader lower part increasingly as it unwinds, when it gains the benefit of leverage. The winding square is on the fusee (which is fixed to its arbor and linked by clockwork to its going wheel base) —that on the mainspring arbor is used only when setting the contrivance up.

Going Barrel

The French were using the alternative, cheaper and very effective expedient of the going barrel whilst the great age of English clockmaking (say from 1670 till 1800 and after) almost always used fusees. The going barrel is a cylinder for the spring, with the base toothed and acting as a great wheel. Its dimensions are so calcu-

lated that the spring's weakest outside coils are restrained by the barrel and only the more constant driving force of the inner and middle coils is used. As a rule, this is achieved when the unwound spring occupies about half the area of the barrel exclusive of the arbor; if it occupies more, the spring will not be able to be fully wound, and if it occupies less, the regulating effect of the going barrel will be reduced.

Traditional French movements were very finely made and light in mass, their springs relatively long and weak, and the clocks were capable of keeping as good time as the heavier English clocks with fusees. Cheap modern clocks use going barrels or unenclosed springs and quite often exhibit a losing rate as they run down.

Repairs

Springs can usually be mended when broken at the outside end. It is a matter of heating the tip to bright red, allowing it to cool

Space in going barrel

BETWEEN PLATES
Clickwheel fixed to arbor,
gearwheel free, attached
to open mainspring

OUTSIDE PLATES
Click, clickspring and bracket
screwed to plate. Clickwheel
located on going barrel square

slowly, and drilling or bending the end, according to which of the many methods of fastening is involved. This is the commonest place for breakage. Breaks in the length of the spring can occasionally be repaired, but it is not good practice in the long term and such a spring is better replaced. Breaks at the inner end demand replacement. When trying to obtain a replacement, send the whole of the original spring. If trying to 'make do' (as occasionally you may have to) with only similar springs, remember that the thickness of the metal and the height of the spring are the critical factors—the length principally governs duration rather than power output. As a guide there are generally upwards of ten coils in the barrel.

Click mechanisms for going barrels and open mainsprings vary widely, usually comprising some form of clickwheel on the arbor, and click and clickspring on the movement plate or the great wheel. They are easy to under-

stand from observation and can often be replaced with home-made parts filed up as necessary, if the supplier can offer nothing suitable. Obviously it is essential that click mechanisms are not worn, and vital that they are securely screwed or riveted. Damage here is a common cause of broken mainsprings —and vice versa. If a mainspring needs attention, carefully inspect the associated clickwork for firm and positive action. Check that the angle of the click is such that the thrust of the mainspring passes through the click to its mounting, and that the profile of the click's tip matches the gap between two wheel teeth. Make sure that neither click nor clickspring grates on the movement plate, because this rubbing causes erratic action and wear. Ensure also that the click is the thickness of the wheel; if it is more, or less, click and wheel will soon be worn unevenly and replacement will probably be necessary.

ITR&R - C

Oscillators—
Pendulums

The oscillator governs a clock's time-keeping. In mechanical clocks, if moved and released it will maintain equal swings (vibrations) more or less independently of variations in the power which is applied to keep it going. Each of its vibrations takes virtually the same time whether it is big or small. In mechanical clocks it is, generally, a pendulum or balance wheel with spring, though other devices have been used. In electric clocks, the AC mains frequency or the quartz crystal would be examples, though the oscillators of mechanical clocks are also used in electric clocks, the electricity being a substitute for weight or spring power.

The period of a pendulum's vibration depends on its length down to its centre of gravity, say the centre of the weight (bob). Many lengths have been used, but, naturally, lengths which require simple and standard gear trains are the most common. Those most often met are just over 99cm/39in (1-second vibration), about 25cm/10in (half a second) and 13cm/5in (common on nineteenth-century French clocks); the actual length will, however, vary from the theoretical length according to how the weight is disposed. Clocks of the nineteenth and twentieth centuries exhibit a great variety of trains and pendulum lengths. Although the pendulum does not drive the clock —it is in fact driven by it through the escapement—it must exert control over it, and the heavier the

pendulum bob relative to the rod and to the driving power, the better.

Pendulums formerly hung from knife-edge bearings or from silk thread, but from the late seventeenth century on, at least in England, pendulums have been hung from a thin suspension spring (included in the length), whose other end is attached to a bracket (cock) fixed to movement plate or case backboard. The more solid the mounting, the better, and there must be no distortion in the spring or the pendulum will wobble. Regulation is principally by altering the pendulum's length. This can be done at the suspension spring, or by a rating nut acting on the bob, or by small

Simple pendulum and layout

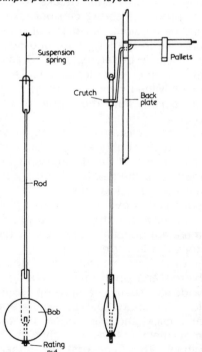

Suspension spring

Pallets

Crutch

Back plate

Rod

Bob

Rating nut

weights on a tray halfway up the rod which alter the centre of gravity. The pendulum is linked to the escapement in the movement by a descending arm known as the crutch. Its slot for the pendulum rod should be as close a fit as possible without binding. Alternatively, the crutch has a pin which runs closely in a slot in the pendulum.

Pendulums may be simple wooden or iron rods with brass-cased lead weights, or they may be in one of the many elaborate compensating forms. These are designed to counteract the tendency of the rod to lengthen and the clock to run slow, in high temperatures. Sometimes the compensation work (which depends on the coefficients of expansion of the different metals used) is imposing in appearance but not designed to work scientifically, if at all.

Repairs

The commonest repair to pendulums is the replacement of a distorted or broken suspension spring. Assortments of these springs can be obtained from suppliers, or you can try making a spring from similar metal to that which is broken. Within limits, a stiffer spring (of the same length) will cause the clock to gain and a weaker one will cause it to lag. Outside those limits, too stiff or weak a spring will stop the clock, either asking for more power than is available or absorbing the power in the spring rather than passing it to the rigid pendulum itself.

Compensating pendulum

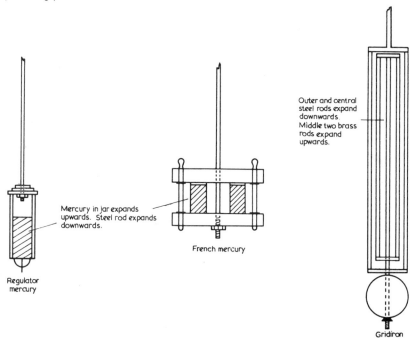

Mercury in jar expands upwards. Steel rod expands downwards.

Regulator mercury

French mercury

Outer and central steel rods expand downwards. Middle two brass rods expand upwards.

Gridiron

Oscillators— Balance Wheels

The most common alternative to the pendulum is the balance wheel and spring, whose clocks may have the merit of being portable. The factors governing the period of vibration here, are the size and mass of the wheel (principally its rim) and the strength and dimensions of the balance spring (where length, height and thickness of metal are all involved). Hence there is no simple formula like the length of a pendulum—many combinations of springs and wheels must be tried, but they will not, provided the springs are not bent, vary from their own particular timings once these are known.

In most movements the balance staff connects through a lever, comparable with the crutch, to the escapement, but there are other more, or less, direct forms of linkage. The wheel should be perfectly poised (as a car wheel is balanced) by screws round the rim or by shaping the metal during manufacture; there is a science of coiling balance springs so that they complement the inherent design of their balance wheels, and the latter vibrate over the same period regardless of variations in the size of their swings. Balance staffs are carefully lathe-turned and end in very finely shaped pivots revolving in jewelstones and resting on polished endstones, for obviously friction must be reduced to a minimum. Alternatively, in cheaper forms, the staffs end in conical points which run in inverted cone bearings on the ends of adjustable screws mounted in the plates.

Regulation is, of course, by moving the index, which alters the functioning length of the balance spring. More drastically, it is by freeing the spring in its stud, moving it along so as to shorten or lengthen it, and moving the collet on the balance staff, to return the wheel to its previous position of

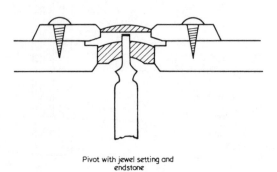

Pivot with jewel setting and endstone

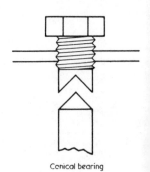

Conical bearing

rest. Compensation is generally by use of a bimetallic rim with open ends at opposite sectors. It requires no attention, but these wheels are delicate and must not be bent. The screws sometimes spaced round the rim are best left alone by the amateur, though information on them will be found in watch-repairing manuals.

Repairs

Repairing broken balance pivots (or more usually turning a new staff complete) is a job for the expert. Be wary of buying, for example, a carriage clock with a broken balance pivot—detectable from the balance's rocking from side to side as well as rotating on its axis—unless you are prepared to spend a few pounds on having this work done or on a new escapement which you may be able to fit yourself; the replacement may well be cheaper but, of course, will seriously detract from the clock's authenticity. Bent pivots can occasionally be straight-ened—as will be described shortly of pivots in general—although the odds are not good for balance pivots; still, there is nothing to lose by trying.

Bent, but not badly tangled balance springs can often be straightened with patience and a steady hand. To remove a balance spring, turn a prod or fine screw-driver in the collet opening to spring the collet loose. This is safer than prizing the collet up from below, though this may be un-avoidable in stubborn cases. The spring must not rub the wheel or balance cock. If it does, and is bent, it can be flattened by holding the outer coil down on the work-ing surface and pulling the collet gently upwards to reverse the dis-tortion. Sometimes the fault will be found to be in the pinning of the spring in the stud, or in a twisted pinned section. These troubles can be rectified with patience. Note that the pin should have a flat-tened surface to lodge against the spring in the stud.

Balance and balance spring

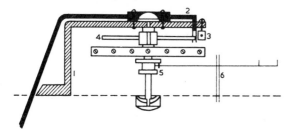

1 Balance cock
2 Regulating index
3 Spring pinning stud
4 Spring and split collet on balance staff
5 Roller (not always present) and impulse pin
6 Lever and pallets

Escapements

The escapement is the means by which the oscillator, with exact regularity, interrupts the train and so governs its speed, and it is also the means by which the oscillator is kept vibrating. There are, of course, clocks with centrifugal and other governors where there is no interruption of the motor, and on the whole, electric clocks do not have escapements since their oscillators actually drive the trains. But the vast majority of mechanical clocks have an escapement of some sort linked to pendulum or balance wheel.

There is a broad similarity between the various forms of escapement. They usually comprise a pivoted steel arm (with the crutch on its arbor, or with the balance lever as tailpiece) with two tips or pins known as pallets. The pallets embrace the fastest wheel of the train (the scapewheel) and move alternately in and out of its ratchet-shaped teeth. As one pallet, under the influence of the pendulum or balance, swings away from a tooth, the tooth slides against its shaped foot and gives the pallet a little push (impulse) which is transmitted to the oscillator to keep it vibrating. Meanwhile, the scapewheel advances the space of half a tooth, when it is then obstructed (locked) by the other, descending, pallet. Sometimes the pallet is so shaped that the scapewheel does not move once it is locked (dead-beat escapement) and in other cases, generally more robust but less accurate, the overswing of the pendulum forces the scapewheel momentarily backwards against the train (recoil escapement). The recoil escapement gives a strong impulse to the oscillator, and then imposes recoil to limit its vibration.

Variations of the true dead-beat escapement (which is found mainly in turret clocks and specially accurate 'regulator'

Pendulum escapements

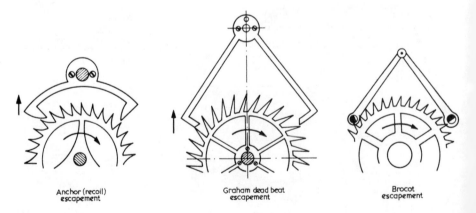

Anchor (recoil)
escapement

Graham dead beat
escapement

Brocot
escapement

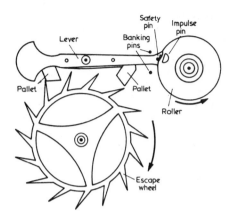

Offset lever escapement

the pallets. Good quality lever escapements with balance wheels are found in later bracket and small mantel clocks and in many carriage clocks. The 'club-tooth' lever is the more modern form. The pin-pallet form of escapement is general in unpretentious alarm and domestic clocks mass-produced in the twentieth century.

Another very common form of balance-wheel escapement on nineteenth century clocks, especially carriage clocks, is the cylinder escapement. In appearance it is rather complicated, but is readily understood if you see only one tooth, whose curved top impulses the balance as the tooth pushes its way into the cylinder. (A French recoil escapement, known as 'tic-tac' and used with light pendulums, has in fact 'anchor' pallets embracing only one tooth.) The cylinder escapement is fragile and involves excessive friction, leading to wear and imperfect time-keeping, so that it is no longer commercially made.

clocks) are used in most Vienna and 400-day clocks. The escapement visible in front of the dial in many nineteenth-century French clocks is usually the Brocot type. Forms of recoil escapement are found in the majority of long-case and bracket clocks with pendulums: the amount of recoil depends, of course, on the shape of

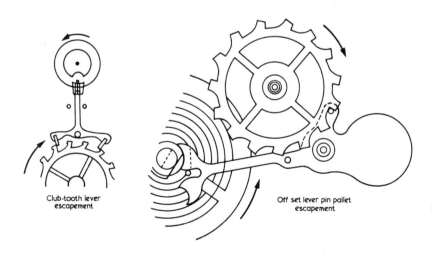

Club-tooth lever
escapement

Off set lever pin pallet
escapement

Adjusting Escapements

The escapement is the most fragile and delicately adjusted part of the clock, and its performance is vital to time-keeping—and to keeping the clock going. There are special regulations to be made to each of the various escapements and it is impossible to list them all here. Some points are common to most escapements, however.

You will see that how far the pallets engage with the scape-wheel teeth is critical: if they are too far from the wheel there will be imperfect locking and poor impulse, and if they are too close the escapement will not be able to unlock at all. Depth—closeness to the wheel—may be adjustable by a set-screw in the plate, in which the pivot hole of the pallet arbor is drilled eccentrically. It may be possible to adjust this, but approach the idea warily; these bearings are usually fitted very tightly and a sudden or excessive movement can damage a pallet pivot. If there is no such bearing, more extensive work will be needed to alter the pallet cock—though this often has slotted holes for its fixing screws to facilitate adjusting it higher or lower. Engagement also depends on how far apart the pallets are, which varies according to the wear on their surfaces. Worn pallets should have the wear stoned out and the arm closed up after application of heat, but it is safer and quite acceptable to solder a small piece of steel (part of an old spring will do) over the pallet face to make up the thickness which has worn and been stoned away.

Lever escapements with jewelled pallets can be altered by very careful moving of the pallets (which are mounted in shellac) whilst they rest on a heated metal block; tiny movements are called for and, in general, if you move one pallet out then the other will have to be moved in by almost the same amount. This is an intricate procedure and should not be attempted until you have built up considerable working knowledge of escapements.

Repairing worn anchor pallet

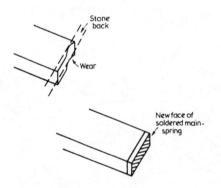

Cylinder escapement chariot

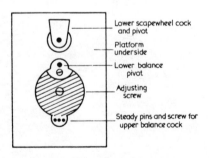

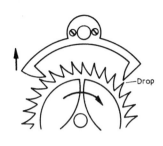

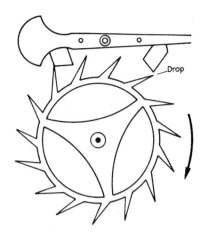

Escapement 'drop'

If replacement pallet pins of a pin-pallet are fitted, they must be of the original size and of hard steel.

The pallets of the Brocot pendulum escapement may be of steel or jewel and can be replaced by steel. These pallets must be half of a circle which is itself minutely less in diameter than the distance between two wheel teeth. This ensures freedom without wastage of power.

This freedom, known as 'drop', is the distance a scapewheel tooth has to travel before being locked immediately the previous tooth has been released from the other pallet. Drop is essential, but it has to be kept as small as possible consistent with the regular freeing of the scapewheel teeth. It will be impossible to set it properly, or to make any other useful adjustment to the escapement, if there is too much looseness (shake) in the holes of the pallet arbor's pivots. Worn holes here are extremely common and must be tightened, normally by bushing, as shown later.

The depth of the cylinder escapement is varied by moving the 'chariot' on the underside of the escapement, which carries the lower pivot of the balance wheel and also the balance cock.

The parts are no longer produced in quantity and repairing pivots or cylinder is a job for an expert. A good cylinder escapement should be repaired for the sake of authenticity, but often there is a case for replacing the escapement with a new lever escapement, for the latter are made in standard sizes, look well and perform excellently.

A final caution. If on any escapement you must tidy up a scapewheel—straightening up bent teeth—do as little as possible and, in particular, try not to touch the locking (usually radial) surfaces of the teeth. These are cut with great accuracy, sustain little wear, and control the regularity with which the escapement functions. Altering them can result in unequal drop on the teeth which will cause wasted energy if it does not cause actual mislocking.

Striking

An hour-striking clock strikes 78 blows in 12 hours, or 90 blows if a blow is also given at half-hours. The time for the train to run is proportioned according to the blows to be struck. How is this arranged, and how is it made to correspond to the time shown by the hands?

Countwheel

The older system, known as the countwheel system, has an arm, or detent, passed by a wheel with a notch or pin in it (the locking-wheel) once for each blow. The detent can only collide with this pin or fall into the notch, however, if another detent on the same arbor is also able to fall into another notch, on the more slowly moving countwheel. The countwheel is part of the striking train with the pinwheel and revolves once in 12 (occasionally 24) hours. The raised sections between its notches are proportioned in ratios of 1:2, 1:3, 1:4, etc, up to 1:12. Thus the locking which could occur for each blow is in fact overridden in such a manner that the striking train runs for progressively longer periods and gives a progressive series of blows to the bell. At 1 o'clock, and between each hour section if half-hours are struck, the notch is wide enough to let the lockingwheel revolve once, so that only one blow is struck.

There is no fixed connection between the time shown and the blows struck. If the clock is set up correctly they will carry on correctly. Otherwise, the striking train must be released or 'struck round' until it corresponds to the hour shown by the hands.

Rack

The rack system cannot become out of sequence with the going train. This is because the period of striking is governed by a proportionately stepped (or curved) 'snail' which is either fixed to the hour-hand wheel or advanced one step at each hour by the minute wheel. Just before the train is released the tail of a pivoted piece called the rack falls onto one of these steps. Once the striking train runs, the teeth of this rack are gathered up by a pallet on one of the striking train wheels (the locking wheel), one tooth for each blow struck. Striking stops when the rack is up and back in place; either a tail on the gathering pallet catches up a pin on the rack, or a hook falls beneath the foot of the rack and on the hook's arbor is a locking piece which thus falls into the path of a pin on the lockingwheel. At half-hours it is usually arranged that the rack is not allowed to fall when the train is released. Therefore, only one blow is struck. This system is, of course, suited to repeating clocks; if you release the train by pulling a cord or pressing a button, it will strike again the last hour struck— whereas if you do this with the countwheel system you get the next hour to be struck.

Strike Release

The details of release and locking vary in both systems. There is usually a pivoted lever, the lifting piece, which is raised by a pin on

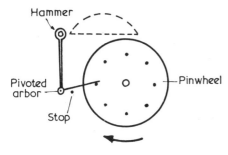

Hammer action

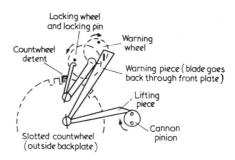

French countwheel striking

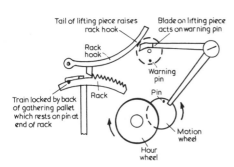

English rack striking

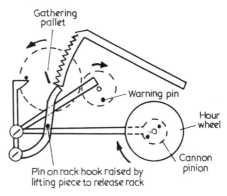

French rack striking

the minute-hand pinion (cannon pinion) or by a shaped cam on the arbor, and which directly or indirectly raises the locking piece out of the train. As a rule, the train then runs for only an instant (the 'noise' often heard 2 or 3 minutes before the hour, which may also be the rack falling on to the snail). This is because the lifting piece has an extension, or acts on another piece (the warning piece) which itself intercepts a pin on the wheel (the warning wheel) next to the fly or fan. Not until the lifting piece is dropped from the lifting pin exactly on the hour is this temporary locking or 'warning' set free; by then the main locking has been passed and the train can run.

In repeating and some other clocks there may be no lifting piece. Instead, the lifting pin pushes aside a sprung lever which, on its release, jumps back and knocks the rack hook out from beneath the rack, so freeing the train. There is then no warning. The purpose of this in repeating clocks is to ensure that the clock is not prevented from striking for some minutes before the hour as a warning system entails. For the same reason, the snail in these clocks is mounted freely with a jump spring and moved round by the minute-hand pinion only as the clock is on the point of striking.

Adjustments to striking are outlined on page 90.

Chiming

To many people a 'chiming clock' strikes the hours. To others it plays a tune at the quarters. Even this is not quite right, for there is sounding the quarters from the striking train (quarter striking), and sounding them from a separate train for the purpose (chiming).

Quarter Striking

Quarter striking is obtained by various means which cannot be set out in detail here. As a rule, it is restricted to two or three bells and requires a spring and gear train calculated for the large load. The rack system is almost always employed, and there are four lifting pins, instead of one or two, to release the train. The commonest principle is to arrange for the first three quarters to be struck on the bottom three teeth of the rack.

At the hour, the rack is fully released, and a pin on the underside of the minute wheel (ie motion wheel) moves a pivoted arm which inactivates all the bell hammers but the one for the hour. Quarter-striking carriage clocks use a more complex arrangement involving one rack for the quarters and one for the hours; both are on the same arbor, but the hour rack is held up save at the hour. A fuller manual should be consulted for detail.

Chiming Systems

For chiming from a separate train, there is again the choice of countwheel or rack methods, the latter being generally outmoded as heavy and expensive—though it is a magnificent mechanism. In either, the sequence of events is that the lifting pins (four) let off the chiming, but the hour-striking train is itself let off by an exceptional movement produced by the chiming train at the fourth quarter: this is the knocking out of the hour rack-hook as a result of the deeper fall of the quarter rack, or of a specially high fourth section on the chime countwheel. The hour train (normally rack system) is held at warning throughout the chiming and will run once the warning (operated from the chiming train) is dropped, provided that this co-incides with the release of the striking rack.

Rack chiming cannot go out of phase if properly set up. Countwheel chiming of course, can do so since the countwheel, with its four sections governing the locking, can run independently of the going train and the hands can be advanced without the countwheel's completing a run. Many

English rack chiming

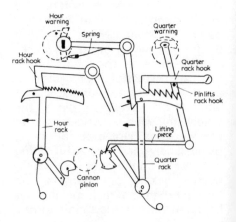

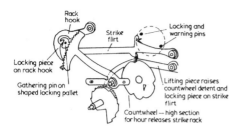

Countwheel chiming

Rack hook

Strike flirt

Locking and warning pins

Locking piece on rack hook

Gathering pin on shaped locking pallet

Lifting piece raises countwheel detent and locking piece on strike flirt

Countwheel — high section for hour releases strike rack

older clocks of this type have a pull-cord for running the chime round to the correct quarter. The modern preference has been for self-correcting devices. These depend on special locking of the chiming train after the third quarter. This locking can be released only as the hands approach the hour, so that the chiming is held waiting in silence if it is out of phase.

Chiming Sequence

The periods of chiming are exactly proportioned, just as are those of striking. The full series is composed of ten sequences on the bells or gongs—one for a quarter past, two for half past, three for a quarter to, and four at the hour. In all the commoner chimes, this total of ten sequences consists in fact of two series of five sequences repeated—the repetition starting with the last sequence at the third quarter. The series of five is set out on some sort of chime barrel, like the cylinder of a musical box, with pins or raised nicks to catch the hammer tails and, because of the repetition of the series, this barrel revolves twice in an hour.

Usually it is detached from the movement and connected by

external wheels ('ratio wheels') to the chiming train. These or the barrel can be freed so that the barrel can be turned independently of the train; this is, of course, necessary so that the barrel is correctly placed for (say) the first quarter sequence of the chimes to correspond to the first quarter position of the chiming countwheel or quarter rack.

Getting the barrel into phase may seem difficult. Remember that when the chime is not in action, all the hammer tails must be quite clear of the barrel. There will not be many places on the barrel where there is such a clear space. The clearest space is likely to be the start of the chiming series. It may then represent before a quarter past the hour, or before the third part of the third quarter. You can assume either in setting the countwheel or running the train (keeping the chime barrel disengaged) up until it reaches this point—although it is simpler to use the first quarter as the starting-point since before it the train will stop running. When it comes to old clocks whose chimes are unrecognizable, some books set out the sequences for quite a number of chimes, but if you cannot find yours you will have to settle for the best sounding sequences that you can arrange.

Adjustments to chiming are outlined on page 90.

Alarms

Alarm work involves a separate short train (often just a barrel and one wheel) but not necessarily a separate power-supply; if the same supply is used, some simple stop mechanism may be incorporated so that the alarm does not run the clock down if unattended. The hammer ends in a simple pair of pallets, much like those of a recoil escapement. These act on the last wheel of the alarm train so that the hammer is, in effect, a small pendulum with an over-powerful spring.

Setting and Release

The alarm train is, of course, held wound and waiting until it is released by the going train. There are several forms of release mechanism but they all work on similar principles. Basically, an arm is arranged to obstruct the alarm hammer under pressure from a small spring. The other end of this arm, which is pivoted, presses on a wheel with a notch or lug in it. This alarm or let-off wheel is free on its arbor, so that it is carried round by the going train but its arbor does not move, being friction-tight in the plates so that it can be turned for setting but will not move with the alarm wheel. On the end of this same arbor, above the wheel, is fixed a pin or a cam with a corresponding notch to engage with the notch or lug in the wheel. The arbor has fixed to it the setting index—either a small hand to show on the dial or a numbered brass ring (in older clocks) in the centre of the dial which is turned till the desired number lines up with the tail of the hour hand. The alarm goes off when notch and lug or pin coincide, so that the alarm wheel jumps up and releases the pivoted arm which has been obstructing the alarm hammer.

The various arrangements, in practice will be intelligible if the principle is grasped.

Single Mainspring

Modern alarm clocks often use one spring for the going and alarm trains. In this case, the cover of the mainspring barrel is separate and acts as the great wheel for the alarm train, the spring driving the cover in one direction and the barrel in the other. There are several forms of clickwork. In one of the commonest, the cover is fixed to the arbor and so turns when the clock is wound, but the intermediate alarm-train wheel, with whose pinion it engages, has an enlarged hole at the winding end, and the pivot is held in place by a spring. During winding, the cover rocks this pinion so that it does not engage but slips past and the cover revolves but the alarm train as a whole does not. As soon as the winding pressure is removed, the force of the spring and mainspring rocks the pinion back into engagement with the cover and the alarm train will run when released. The position is then that the force of the mainspring can be released through either end— through the barrel to the going train, or through, the arbor and cover to the alarm train (or, of course, to both at once).

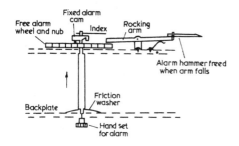

Principle of alarms

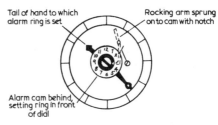

Alarm set by dial ring

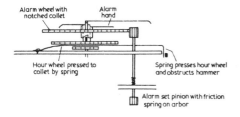

Modern centre hand alarm

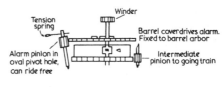

Alarm and going from same spring

Adjustment

Three principal points arise with servicing alarms. The first is that the alarm set square and arbor must present appreciable frictional resistance to the alarm wheel. If not, the clock will persistently sound the alarm at the time showing and the alarm hand will travel round with the hour hand. To correct this fault it is necessary to tighten or replace the tension spring between the alarm set square arbor and the movement plate. It may be a coiled spring or a domed washer. Secondly, adjustment is often needed to secure effective release and cut-off of the alarm—this is usually a matter of bending the intercepting arm or spring. Thirdly, an alarm cannot be set backwards, because the notch permits movement in only one direction. Damage may have to be made good to the alarm set square, the motion wheels and the alarm pin or lug if setting has been abused.

To replace the index hand (if the clock has been dismantled or the hand has come off) simply turn the set square slowly until the precise moment when the alarm train is released, then immediately press on the hand to whatever time the clock itself is showing. As a rule, play in the motionwork will not allow accuracy greater than about 5 minutes.

Cases

Clock cases are used for support, for cover and for appearance. Each of these functions merits attention. Thought has also to be given to the material of the case; this is closely connected with the design and also with the scope and nature of any possible repair. Most old clocks commonly met are cased in timber, gilt or lacquered brass or bronze, or in some form of slate or marble. In general, the older the case, the more substantial it is and the more scope there is for repair. Many modern cases use very thin metal, wood or plastics; they rely on bent lugs or welded seams rather than screwed joints, and the material is given a sprayed factory finish which is hard to touch up.

Long-cases

Long-cases invariably have a basic structure of a backboard and side-pieces terminating in cheeks across which the movements rest or are screwed. The movements are most often shackled to the seatboards, which rest on the cheeks, but are sometimes screwed through the pillars (in early clocks and in reproductions) and sometimes simply stand on them. The trunk doors are customarily hinged on the right but a few are met with hinges to the left. Suitable hinges and finials are available now from specialist advertisers.

The hoods normally slide forwards, but on the oldest clocks slide upwards. The hinged door for the dial—often with a wooden catch operable only through the trunk (which was locked)—is not found on the oldest clocks and also often not found on eight-eenth-century 30-hour clocks (which are not key-wound). Here again, hinges are available, as are fluted or 'barley-sugar' columns for the corners, together with brass caps and feet; care is needed, as with hands and dials, to find suitable historical patterns.

Backboards have often split through warping and repeated screwing to the wall; if the original is to be retained, it should be strengthened with stout battens. This is preferable to introducing new timber, and anyway, obtaining suitable wood of these dimensions is no longer easy. The base of a case often has to be replaced because it is rocking and rotten. Structurally, simple and invisible carpentry may be all that is needed. On the other hand, de-pending on the piece, the job may be better given to a skilled cabi-net-maker. As so often, questions of age, finish, general condition and value govern such decisions. So far as possible, dust should, of course, be denied entry by filling or by replacing mouldings, which may have to be made up to the correct shape.

Bracket Clocks

The same applies to English bracket clocks, where the weight of the movement is normally sup-ported on a simple table within the case, and the movement itself secured similarly or, from the eight-eenth century onwards, by stout angle-brackets attached to the back plate and the sides of the case. In both bracket and long-case clocks there may be silk side-panels behind brass or wooden fretwork to hamper dust but to emit the sound of striking. It does much for a case to replace the silks in not too garish a hue—the newly uncovered edges may reveal the original colour used.

French Clocks

Round French movements are found mainly in slate (or marble) or gilt metal cases. The white marble or limestone cases can be very hard to clean. Metal polish, fine wire wool and benzine, and car colour-restorer seem among the more effective materials to try. Black cases are best rubbed with benzine and warmed black shoe-polish. All types can be finished with a thin polish made of bees-wax melted and mixed with tur-pentine (not white spirit). The mixture is inflammable—take care and use a double saucepan. Cracks and chips can be filled with plaster of Paris, plaster filler or resin filler for strength. A complete split needs to be reinforced with steel rods before sticking and filling.

These movements are mounted with long lugs from front to back, the case being clamped between them; the movement will turn if these mountings are loose, and the lugs often need to be riveted on or tapped for new screws, or indeed, replaced with brass strip. Some suppliers will fit a new glass into a front or back bezel—trying to snap one in can be a costly mistake.

(left) *Long-case*; (right) *bracket, seen from back*

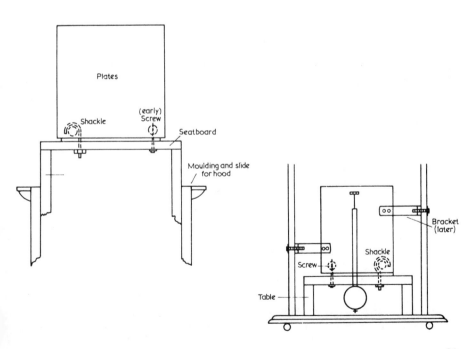

81

More Cases: Dials and Hands

Carriage Clocks

Carriage clocks are in brass cases with the movements screwed to the bases in a variety of ways, and the bases secured to the corner pillars by screws accessible from inside the base. The doors usually pivot on pins and replacement pins can be driven into the holes, the old stubs having been drilled out if necessary. Carriage-clock glasses are available from suppliers. Very careful measurement is needed when ordering them, taking in the rebates in the pillars and allowing for any distortion in the case. Where curved and oval glasses are involved, it is wise to send the original to the materials shop. Synthetic glass is subject to scratches and never looks right. You are unlikely to be able to get a good polished bevelled edge on glass you cut yourself; the suppliers' glasses are not cheap, but they are the best answer. Three or four styles (partly according to date) of blued steel hands are made for carriage clocks and it should be possible to obtain a reasonable set of the right length. Handles, unfortunately, are another matter; some are made, but they are a very poor likeness of the traditional styles.

Wall Clocks

Vienna clocks are heavy and their backboards suffer like those of long-case clocks. Once a back has been repaired, there is much to be said for fitting battens behind the clock and attaching a triangular brass hanger if there is not one already. The movements usually slide on metal brackets, often cast with the suspension cock and screwed, none too firmly, into the backboard. Sometimes the holes have to be plugged since better screws will not go through the casting. Many nineteenth-century and American wall and shelf clocks allow for the glazed front of the whole case to open, the movement being mounted on lugs screwed to the backboard, often with a gong between it and the board, making space rather tight. Sometimes the lugs can be moved and sometimes the holes can be plugged. As the back tends to be rather thin softwood the arrangement is never very satisfactory.

Finish

When it comes to finish and appearance the amateur needs to consult reference works for styles and experts for specialist work. It all depends on your own skill and experience in related fields and the value which is at stake. I would class marquetry in a long-case clock as seldom worth the risk— although of course small pieces of marquetry can be filled in by recourse to craft shops. Similarly, gilding in a French clock is better left to experts; however, much can be done to giltwork with a brush and warm soapy water, and indeed small areas and ornaments can be touched up with restoration wax or similar material, or with gold leaf and size if you have had some practice first. If little gilt is left, you may care to remove it and go over to lacquer, or you may have a lacquered case which you have cleaned and stripped. Special clear lacquer can be obtained to brush on in a warm room—do practise on scrap metal first—or you can try a cellulose lacquer aerosol which will produce a high and durable gloss. Keep aerosol coats very thin or there will be trouble with running; however, the beauty of lacquer is that you can always strip it off and try again.

Generally, a stiff polish of beeswax and turpentine is good for older wooden cases. To produce a high gloss on a large area of French polished wood is no easy matter and, in any case, is quite inappropriate unless that was the original finish. You can, however, take on small cases where not too high a polish is required, and you can attempt touching up small areas with stain and polish after removing the original coats with finest steel wool. On dark wood unfinished French polish or oiling are more pleasant to look at and more in character than modern varn- ishes. If you have a simple painted or varnished long-case, try to resist the fashion for stripping and leaving it 'natural'; it is a mistake to suppose that these cases were often left natural originally.

If you have a valuable ebonized case, consider expert treatment. Alternatively, black French polish can sometimes be obtained, but you will not be able to bring it to a grainless finish without having acquired skill in true French polishing. (Practicable ebonizing procedures are described in information bulletins issued by manufacturers of materials.)

Dials and Hands

Dials and hands can now sometimes be obtained through, or made by, suppliers advertising in the periodicals mentioned at the end of this book. Materials are advertised for silvering and blacking the figures of an old chapter ring, or you may like to try the traditional methods set out in several manuals. Do not use metal polish on a silvered dial or ring, or it will be silvered no longer; clean it up with a paste of cream of tartar and water on a soft rag then lacquer it. Whilst you can do minor touching up with oil paints, complete restoration of a painted iron dial is best attended to professionally. For carriage and French clocks, whose enamels often cannot be repaired, there are reproduction dials on the market; however, a carriage clock with a cracked or reproduction dial cannot have the value of the perfect article. In this connection, look to see signs of moved dial feet or extensive masking with patterned metal—both can indicate a damaged or replaced dial.

Hands can be made, filing from steel and blueing the bright metal in heat (see page 87), but it is a long and difficult job—and always was. Good hands in many styles are available. Try to fit replacements appropriate to the clock and of lengths just sufficient to reach the chapter rings. Obtaining the right lengths in the right style can involve a long search which may have to end in compromise.

Tools and Materials

The tools and materials you need naturally depend on how far you intend to go and how much you wish to invest. You do not need every tool on the market to start with—or finish with. Many superb gadgets exist for doing many times what you will quite possibly never have to do once. On the other hand, there is no doubt that having the right tool, of good quality, gives a certain pride and can make the difference between successful and botched work.

Immediate requirements are a set of jeweller's screwdrivers, a couple of larger screwdrivers (one with a long blade for reaching into cases), one very small and one medium-sized pair of pliers (snipe or long-nosed), small and large tweezers (preferably non-magnetic), a light hammer, and a small pair of top-cut nippers. All these can be bought from a good hardware or tool shop. In the way of materials, you must have oil (and for lubrication nothing but clock or watch oil will do, save for mainsprings—though a bottle of it will last for years), some ammonia and metal polish for cleaning, and the finest grade emery-paper that you can obtain. Buy a little of the best quality rather than a lot that is indifferent; poorly jointed pliers and unaligned tweezers are a particular nuisance. This selection will let you make a reasonable job of cleaning and asembling a movement. What you need for the case obviously depends on what it is made of.

For actual repairing and restoration you need rather more. You will certainly have to work on holes and pivots, so assortments of fine files, broaches and punches must be obtained. Broaches are tapered lengths of hard steel with five sides, and are used for enlarging holes to a fit. Punches should include some solid and some hollow. You can buy 'staking tools', at various prices, for keeping punches vertical—a cheap holder is also made for the purpose. You could either buy wood handles for files and broaches, inserting the tangs at red heat, or use a pin-vice to hold them; they are dangerous without handles.

At this stage you might build up a selection of drills—twist drills for the bigger work, spade or fluted drills for finer jobs—they can be bought in assortments. A hand drill is inclined to be too heavy and to wobble; there are archimedean drill stocks and various powered (some battery) alternatives. You could invest in a set of fine taps and dies—the type of thread is not very important as you will use them mainly for fitting new screws where old ones are lost or holes are worn, and the old screws and holes do not conform to modern pitches.

If you are going to make a habit or hobby of working on clocks, you will be well advised to obtain a mainspring winder of suitable size. A collection of keys, or a star of keys in several sizes, is extremely useful and can be had from a supplier.

You will need a bundle of peg-wood for cleaning holes and pinions, and your cleaning materials could also be supplemented by a block of tripoli compound (cheap and useful), a variety of brass and hair brushes, possibly material for silvering, and perhaps even a small polishing and grinding motor with a flexible drive and a set of buffs and burrs for use with it. This sort of thing, like a special workbench or adjustable light, or in time a lathe, is, of course, a more ambitious investment.

Humbler needs still to be met are clock pins (iron or brass), bushes and screws, and pendulum suspension and balance springs—all can be had in assortments. You may also need clear lacquer, since even on a wooden case there are usually metal fittings which benefit from cleaning and then need to be sealed.

All these items can be obtained from specialist suppliers, many of whom advertise in the trade papers, telephone directories and in the horological journals. Larger suppliers produce extensive catalogues and run mail-order services, but note that there may be a minimum order charge.

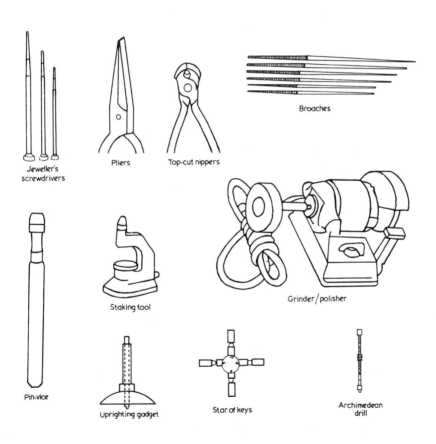

Jeweller's screwdrivers

Pliers

Top-cut nippers

Broaches

Pin-vice

Staking tool

Grinder/polisher

Uprighting gadget

Star of keys

Archimedean drill

Dismantling and Cleaning

Dismantling

There is a fairly standard order for taking clocks apart: remove the case, take off the power-supply, remove the oscillator and escapement, take off the hands and dial, remove all parts outside the back and front plates, separate the plates and remove the trains, keeping them separate. With a long-case clock, first stop the pendulum, then remove the weights before the pendulum. Steady the movement lest it tip.

In all this, the action needing special comment is removing the power. Springs must be let down carefully, holding the winding squares in a large key or hand-vice and pushing the click aside against its spring so that the mainspring comes down slowly and is always under control; otherwise, it is a danger to you and to the clock. (With a fusee movement, it is the mainspring square and click which are used, not the winding square and fusee click, which is inaccessible.) In a few clocks—particularly alarms with only one mainspring—this procedure is not possible; you must, therefore, take the power by placing a finger on a wheel, remove the escapement and let the trains run down—which takes time and is not very good for them.

Do not hurry. Take the opportunity to inspect parts for damage as you remove them. Keep all screws and small springs with the parts to which they belong. If necessary, lay out the parts on paper with a diagram and make notes—a note of which way up the wheels go can save a good deal of time, for instance. Clean the parts a few at a time if it is a strange and complex clock, returning them to their place on the paper. It is often particularly helpful to have a sketch of the layout of the front plate. Note that some parts may be marked with punched dots to show that they belong to the same train.

Cleaning

For the amateur, traditional cleaning is best—indeed, many hold that it is always best, if only there were time for it. The method is to soak brass parts (and arbors) in a solution of household ammonia and soap—washing-up liquid serves well and a roasting pan is a useful receptacle. Start with the solution fairly warm. The time depends on how dirty the parts are and how dilute the ammonia is; 2 or 3 hours is usual. Make sure they are completely covered; 'high-water marks' can be very difficult to remove and re-soaking is the best answer if they arise. The parts will emerge a dull yellow. Brush them out under a running tap, giving the wheel teeth an extra hard scrubbing, and then turn to finishing them. For older bracket and long-case clocks, a high polish may not be appropriate—in the trade these movements were often cleaned merely by soaking in paraffin. A pleasant finish will be given by hard rubbing with a rag charged with machine oil and rubbed on a tripoli block to pick up the abrasive. The resulting mess can be removed with methylated spirits. For a finer finish, liquid domestic brass polishes are quite satisfactory; impregnated wadding will add little to the cleaning, and 'long-term' polish, whilst it works, really needs to be preceded by a harsher brass polish.

Steel can be attended to with fine files and the finest grade emery-paper glued round a stick of wood (say 2.5cm (1in) wide and 6mm ($\frac{1}{4}$in) thick) to form a buff—buffs can be obtained ready-made from the materials' shop. Pinions are difficult to clean but an oiled edge of emery-paper and a piece of shaped wood will help. Ensure that pinions are dry after cleaning. Items which are of blued steel can either be painted with blue steel enamel (from the suppliers) or be properly re-blued with heat. This involves having them brightly polished and entirely free from grease (including finger-marks), and heating them slowly on a brass tray (or better still in brass filings) until just before they reach the desired shade, when they are plunged into oil. It takes practice but is more pleasing in effect than any painting.

Before assembling, all holes in the plates should be pegged out—their hard deposits of oil will not necessarily have come away in the soaking. Pegging them out consists of twirling pointed pegwood sticks (from the supplier) in each hole until the sticks no longer come out blackened with oil. You will have noticed during stripping which holes need to be tightened but may now also see others which are oval, and these must be dealt with as described shortly.

Remove a mainspring barrel cover (by tapping the arbor from the back rather than by prising it off with a screwdriver) and make an inspection. Turn the arbor and see that the inner end of the spring catches firmly on it. Check that the outer end is secure. If all is well and the oil does not appear too congealed (and there is no rust) consider applying a few drops of machine oil to the coils and leaving well alone.

To remove the spring without a mainspring-winder, secure the barrel, open end up, between pieces of wood in a vice, and then twist the spring out with pliers—be very sure the barrel is held firm. Wear leather gloves to replace the spring in the barrel by hand.

If you are unsure, do not separate the balance spring from the wheel—do the best you can to clean them up dry. If you take the springs off, they are best soaked in benzine or petrol and dried between blotting paper. Never let them come near oil. You must, of course, peg out jewelled holes, but real care is necessary for they are very brittle.

Hand vice for letting down springs

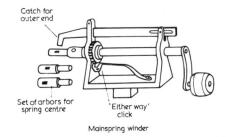

Catch for outer end

Set of arbors for spring centre

'Either way' click

Mainspring winder

Bushing and Pivoting

As a gear train is essential in a mechanical clock and as it involves continued friction of tooth against tooth and pivot against hole, every clock requires periodical servicing, the trueing of holes and renewing of surfaces. This is necessary for all arbors, or the wheels will gradually cease to mesh properly, and vital in such holes as those of the pallet arbor where excessive shake will make the escapement unreliable and eventually inoperative.

Drawing and Bushing

Holes naturally wear away and become oval in the direction of pressure, losing their original centres as minute particles of either surface become embedded and act as fine files, however well lubricated. The repairer has to restore the true centres of the holes and to ensure that the pivots running in them have proper 'sideshake' and 'end-shake'. The two objectives are achieved by 'drawing' the hole back to its centre and 'bushing' it—riveting into the enlarged hole a small cylinder of brass (to be had from the supplier), with the right hole for the pivot. This 'right hole' is a matter of feel rather than of engineering measurement and will be found by experience, but there is no reason why you should not make a satisfactory job of drawing and bushing your first hole.

As the back wall of the hole will be little worn (being relatively free of pressure) it is possible to judge the centre of the original hole.

Select a bush which is a close fit to the pivot, and estimate how much of this rear wall has to be removed to accommodate the bush with the hole in the true centre. (The bush must be thick enough to more than reach the worn wall.) Then with a round file, take the hole back to that point and gently make it round with a broach, keeping the broach carefully vertical. All this work is done from the inside so that the enlarged plate hole has a taper and the tapered bush will seat against it and be unable to fall out.

Tap the bush in level, filing flush if necessary with a guard under the file to avoid scratching the plate. Ensure that the finished bush is not longer than the pivot or the latter will burrow a hollow in it. With a punch, rivet the bush in from the outside of the plate and then try the pivot for size. The pivot should be a little large, so that you must very lightly broach the

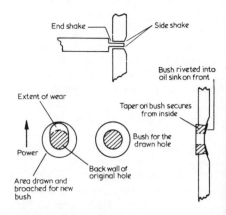

End shake — Side shake

Bush riveted into oil sink on front

Taper on bush secures from inside

Extent of wear

Power

Bush for the drawn hole

Back wall of original hole

Area drawn and broached for new bush

Badly worn wheel which might reverse on its arbor to offer new surfaces

bushed hole. Use oil on the broach as this will help to burnish the hole. Be very careful to keep the tools and the bush upright—this is best done by constant rotation of the work. When you have done the job, try the wheel and its neighbours between the plates—this is most important, or you may assemble the movement and find that the wheel will not turn freely.

Pivoting and Wear

Wheels affected by badly worn holes are often deformed, part of one side of each tooth being worn away. Ideally, the solution is a new wheel, and there is little option with pinions, but it is sometimes possible to reverse a wheel on its arbor. Pivots wear anyway, but particularly where there is too shallow a hole, as a result of which a knob, the size of the original pivot, protrudes whilst the acting pivot is reduced. Pivots can be improved by fast but light filing

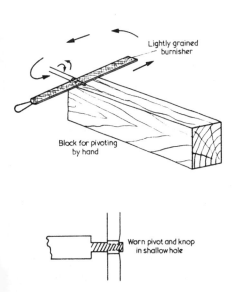

Lightly grained burnisher

Block for pivoting by hand

Worn pivot and knop in shallow hole

with a virtually toothless file (or, better, a blank steel strip that has been roughened with medium emery) in a hardwood block with a notch in it such as to leave the pivot proud. The pivot must be kept revolving during this process. The fine pivots of balance-wheel escapements and of the faster wheels of French and carriage clocks are best left to the expert.

Broken pivots strictly call for replacement, preferably of the whole arbor, and you should send the plates with the wheel. However, the really large pivots of a mainspring or great wheel can sometimes have the studs flattened and holes drilled to receive steel wire. The holes should be rather deeper than the length of the visible pivots. The difficulty is to get the holes central and straight without a lathe, but there are tools which will assist with this, as with the vertical location of bushes.

Bent pivots, if not too fine, may sometimes be straightened, and there is nothing to lose by trying. The end of the arbor will have to be heated to cherry red (as it will if it has to be drilled) and allowed to cool as slowly as possible—preferably it is wound with iron wire to slow the cooling process. You can then try to straighten the pivot with pliers or tweezers, or with a fine hollow punch placed near the pivot and used as a lever. Several attempts may be necessary, trying the wheel in the plates between its neighbours each time. Afterwards, the metal needs to be heated again and plunged into cold water whilst glowing, to restore its hardness, and it will then have to be polished.

Setting up and Oiling

Even if you know where all the parts go and believe you can get them in, there are certain points in reassembly and starting the clock where special knowledge is called for.

Setting Striking and Chiming

The golden rule is that, whatever the system, the pinwheel or chiming barrel must be so placed that no hammer tail reaches it when the train is locked. Chime barrels can usually be turned after the movement has been assembled. Striking pinwheels are generally between the plates and they must be positioned, and if necessary repositioned, during reassembly until hammer tails are well clear of the pins when the train is at rest.

Matching Sounding to Going

Motion wheels, like locking wheels, are often marked to show engagement. This is usually to ensure that the clock sounds exactly on the hour or half-hour, and that the snail's steps correspond with striking. Some experimental turning of the wheels may still be needed.Where a clock cannot be made to strike correctly on the hour, it may be necessary to turn the hand on its squared collet and then to rivet it in place. Only as a last resort should lifting pins be bent or moved, for there must be a presumption that they started off in the right place. This applies particularly to a half-hour pin

designed to release the train but not the rack.

When an hour hand is fixed to its wheel and shows an hour when the minute hand is not pointing to 12, it is usually necessary only to loosen the motionwork, hold the minute wheel still and turn the hour wheel a tooth or two in relation to it.

If, after every attempt with the motion wheels, a rack does not fall correctly, it is possible that the angle of the rack to its tail has been altered during cleaning (or that the rack has been bent). Rack and tail are often friction-tight and can be moved, for their angle determines how many blows are struck for a given position of the tail. This fault may also be indicated if the gathering pallet does not pick up the rack teeth cleanly. Make sure that rack and tail are tight enough not to slip in normal operation.

Setting up Springs

Fusees and stopwork have to be set up so that the mainspring is partially wound even though it can deliver no power. For a fusee, wind all the line on to the barrel neatly and hold it there whilst you wind the barrel square round once and then slide the main barrel click into place, screwing it up firmly. Stopwork is an arrangement in various forms to prevent the spring from completely unwinding and also to prevent its being overwound. It usually consists of a finger or wheel on the barrel arbor, engaging with a free wheel which has a projection or several uncut teeth. Hold the barrel and wind up for about half a turn before fitting

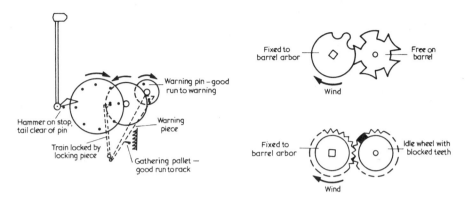

(left) *Setting up striking (and chiming) train*; (right) *two forms of stopwork*

the stop wheel in such a way that the spring cannot unwind.

Setting in Beat

Clocks will not run reliably unless their oscillators are 'in beat'—indicated by entirely regular ticking or, visibly, by the pallets hanging or swinging an equal amount to either side of the centre of the scapewheel. A balance wheel and spring must be turned until in beat, which may mean turning the spring round on the staff so that its vibrating length remains the same (see page 68). Several attempts may be needed, especially if the design is such that there is no straight line through the balance wheel and lever to the scapewheel.

Pendulum clocks, as they are ruled by gravity, generally have to be set in beat where they stand or hang. Adjustment is by moving the crutch to one side or the other in relation to the pallets, until the ticking is even. In most clocks this means careful bending of the crutch. In many French clocks the crutch is friction-tight on its arbor and can be turned rather than

bent, if you hold the pallets to protect them. On some Vienna regulators and good-quality modern clocks, the crutch is adjustable—the pin fitting into the pendulum's slot is mounted on a screw, or the crutch is in two halves which are movable in relation to each other. Four-hundred-day clocks are set in beat by turning the pendulum suspension assembly.

Oiling

Everyone knows that clocks need oil. But they are not cars. It is as bad to overdo it as to omit it, and you must use only clock oil. Before replacing the under-dial work on the front plate, place a minute drop of oil in each pivot hole (not enough to fill the recessed oil-sink). If you leave this oiling till later, you will not be able to reach all the holes. Then, before you put the dial on, oil the other rubbing surfaces, except that oil should *never* be applied to the teeth of wheels and pinions, or to a balance impulse pin, since it will merely collect dirt and cause wear.

Long-case Clocks

From the end of the seventeenth century the long pendulum, anchor escapement and case with a trunk were a standard combination. It was to remain basically unaltered until it died out, in its traditional form, in the mid-nineteenth century. There were, of course, important changes of detail—the proportions of the case, the shapes of applied moulding, the design of dials and hands, the introduction of arched tops and dials. These are useful for dating a clock or parts of it (for many are 'marriages' of differently dated components) and can be looked up in the standard books on the subject.

There seem to have been from the start two distinct long-case clocks: the 30 hour and the 8 day. Clocks going for a month or a year are also found but were, even in their own day, expensive rarities.

The 30-hour clock descends from a long line of 'day' clocks driven by weights, with the trains originally one behind the other between strip plates wedged in iron- or brass-posted frames, and having a large bell on top. Later, similar trains were placed between full plates with the gear trains side by side, as with key-wound 8-day clocks from the 1670s (but 30-hour clocks for some reason usually have the striking train on the right).

Whilst the sumptuous specimens and the work of small provincial makers alike evince many novelties, the long-case clock mechanism is in outline pretty standard—a seconds pendulum with recoil escapement, rack striking for 8-day clocks and, more often than not, countwheel striking for 30-hour versions. A day-of-the-month indication is common from about 1685 onwards; it consists of a pin on the hour wheel turning a wheel of ratio 1:2, this turning a large thirty-one-toothed ratchet, with the figures on it, every 24 hours; alternatively the pin on the hour wheel turns a smaller ratchet, but with sixty-two teeth, every 12 hours. If missing, these parts can reasonably be cut and filed by hand. (In short months the ratchet has to be advanced by the owner.) In later models there is often some moving device, which may or may not have precise horological significance, in the break-arch and worked from the pallet arbor or by a cam and lever from the hour wheel. Seconds hands on the extended scapewheel arbor were introduced some 10 years after the seconds pendulum (c1665) and rapidly became normal. Centre seconds, which involves a more complicated train, is not common.

Many parts for long-case clocks, including finials for cases, are available in blank or finished form. A missing wheel is rather a serious problem and probably a job for the professional, although wheels with few teeth can sometimes be made by hand. A movement with badly worn pinions throughout may run for a while on heavier weights, it should not be allowed to, and ultimately you will have to have new pinions cut, which will be neither cheap nor original. So caution is advised in purchasing.

The lack of a countwheel can be made good by using a cardboard blank disc and marking where the detent falls on it for each sequence of blows. There should be 78 equal divisions round the disc. When your disc works, transfer it to sheet brass. If the associated gearing is missing, some manuals tell you how to replace it; the ratio is usually 1:6 from a pinion on the back of the greatwheel arbor—knowing this, you can also make a new pinion if need be.

Movements have to be cleaned, but a high polish is not usual. The structure of long-cases is usually amenable to simple repair, but a suitable finish may not be achieved at the first attempt and consultation of a book on restoring antique furniture (or of a craftsman) is advisable. If you are completely new to working on clocks and contemplate renovating a long-case clock, it would be worth reading the articles specifically on this subject in *Horological journal,* March-May 1979. These also form an excellent introduction to working on clocks generally.

'Regulators' have not yet been described. The term is used rather widely. The true long-case regulator is designed purely for accurate time-keeping, does not strike and has separate chapter rings for hours, minutes and seconds (which are usually central). Common features are a dead-beat escapement, a compensated pendulum, jewelled holes, and wheels and pinions with many teeth (high count) to reduce play. There are heavy plates with at least five pillars. The regulator tends to have a simple, architectural elegance— though there are exceptions. You would be unwise to work on one of these lovely pieces before you have gained wide experience of working with clocks.

(left) *30-hour posted movement*; (right) *an English regulator*

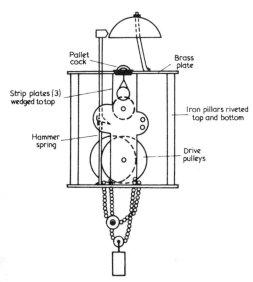
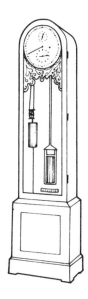

Bracket Clocks

Most clocks so called have not and never have had brackets made for them, and probably always stood on any piece of solid furniture or a shelf at a convenient height. However, clocks with their own brackets were made, particularly in the late eighteenth and nineteenth centuries, and the term was thereafter applied more generally in contrast to long-case and wall clocks. The oldest bracket clocks approximate in appearance and design to the scaled-down tops of long-case clocks, with whose fashions they interplayed in a complex manner. The term is now reasonably extended to include fusee standing clocks with solid movements of a traditional character but cases in a variety of shapes, always of wood, up to about 1830. After this time, table and shelf clocks become of great variety, there is much importation and, to my mind, the term 'bracket clock' is usually inappropriate except with a reproduction. 'Mantel clock' is more useful for the later forms. But you must face human nature and accept that you may follow an advertised 'bracket clock' across the country only to find that it is a Westminster chimer of the 1930s.

Bracket clocks cover a very wide range, even if you restrict them in this way. The preference was for pendulums of about 25cm (10in) long and rack striking or chiming which enabled repetition work to be fitted for use at night— and, no doubt, for show. The earliest clocks, however, date from when rack striking was barely established and use countwheels, generally engraved; these are outside the price-range of most ordinary collectors now. Developments in the long-case—design of the dial, rings round keyholes, use of finials, introduction of the break-arch, and so on—appear in bracket clocks and are some guide to dating. The various shapes of case tops are particularly distinctive.

Seconds hands are rare until the end of the period and day-of-the-month indicators are less universal, no doubt because this function was performed by the main house clock. Instead, you quite often find that the dial has an elliptical slot above the hands. In the slot, between the dial and the front plate, swings (or used to swing) a 'dummy pendulum' (a brass circle, rose, star or other device) fitted to the pallet arbor and swinging when the clock is running. If the slot is wider than now seems justified, this is because it was made for the pallets of the old verge escapement, whose light pendulum had a much bigger arc than that of the pendulum for a recoil escapement.

Bracket clocks often have glazed back doors and possibly glazed side-panels. They may well have been placed against mirrors to reveal their glory, for the back plate may be beautifully engraved all over. The extent to which bell standards, pallet cocks, and so on, interrupt this engraving, may indicate how far the movement has been altered. In the nineteenth century engraving continued, but increasingly it was restricted to the edges of the plates and suggests mechanical cutting or stamping rather than hand engraving.

Bracket clocks tend to be highly wrought and finished in great detail. They are more difficult to clean well and, as the parts are smaller, more difficult to repair. Damaged wheels and pinions here will generally have to be replaced. A broken pivot may well entail a new arbor. Parts and ornaments can be obtained, but less easily than for long-case clocks, because there is more variety of size and type.

Handles, frets and the like should be stripped and relacquered, or sent for regilding if appropriate. Gold paint is never satisfactory for the whole article, although paint or wax may be used to touch in. Plates need to be polished as well as cleaned. If they are unengraved, but grained, more modern back plates require hard rubbing, absolutely straight down (lifting for the 'up' stroke), with medium emery on a cork sanding block. As it will be very sensitive to oil and fingermarks, there is something to be said for then lacquering the back, but it is essential to clean out the holes afterwards. This finish is not appropriate, as a rule, to pre-nineteenth-century back plates, which were not finished with a grain and should be kept in their original state as far as possible.

One-piece silvered dials—that is, without a detachable chapter ring—started to appear in about 1770. They are very difficult to restore by the usual silvering methods as the finish is inclined to come out patchy and heavy; since the dials mean so much to the appearance of these clocks, they are better dealt with by specialists, but it is worth trying to brighten them up with cream of tartar paste first.

The mainsprings are about 50mm (2in) high and extremely powerful. If you are obliged to have one out of its barrel because of breakage, think twice before removing it (unless you are experienced with a mainspring-winder) and consider sending the barrel and spring to your supplier with a view to replacement of the spring.

Regency bracket clocks

Vienna Regulators

This is a term often used for a good-quality pendulum wall clock with a glass front to its case and small brass-cased weights. Strictly speaking, however, a Vienna Regulator was made in Austria in the first half of the nineteenth century. It had a dead-beat escapement, a long pendulum (but beating less than seconds), a regulator dial (ie separate chapter rings for hours, minutes and centre seconds), the pendulum suspended from the backboard, maintaining power to keep the power on during the process of winding, and no striking. Such clocks, whose cases tend to be plain and made with a great deal of glass, are hard to come by and valuable.

Later clocks often so-called, are of similar dimensions, but have concentric hands (save for a small seconds hand attached to the scapewheel arbor which will not in fact record seconds), generally more ornament on the dial (which is often tinted rather than white), and, frequently, striking (rack) and even chiming trains. Whilst they are not in the same class as the true Vienna Regular, these clocks are still finely made and of pleasant appearance. Of recent years, they have ceased to be available in junk shops and have become expensive. Moreover, good reproductions are being made which is a sure indication that the real thing is in demand.

Very different still are the pint-sized reproductions made in the early years of the twentieth century. These are mass-produced units, spring driven, generally with a coiled gong screwed to the back for striking, and with a pendulum in imitation 'gridiron' compensation form—the bob usually being faced with enamel carrying an ornament or the letters A/R (Advance/Retard) to show how the rating nut is to be turned. The many wooden finials and ornaments on their cases—as on the larger weight-driven clocks—seem sometimes to have been detachable for ease of transport or storage, and sometimes to have been glued; some are frequently missing and replacements have to be turned on a lathe, or else all ornament has to be removed and the holes filled in. These little clocks are sometimes after the American pattern (for example those made by the Junghans factory in Germany which deliberately followed American methods and models), with skeleton plates, an offset escapement with strip pallets and striking on an internal countwheel (itself toothed and part of the train), and sometimes—the better ones—of continental type with solid plates and rack striking. They were produced in enormous numbers and neither their shape nor their sound would be universally regarded as pleasurable. On the other hand, they are a good clock to overhaul for practice—both the movements and the wooden cases—and when brightened up throughout, can be attractive in suitable surroundings.

The most complicated of these clocks are the striking and chiming 'regulators' directly descending from the true Vienna Regulator.

They are beautifully made, having fine pivots and nicely crossed-out wheels, with much attention to detail—you have only to consider how small the driving weights are and how heavy the pendulum weight is to perceive their quality. They require scrupulous cleaning and polishing—the movements are often visible through the sides of the cases—and the escapements have to be carefully adjusted for minimum drop. The pallets are almost always removable from the

True Vienna regulator

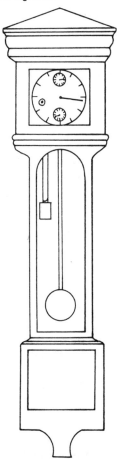

pallet arms, and have only to be reversed to present a new surface free of wear. (They are not, however, interchangeable right to left.) If one is missing, replacing it is a specialist job; the steel is glass hard and the pallet must be part of a circle with a particular circumference. The pallet arbor is normally in an eccentrically screwed hole to permit adjustment to depth. The pallets and crutch should tick steadily but slowly with the pendulum removed. Do not attempt to use long-case lines (let alone wire) for these clocks. Most often their barrels are grooved and will in any case only receive fine gut lines made for them. If these are unobtainable, gut cello 'D' string is a reasonable substitute until you can find some.

Vienna clocks of whatever grade have to be set most exactly in beat, and obviously this is more easily secured with the case vertical and the pendulum rod in the centre of the scale at the bottom of the case rather than by moving the case at an angle. (Many cases have thumb-screws with points to ensure that they do not move sideways on the wall.) The better clocks have a crutch-pin which can be moved by turning its threaded rod. Otherwise the long crutch must be bent in the usual way (see page 93), and, of course, this may take time since the crutch is not easily accessible behind the movement, particularly if there are gongs there as well. Check that the fastening of the casting or brackets to the case is firm, and do not underestimate the weight of these clocks when fixing them to the wall.

French Clocks

French mantel clocks of the last 200 years are generally identifiable by their small round movements and ornate cases, which are made of gilt bronze, marble or porcelain, or, less often, of wood. The movements usually have bezels at the front and back, and the cases are clamped between them by metal straps and screws passing through the back bezels.

These movements are much lighter in construction than the contemporary English ones and they were standardized, mass-produced and exported (hence the dial may not bear the French name) much earlier. A highly efficient design was evolved in the eighteenth century and was hardly changed for upwards of 150 years, apart from modifications to permit striking on more than one bell, a visible escapement, and centre seconds. This movement ran for 8 days and rarely had a fusee. It used large going barrels, often with stopwork, and small, delicately cut wheels with fine pivots. The pendulum was short and relatively heavy, and well into the nineteenth century it still often hung on a silk thread, which was taken in or let out for regulation by a square on the back plate or passing through the dial. Later the Brocot suspension spring became general, and this could also be regulated from the front, the spring moving up and down between close chops, or the chops moving up and down a fixed spring. A recoil escapement with solid,

angular, polished pallets was commonest, the Brocot escapement also being used widely.

Countwheel striking persisted into the nineteenth century. The countwheel fits on the extended arbor of the intermediate wheel in the striking train and is outside the back plate. Eighteenth-century countwheels usually have the hour numbers engraved on them. The countwheel detent is generally a small projection—passing through a slot on the backplate—on the locking piece, being on the same arbor as the lifting piece at the front. Repeating work and other complications are rare, even in those movements with rack striking, but a separate round calendar unit patented by Brocot was widely used in deluxe clocks in the second half of the nineteenth century and results in rather ungainly proportions. (Its complicated mechanism is described and illustrated in some manuals.) The bell is almost invariably screwed to a standard rising from the back plate, and the hammer is an engraved disc on a brass wire. Coiled gongs rather than bells indicate a date after about 1840, though bells also continued long after this.

White (occasionally coloured) enamel dials were used long before they were in England—they appear from about 1725 on.

A rough indication of date is whether the dial is flat (eighteenth century and early nineteenth century dials tend to be deeply domed), the size and fineness of the figures, and whether Arabic figures for the minutes (indicating an early date) are present. Subsidiary seconds are unusual but centre seconds are more common than on English movements. Reproductions of these clocks were made in great numbers, not only in France, in the late nineteenth century and dating can be difficult. Deep engraving of the plates (rather than a stamped motif) and very yellow metal suggests work from before the middle of the nineteenth century.

These clocks are very compact; their pivots are easily broken. and are not readily repaired without a lathe. The escapement, which often has a frictional crutch, needs to be exactly in beat—there are many teeth on the scapewheel and the pendulum has a very small vibration. Small adjustments can be made by turning the movement slightly in its case, but it must then be tightly clamped into place or it will turn, and beat will be lost during windings. Brocot suspension springs are readily available and a bent spring must always be replaced. Whilst efforts can be made with porcelain adhesives, and stick-on dials are available, it is very difficult to repair a damaged French dial satisfactorily. The hands are less indicative of date than English hands and tend to be much more ornate; they are frequently brass or gilt. It is better to try to repair a broken one, with silver solder and a blow-torch, than to fit new, stamped, blued steel hands even if they seem in good taste.

There are, of course, many other kinds of French clock but the clock centred on a standard round movement is by far the most common for the repairer. The French case as an art-form, and its proper restoration, is a specialized subject for which there is no parallel in English clocks. If you have reason to think that a French clock is valuable, it is only sensible to take reputable professional advice and to consider professional restoration. It is no good going to work on a rare porcelain panel with paint and a tube of glue.

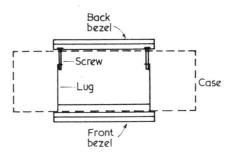

Mounting of round French movements, seen from above;

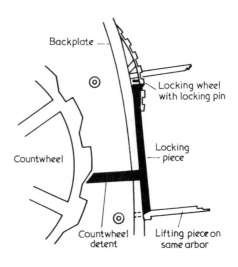

French countwheel locking (seen from behind the movement)

Carriage Clocks

Though there are valuable English examples and versions from other countries, most of the brass-pillared, glazed clocks known as 'carriage clocks' are French. The heyday of production was from about 1830–1910, though they have continued to be made until the present day and the boundary between 'genuine' and 'reproduction' is hazy. The name is obscure —the corresponding French term merely means 'travelling clock'.

The typical carriage clock has a platform escapement (lever or cylinder, or sometimes more elaborate escapement) screwed across the tops of the rectangular plates of an 8-day movement. (Clocks running 15 days and longer do occur, however.) The movement may have an alarm and striking or quarter-striking mechanisms, which were often sold as options in a manufacturer's range. Good English specimens frequently have a fusee, but French ones never do. More expensive clocks may have centre seconds and calendar work.

The plates are usually fixed to the base by screws through the pillars, but older clocks have angle-brackets or screws into the plates themselves. Striking is generally on miniature gongs; a bell indicates an early clock, as does an unglazed metal door. On clocks from the Comté region, all the striking mechanism may be on the back plate and visible through the door. The early mass-produced form of case was a single casting for top and sides, the top glass being secured by pins or screws and a concealed bezel. The later standard construction has the top glass clamped by the screwed handle bearings between the top surround and clips on the top casting, and the pillars can be detached from the top as well as from the bottom. Carriage clocks were made in a variety of standard shapes and sizes once production got really under way. Full details will be found in Charles Allix's book on the subject.

Carriage clocks are always desirable and often extremely valuable. Their prices have rocketed far higher than inflation in the past 15 or so years. To pick up a dilapidated example cheaply and to make it beautiful and going is the dream of many an amateur repairer—and it can come true. But some caution is needed. The movements are fine and fragile and they are entirely visible. You cannot get away with second-rate work on a carriage clock for it will show, in appearance or time-keeping or both. All parts, brass and steel, require polishing, and cases must be evenly finished, whether lacquered or professionally gilt.

The platform itself must be dismantled and polished. Great care is needed here. If possible, a good cylinder escapement should be retained. If not, a new lever platform escapement, with similar pinion, will have to be bought and fitted. Place it on the movement and scratch its underside along the plates to show exactly where screw-holes are to be drilled; do this while the movement is running with the platform held in place—

there is little room for guesswork. Thereafter, until testing, work on only the platform, stripped of balance, scapewheel and lever, or you risk damage.

For quarter striking, consult a book which includes diagrams. These are reliable movements if correctly assembled, but they are intricate. With alarms, pay especial attention to the friction spring between the alarm set square arbor and the back plate. If it has become flat or compressed, the alarm will not sound reliably on time.

A movement is most easily inserted in its case when held by the base and gently lowered in, leaving the door to be eased into place before screwing the base to the pillars. Sometimes, repeater buttons (which press on an angled lever to knock out the rack hook) cause difficulty by barely engaging with the movement or slipping away when the case is screwed up. It is simplest to enlarge the inside button with a little soldered brass, which will be invisible in the case. Do not case the movement until you have had it around under a glass cover for a few days to check its time-keeping and striking—it is tiresome and also risky to keep taking it in and out. Once it is in, if the movement is of a striking clock listen carefully to how it sounds; wedge any loose and rattling glass panels with slivers of cork or paper. Never stick carriage-clock glasses to the case; wedge them or replace them.

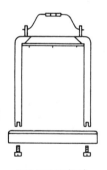

Early mass-produced
structure

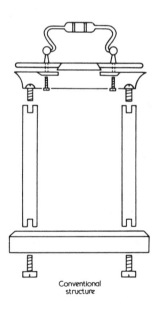

Conventional
structure

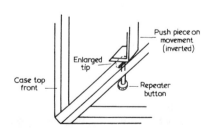

Push piece on
movement
(inverted)

Enlarged
tip

Case top
front

Repeater
button

Four-hundred-day Clocks

The 400-day or Anniversary clock was developed in Germany at the end of the nineteenth century. It is designed to run for over a year on one winding; this is arranged by having three intermediate wheels between the centre wheel and the going barrel. In modern 'electronic' models the pendulum (which on 400-day clocks usually vibrates in 6–10 seconds) is maintained by a battery-driven balance-wheel movement which in fact keeps the time; the pendulum is purely ornamental and the battery lasts at least a year.

The clock typically has a small round or rectangular movement hidden behind a metal or enamel dial and rising from pillars at the base. In the electronic versions the movement is cased, but in most others it is visible from the side through the covering glass dome. Down between the pillars hangs the heavy brass pendulum bob, suspended from a long fine spring strip. There is no pendulum rod and the bob merely hooks on to the spring. Bobs vary in design, partly according to date, those based on a sphere or a disc or wheel being early and those with four balls being from the revival of the clock after World War II. Timekeeping is determined primarily by the length and torsion characteristics of the spring (these being fixed), and secondarily by the distribution of the weight of the bob (this being varied by turning a screw which moves the balls or subsidiary weights towards or away from the centre). With the spherical bob there is a series of discs which can be raised or lowered on rods above the bob. Most older clocks have no latch for the pendulum in transit and so are delicate to move. Modern clocks encase the spring in a tube and have a clamp which can be raised from the base to secure the bob if the clock is moved.

The vast majority of these clocks are simple timepieces with a characteristic dead-beat escapement. There are, however, some with most unusual escapements, striking mechanisms, skeletonized plates, compensating pendulums, etc—you name it, somebody's tried it! The clock itself is often said to be a poor time-keeper, but short-term tests seem not to support the view; few of our domestic clocks (prior to the quartz movement) do not have their hands adjusted, usually when being wound, several times a year. Properly set up and adjusted, 400-day clocks should be accurate within a minute or two a week; within a month, as they are untouched, someone will be saying that they keep bad time when many other clocks do no better.

Four-hundred-day clocks, even old ones, are often available cheaply and are good for the amateur to work on. The movement must be well cleaned and polished, being visible, and the plates may be lacquered, leaving the holes to be cleaned afterwards. The powerful springs are best left in their barrels for oiling. The pallets are often reversible, like those of Vienna clocks. The escapements are similar also save that this escapement must be set to lock deeply, almost to the root of the tooth just past; the pallets are adjustable and depth is adjusted by an eccentric screw in the plate.

The most critical adjustment is of the fork which is clamped to the suspension spring and connects with the pin rising upright from the pallets. If this fork is too high on the spring, power will be lost and the pendulum will stop; if it is too low, it will 'flutter' as the movement vibrates the spring instead of the whole pendulum. A difference of a millimetre is everything here.

Older and newer suspensions vary somewhat in detail, as does the ease with which the spring and bob can be removed. The suspensions are U-shaped saddles for the suspension-spring pin and they are fixed to the back plate in such a way that they can be turned to set the clock in beat. To set it in beat, it is simplest to adjust to the point where the bob swings an equal amount either side after the pallets have moved. The pendulum must hang vertically seen from any direction—newer clocks have screwed feet with which to adjust this.

Glass and plastic domes are available for modern sizes. Large old versions are more difficult, but a cylindrical glass is easier to find and, whilst it may not be ideal, will often serve. Forks can be had from suppliers—they differ according to date, but modern ones are usually serviceable, although, of course, you can make your own. Likewise, modern brass suspension spring tips can usually be adapted.

Suspension springs can be obtained in assortments and, as the length is dictated roughly by the movement, experiment will eventually locate the right one. Still, it can be a long business, and it might be wiser to consult Charles Terwilliger's book which gives specifications for the great majority of models and means of identifying them. When it comes to dealing with an unusual escapement, you are on your own—but count yourself lucky, for the clock will eventually be sought after by collectors.

400-day bobs and suspension

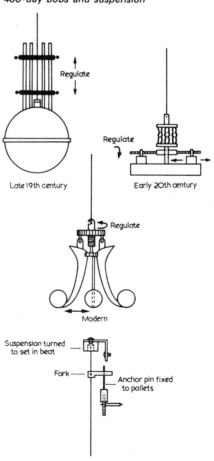

Regulate

Late 19th century

Regulate

Early 20th century

Regulate

Modern

Suspension turned
to set in beat

Fork

Anchor pin fixed
to pallets

Furniture

John Newell

Illustrated by Robin Wiggins

Introduction

The cost of new furniture has increased five or six times since the end of the war. A genuine antique may have increased fifty-fold in value. Even items made between the wars now have a sales value far in excess of their intrinsic worth. Cabinets, chests of drawers, even hard chairs, which a short time ago would have ended up in a junk shop or on a rubbish tip now find eager buyers who are prepared to renovate and repair them, not only to save money, but because the wood is more seasoned and of better quality than that used in many of today's pieces.

Furniture is subject to hard wear. Deterioration and damage in the average household are inevitable, but there is no need to make do with a shabby table or a cupboard with ill-fitting doors, still less to replace them with something new and probably expensive, before considering a simple repair.

It is always advisable, however, to consider whether a repair is justified, or whether it is prejudicial to its worth. A really old and good-quality piece, even if scratched and chipped, will probably be spoiled if the surface is stripped down and a veneer or synthetic polish put on it. Any attempt to disguise the consequences of great age is to be regretted. An antique may not be strong enough to withstand daily use, but it probably has its place as a treasured show piece, and anyway it has a sales value to a professional renovator who will know just how far renovation should go.

But the majority of broken, damaged and deteriorating pieces are essen-

Renovation or repair can transform shabby or broken chairs

tially utilitarian, subject to hard daily use. The main object is to ensure that they are strong and attractive to look at. For these pieces a few hours' work can transform them, prolonging their useful life and saving the modest cost of materials used in renovation over and over. Two objectives should be kept in mind: first to ensure that the repair restores the strength and function of the furniture, and second to ensure that everything that is done is so unnoticeable that the observer is unaware that the original blemish-free appearance has had to be largely restored or replaced.

Simple repair work on other

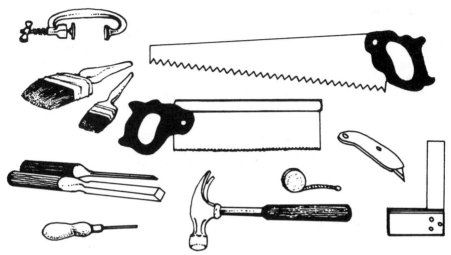

Essential tools make work better and easier

people's rejected pieces of furniture can provide you with much needed items. At auction sales there are often lots covering the residue of the sale — collections of so-called junk items of little interest to dealers. Such old and broken pieces are taken in part-exchange by furniture dealers, or sometimes simply because the customer says that he will buy new furniture only if the dealer takes away the old stuff.

Many dealers burn some of these items because it is cheaper than paying the local authority to take them to a rubbish tip. Simple items, such as kitchen chairs, children's cots and small tables can be picked up for the proverbial song. They will be dirty and probably damaged, but for literally pence spent on repair and cleaning pounds can be saved.

For this interesting and not very taxing work — one is justified in calling it a hobby for a winter's evening or a leisurely weekend – good quality tools and equipment can make all the difference between a satisfying

repair and an amateurish, make-do job.

In the following pages a few special tools and materials for unusual projects are mentioned in the description of a particular work. But for the general run of tasks the following are really essential :

Adhesive tape — gummed brown paper, cellulose.
Bradawl for making guide holes.
Chisels, at least two sizes.
Cramps.
Drill and set of bits.
Glasspaper — coarse, medium, and extra supplies of fine grade.
Hammer.
Knives — including the craft type with detachable blades.
Paint brushes.
Rules — steel straight edge, flexible tape.
Saws — tenon and panel.
Screwdrivers.
Steel wool — fine grade.
Try square for checking right angles.
Wooden mallet.

Materials

As regards materials it is better to buy as you prepare for a particular repair. Paints, spirits, adhesives, etc., which may deteriorate once the container is opened and the contents partially used, are best bought in the smallest quantity applicable for the job. This will avoid waste, as well as disappointment when tackling another repair months later.

It would be wrong to under-rate the advances made by manufacturers to cope with the demand of do-it-yourself enthusiasts. The aim is usually to make an allegedly tiresome job easier, quicker, and provide a better result. However, the craft of furniture making is an old one and its members discovered near-perfect techniques a long time ago.

Many of the materials used in manufacture and repair have stood the test of time, and cannot really be bettered, even if they sometimes involve more and slower work.

Generally speaking, it is a virtue to be a little old-fashioned in one's approach, and the shop salesman's claim that a new product is 'as good as' or 'better than' needs proof in an example of the results.

The basic materials required for the general run of furniture repairs and renovations are as follows:

Bleach – domestic type.
Fillers – usually based on plaster of Paris.
Insecticide, for woodworm.
Methylated spirit.
Paints – gloss, matt, enamel, aerosol.
Panel pins, various sizes.
Plastic wood in different shades.
Polishes – french, polyurethane, wax.
Screws – various sizes, and preferably in a brass or chromium finish.
Stains – water and oil.
Stripper.
Turpentine and turpentine substitute (white spirit).
Varnishes – clear and coloured.

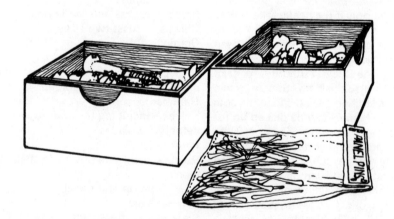

Screws and panel pins are cheaper if bought in quantity

Types of furniture wood

Before attempting any renovation or repair to a dingy, shabby piece of furniture, try to identify the wood. Layers of varnish, and possibly paint, may be concealing attractive wood, especially if the furniture is fairly old. If it is modern it has probably been covered with a veneer, which presents a more difficult problem in making any change in the appearance of the surface.

Generally speaking, good furniture is made from hardwoods, with one exception: Douglas fir, which is a golden brown softwood, has in recent years been quite widely used for modern items. It has a tendency to split.

Furniture hardwoods

Afrormosia, a richly-coloured African timber, used only in costly furniture.

Ash, white or cream, often used in plywood and veneers.

Beech, an almost white wood widely used in chairs.

Elm, used mostly for outdoor items, but occasionally for robust pieces such as linen chests and plant containers.

Japanese ash, a pale cream timber, used for light articles of fairly fragile design.

Mahogany, originating in sub-tropical areas of Africa and the Americas, has a distinctive rich red-brown colour. Many modern items are covered with a mahogany veneer.

Oak, light brown or beige, originates from England, Japan, Europe and the USA. It is used only in heavy, robust pieces with a minimum of decorative work. A characteristic is the sheen of silver flecks. Time changes its colour from light to dark.

Obeche, an African timber widely used in plywood and for so-called white-wood items for kitchens and bedrooms.

Rosewood, from Central America and Indonesia, is regarded by many as the most beautiful of all furniture woods. A purple-brown timber, it can be finished to a perfect gloss and needs no polish. As it is very expensive all but the most costly items are merely covered with a rosewood veneer.

Teak, a red-brown wood from India, is heavy and oily. It is sometimes used for furniture, but in the average home will be found as block flooring, draining boards, or as garden furniture.

Walnut, a medium-brown wood with attractive graining, grows all over the world. It was greatly favoured by the masters of English furniture design in the eighteenth and nineteenth centuries. Unfortunately, English walnut (the most beautifully grained) is now too expensive except for veneers.

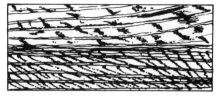

English Oak

Walnut

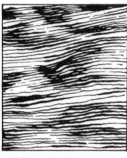

African Mahogany

Ash

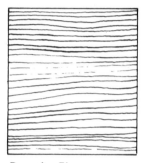

Douglas Fir

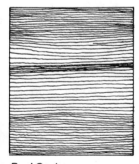

Red Cedar

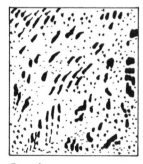

Beech

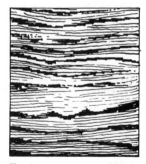

Teak

The different grains of various types of wood

Dealing with blemishes

Bruises

Veneered surfaces are prone to bruising through heavy or angular objects coming into violent contact. The only feasible remedy is to prick some holes in the dent with a fine needle, cover with a damp cloth and rub with a hot iron in order to make the wood swell. It is, however, rather a risky business as the steam may dissolve the glue and loosen the veneer.

The method works better with solid wood. In this case, of course, there is no point in pricking the area but wax polish should be removed to enable the steam to reach the wood fibres.

Burns

Usually burn marks on furniture come from cigarettes. Due to the presence of polish the burn may have penetrated well below the surface. All charred wood should be removed by rubbing vigorously in a circular motion with a tiny ball of steel wool. Plastic wood is the best filler. With the appropriate stain for the wood, experiment with varying amounts of stain in trial lumps of plastic wood until you are satisfied that you have a reasonably good match. Press in with the fingers to achieve a level slightly above that of the surrounding wood. Rub level with glasspaper and then rub in a little linseed oil. When dry wipe away any surplus and, if the patch is still obvious, brush on a little stain. A final treatment with a coloured wax polish to the whole area should produce a satisfactory result.

112

Cracks

Small cracks can be filled with stopping, available under various trade names and in the colours of the principal furniture woods. You can make your own with beeswax, rosin, shellac and powdered pigment of the desired colour. The beeswax is shredded in a small receptacle and a little rosin and shellac is mixed with it; then melt the ingredients by placing the container in very hot water. *Do not* attempt to melt them over a gas flame or electric element.

Carefully pour the mixture into the crack while still warm and fluid; the amount sufficient for the stopping should come slightly above the level of the surrounding wood. When dry and hard rub down and polish.

Home-made stopping is ideal for filling cracks and scratches

Scratches

Proprietary scratch removers are simply stains in a bottle with an applicator. Any wood stain which is a good matching colour will be effective if applied carefully with a fine paint brush. A wax crayon, if the right shade can be obtained, is good for deeper scratches so long as the area is then protected with a silicone wax polish. On dark wood iodine, applied with an artist's paint brush, can be a quick and simple remedy.

Heat marks

The light stains left by hot utensils on polished surfaces are best treated by first cleaning the area with methylated spirit to remove the wax finish and then rubbing in a light or dark tan shoe polish; apply the polish a little at a time and rub well before repeating the process until the right shade is obtained. Thereafter apply a wax polish to the whole area.

If the surface has been lacquered with polyurethane, however, methylated spirit will not remove the lacquer, and the only solution is to rub it away with fine steel wool; then stain and re-lacquer.

Stains

Heavy grease stains, notably from candles, should first be hardened by placing a polythene bag containing ice cubes on the area and leaving it till the ice has melted. Some of the excess grease can then be shifted with the rounded end of a nail file, held almost horizontally. Next lay two thicknesses of blotting paper over the mark and rub with a hot iron.

With veneered surfaces the iron should be below the lowest temperature, ie, unplugged before use.

Ink stains respond to a quick and restrained brushing with household bleach, washing the surface immediately the stain fades. Several applications of bleach may be necessary, but washing it away is essential each time to prevent the surrounding area being too badly affected. A little rubbing with glasspaper and staining completes the job.

Stains from wines and spirits are virtually permanent unless washed off immediately, as alcohol will dissolve and change the colour of most finishes. The visible damage can sometimes be minimised by rubbing in some linseed oil, allowing it to dry, and then repolishing. But complete eradication almost certainly means removing the surface of the whole area with steel wool and glasspaper and refinishing.

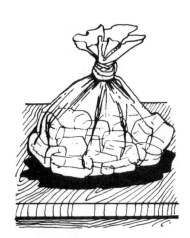

Cold and hot treatments to remove grease marks

Finishes, old and new

Modern waxes and silicone-based polishes are designed to be long-lasting and are therefore quite difficult to remove. Equally, varnishes (and paints) will require effort to get rid of them before refinishing a piece of furniture.

Removing the old finish

Burning off a finish with a blow lamp, however effective on doors, window frames and other robust parts of the house, is not advisable in the case of furniture. Damage to the surface is almost inevitable, and glue in joints will be destroyed.

Chemical strippers, either in liquid or paste form, are completely effective, though somewhat messy, and all traces of them must be washed away with warm water or methylated spirit. If it is necessary to add detergent to the water to remove any signs of grease or vestiges of polish, this must also be rinsed away with pure water. At all stages of removing the stripper and the debris, be reticent with the amount of water: wring out the sponge or cloth before each small area is cleaned rather than dousing the furniture with copious amounts of water which will rapidly soak into the porous surface and which will take hours to dry.

Always bear in mind that these strippers can injure the skin and are toxic. Wear rubber gloves, work in airy conditions, keep children out of the way, and thoroughly clean or destroy all articles used during the work.

If the finish is old or if varnish or paint has been badly applied by an amateur two or more applications of

Always wear protective gloves when using paint and varnish strippers

stripper may be necessary. If some of the original finish remains after washing leave the job until the next day and apply more stripper to those areas.

Some words of warning. Inlays, marquetry, and small carvings are usually glued to the wood. Stripper may loosen them or split them. Keep the application of stripper on such parts to the minimum to be effective and remove it as soon as bubbles appear. If the decorative section is extremely delicate it may be safer not to use stripper at the edges, but to work patiently with steel wool and fine glasspaper.

Types of new finish

With the old finish removed there comes the decision on the new one. The main choices are to bleach, to stain, to varnish or to french polish.

Bleaching

Bleaching is attractive if the wood is naturally light in colour, such as beech. It also has its points if the original stain has left patches of dark colour or if the stripper has itself caused some staining. But do not be too determined to remove all light and shade. The surface of natural wood is rarely perfectly even in hue. Domestic bleach, undiluted and brushed on is usually effective. Hydrogen peroxide is also good. Both these liquids are strong and can be injurious to the skin, so wear rubber gloves, work in the open air or near an open window, and be sure to rinse away with cold water and leave in a current of fresh air to dry.

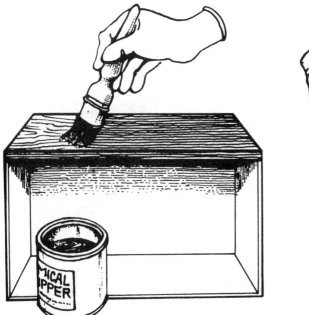

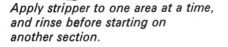

Apply stripper to one area at a time, and rinse before starting on another section.

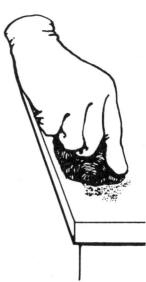

Steel wool will remove paint or varnish from awkward places

Finishes, old and new

Staining

Wood stains are of three kinds : spirit, water and oil. Spirit stain has the property of strong penetration through the surface of the wood, but it is not easy to achieve a uniformly even colour because of the way it instantly soaks into the wood, and the amount on the brush will always affect the hue. It is wise to experiment on another piece of wood in order to get the knack of charging the brush little and often and working rapidly.

Water stains are more easily applied if you work quickly and do not attempt to soak any area. The stain will penetrate quite quickly and the first appearance will be different from that a few minutes later. It is wise to dissolve the stain in fairly hot water to assist penetration, though this may raise the grain, necessitating some light glasspapering after the wood is dry.

Oil stains are usually dyes dissolved in turpentine and some petrol derivative. They penetrate well and will not fade. Their disadvantage is that they tend to soak more readily into the softer areas of the wood and may therefore cause a marked variation in colour. The trouble can be avoided by having a clean, non-fluffy cloth handy to wipe away any newly

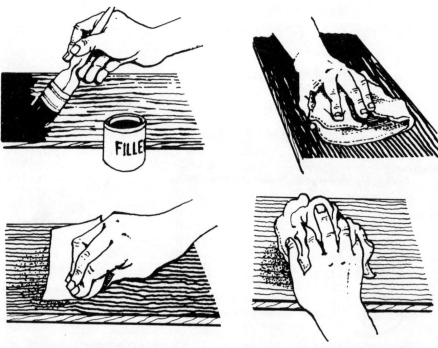

Apply filler liberally along the grain. When almost dry wipe away excess across the grain

applied stain which is apparently producing a darker colour than the rest of the wood being treated.

Varnish

The result of stripping and staining may be depressing at first glance, because the smooth glossy finish has gone. The next step depends on the type of wood — whether it is close-grained or open-grained.

Close-grained woods are ash, birch, cherry, elm, maple, yellow pine which are hard; and cypress, fir, spruce, sugar pine and white pine which are soft.

Open-grained woods are chestnut, mahogany, oak, rosewood and walnut and are all hard.

The only close-grained woods which may need a filler are ash, elm and maple. All open-grained woods need it in order to get a smooth surface. Ready-mixed fillers in light, medium and dark shades of most woods are easy to use.

The filler, which can usually be thinned if necessary to a creamy consistency with a little turpentine or white spirit, is applied with a fairly stiff brush, always in the direction of the grain. Wipe off any excess after about ten minutes with a lint-free cloth, wiping across the grain so as to prevent removing the filler from the crevices. Leave for twenty-four hours to dry thoroughly and then rub along the grain with fine glasspaper until the surface is perfectly smooth. Wipe off all the dust.

You have a variety of choices for finishing; the purpose of them all is not only to enhance the appearance but to seal the surface. Probably the most popular for the amateur are the synthetic lacquers, usually poly-urethanes. They are available in matt, satin and gloss finishes. The most useful are transparent, though it is possible to obtain them in shades which match the wood concerned, but it is rather pointless to use them on wood you have already stained, and as more than one coat of lacquer will be applied it is almost inevitable that the shade will end up darker than that desired.

Polyurethanes are very hard-wearing, resistant to water and heat, and produce a high gloss — some people would say unnaturally high. But for table tops and anything liable to suffer hard knocks these lacquers are probably unparalleled.

Lacquers should be brushed on a little at a time with rapid strokes. Allow to dry, rub over with a ball of steel wool, brush away all debris, and apply another coat. Repeat the process for a third coat.

Waxing

Waxing may be preferred as it gives a rather richer-looking finish than the synthetic lacquers. The wood must first of all be treated with a sealer or oil. Sealers are either based on shellac or polyurethane. Two or three thin coats should be applied, the final one rubbed down after it is dry with fine glasspaper to provide a key for the wax polish.

Waxing is easier with modern liquids but really there is nothing to match the solid polishes made from beeswax and turpentine — and the white waxes, not those purporting to match woods. Apply the polish in a thin layer and work into the surface with wire wool, rubbing quite lightly and with a circular motion. Repeat at least three times, finally finishing off with a lint-free duster.

117

Finishes, old and new

Oiling

An oiled finish is not so popular these days, but is very attractive for heavy pieces which are either genuine or imitation antiques. Oiled surfaces have a rich matt finish, in contrast to the shiny appearance loved by advertisers of polishes.

The best oil to use is boiled linseed, though there are branded oils which are quite good, if rather more expensive than linseed, obtainable from old-fashioned hardware stores. Linseed oil tends to darken wood but this effect can be minimised a little by diluting it with turpentine substitute in the proportion of one part of turps to three parts of oil.

Apply the oil with a soft brush or sponge, working rapidly so that patchiness does not occur. Be economical with the amount of oil, applying three coats with time in between to allow the oil to soak in and dry, the interval depending on the atmosphere, but even in dry warm conditions eight hours should be the minimum.

After the third application, which will probably take longer to dry and indicates that the wood has absorbed all it can, wipe away any surplus with a lint-free duster. You can leave the surface as it is or protect it with wax polish. In the latter case apply as for waxing.

French polish

The best finish is, of course, french polish. There is an aura of mystery about the process, inferring that only an experienced and trained craftsman can produce the unique sheen which was the usual one on small pieces of furniture, both cheap and expensive, a century ago. In fact the secret for success is to use the right material with patient application.

Disappointing results are invariably due to using the wrong french polish. There are six principal polishes, each of them suitable for a particular wood.

General french polish, composed of methylated spirit and orange shellac, is suitable chiefly for floors and unimportant pieces of furniture. It is cheaper than others, but does not give a brilliant appearance and often produces a yellowish tinge.

Button polish, methylated spirit and button shellac, gives a light or medium colour to mahogany, light to medium colour to oak, medium to dark colour on walnut.

White polish, methylated spirit and white shellac, is for natural oak and light walnut.

Garnet polish, methylated spirit and garnet shellac, gives a dark warm finish to oak, mahogany and walnut.

Red polish, methylated spirit, garnet shellac, and bismarck brown, gives a dark red finish to rosewood.

Black polish, methylated spirit, garnet shellac and spirit black, is the finish for ebony.

Brush polish, the nearest to a universal french polish, may be used on plywood which has been stained to simulate a particular hardwood. As the name suggests, it is brushed on, to fill the grain. After it has hardened it is rubbed down with fine glass-paper and then another coat of garnet polish is applied.

But for all worthwhile french polishing jobs on hardwoods the appropriate polish should be used. Any first class DIY shop will stock the type desired or make it up for you.

It is assumed that the surface to be polished has been treated with filler, stain, etc. First rub down well with fine glasspaper to achieve a perfectly smooth finish. Remove all dust.

Make a 'rubber' from a wad of cotton wool about 15cm square and 3cm thick. Fold in half. Fold the corners of the doubled edge to the centre to make a triangle. Place on a piece of non-fluffy linen or cotton rag about 20cm square. Bring back the corners of the rag and twist together over the base of the triangle of cotton wool to produce a rubber

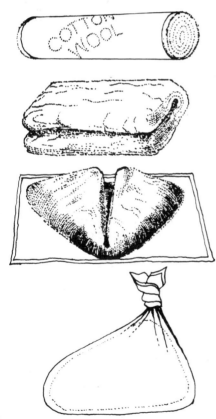

Method of making a rubber for French polishing

which is roughly in the shape of a foot, the twisted ends providing a grip at the 'ankle'.

As polish must be applied sparingly it is a good idea to pierce the cork or stopper on the bottle with a small hole so that the polish may be shaken out, a few drops at a time, on to the cotton wool temporarily removed from its protective rag (never directly on to the exterior of the rag). Replace the rag and begin polishing with a firm movement up and down the grain. When the surface has become slightly glossy leave the job for two or three hours till completely dry.

Take two pieces of fine glasspaper and rub the faces together to blunt the cutting granules. Wipe a little linseed oil over the paper and rub away any gloss on the wood. Recharge the cotton wool with polish, smear a little linseed oil on the pad cover and begin polishing with a circular motion, being careful not to lift the rubber until the whole area has been treated.

The process will have to be repeated two, three, or more times until the surface is even in appearance, though still quite dull.

The final job is to renew the cotton wool, sprinkle just a few drops of polish on it, replace the rag, and rub with straight strokes along the grain.

Gradually the oily sheen will disappear, the shellac will be hardened by exposure to the air and by friction, and the characteristic sheen of french polishing will be your reward for quite hard work. If the appearance is not up to expectations it is well worthwhile going right through the processes again. There will very seldom be failure if you are both patient and persistent.

Other special finishes

Unusual finishes worth trying on single pieces – or, if you are courageous, on all items in a bedroom or sitting room – can turn inexpensive and possibly shabby furniture into something attractive and probably unique.

Clearly it would be wrong to finish something which has good quality unspoiled veneer or is made from solid wood. But some of these finishes work well on whitewood furniture and even on hardboard. Generally speaking, a surface which is already in a dark shade needs to be bleached as a preliminary (see page 115).

Antique bloom
This is a novelty finish to be used with some restraint, perhaps on an occasional chair or the frame around a reproduction of an old painting.

Paint the item with an ivory paint (better than white though not so easy to find). When dry apply artist's glazing compound in which is mixed a little raw umber, burnt raw sienna or lamp black, depending on whether a brown, reddish or grey tone is desired. As soon as the glossy appearance begins to fade wipe away here and there to suggest parts which have aged. Protect the glazing with a coat of clear shellac or transparent varnish.

Artificial grain
This is practicable only on surfaces which are without a readily visible grain, ie, whitewood. First apply a ground coat of stain in whatever shade is desired. Allow it to dry and glasspaper till absolutely smooth. Clean away all dust.

Graining colours, called scumbles, are oil colours dissolved so that they are almost transparent. If the selected shade is rather darker than desired a little turpentine can be added.

Two flat brushes are required – 2cm ($\frac{3}{4}$in) and 5cm (2in) wide. They must be new or very thoroughly cleaned to free them from every vestige of paint.

Apply a coat of scumble very thinly with the 2cm ($\frac{3}{4}$in) brush, working in only one direction. Then go over the area with the 5cm (2in) brush, again working in only one direction.

Before the scumble dries it has to be combed. There are graining combs

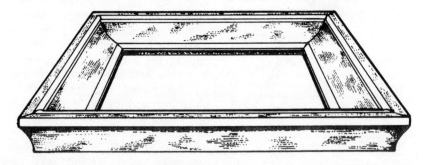

The antique finish is unusual and attractive, easily achieved with a little practice on a spare piece of wood

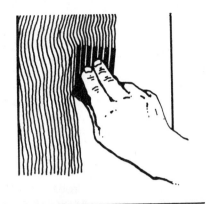

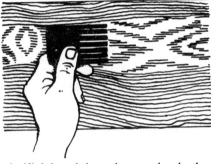

Artificial graining gives a nice look to cheaper woods

of various sizes. The teeth are of steel, so the expense of special combs can be avoided by using any metal comb. If, as is usual, the comb has one half of its width with widely spaced teeth and the other with the teeth closer together, it can be cut in half to provide two combs. Good results can also be achieved by cutting notches in a piece of thin, hard plastic, and glasspapering the points to ensure they are sharp and even.

The comb is held at an angle of 40° and drawn from one side to the other, rapidly but in a slightly wavering line. The teeth will remove most or all of the scumble, and the comb must be wiped clean after each stroke across the wood. It may well be that one comb produces all the graining effect

desired, but usually it is best to use the wide-toothed comb first and then go over the area a second time with the fine-toothed comb, this time pressing more lightly.

The lines made by the combs may appear too sharp. They can be made to look more natural by taking a dry 5cm (2in) brush and, holding it upright, dab lightly over those lines which appear harsh. This process must be done immediately after combing and while the scumble is still wet.

After the surface is really dry go over it lightly with a piece of fine glasspaper, the surface of which has been made less abrasive by rubbing it against another piece of glasspaper of the same grade.

Brush away all debris meticulously and apply a coat of varnish. Copal oak varnish is suitable for dark finishes, transparent varnish for light finishes.

Blond

To produce a light-coloured finish, known in the trade as blond but actually pale gold, the surface of the wood must be removed to get rid of any stains, varnishes or paints, using an appropriate stripper. After washing with warm water apply household bleach, washing it away with hot water once the desired lack of colour has been obtained (this may need several applications of bleach).

Leave the piece to dry. Glasspaper until perfectly smooth and apply an amber-coloured stain. When dry lightly brush over a coat of shellac, followed by a coat of clear varnish. Rub lightly with fine glasspaper and give a second coat of clear varnish. The final step is to rub over with a pumice stone dipped in linseed oil.

Other special finishes

Blonding is really best restricted to close-grained woods. On open-grained woods a filler (see page 112) should be applied after the first coat of shellac and the surplus cleaned away. But filler may not be sufficient to conceal dark stains which may go right through the wood. No amount of bleaching or filler is likely to disguise such stains. It is, therefore, wise to make a test on some part of the furniture which will not be seen before attempting to blond open-grained wood.

Bone white

This finish is attractive for bedroom furniture of delicate appearance. It can be applied to open-grained woods because the attractive grain will show through the white surface.

After stripping to the natural surface and rubbing down, apply a coat of white enamel very sparingly, witho any undercoat. Leave till dry and wipe on a coat of raw umber stain (it may be necessary to get a good hardware store to make this up for you; it consists of raw umber, which is dark yellow in colour, mixed with linseed oil and a drier). Leave for twenty to thirty minutes, watching for it to become tacky. Immediately wipe off the sticky surface.

This will leave lines along the grain which have a glistening appearance. Leave overnight to dry and then brush on a thin coat of shellac. When this is thoroughly dry polish with a silicone wax.

Shaded white

There are several tinges of colour which can soften the harshness of an item being painted white. Glasspaper the surface to provide a key and dust thoroughly. Suitable colours to mix with white paint are light blue, primrose, pink, or light green. The small tins of paint sold for touching up car bodies, etc., are an inexpensive source of this colouring additive. Experiment as to the amount required by pouring a little white paint on to a saucer and add a few drops of colour. Mix well and test on a piece of wood already painted white.

Silver-grey

This is a finish for oak, producing two tones. It will work only on solid oak, not imitations or veneers. After cleaning away all earlier finishes brush on black wood dye which has been dissolved in water. The proportion of dye to water is a matter of taste and experiments should be made on a spare piece of wood (which need not be oak).

When dry apply a filler (see page 112) mixed with an equivalent amount of white lead paste and turpentine. Allow the filler to set for about half an hour, and wipe off any excess across the grain of the wood. Leave to dry for twenty-four hours and then apply clear varnish, brushing first across the grain, and then, without replenishing the brush, with the grain. Leave to dry and repeat the two brushings of varnish. The unnaturally shiny look can be modified by rubbing over with a pumice stone dipped in linseed oil. When this is dry rub vigorously with a lint-free duster.

Two-tone

A finish to give two shades imitating oak, and eminently suitable for whitewood. Glasspaper to get a smooth finish and brush on oak stain, light or dark, according to preference. Leave to dry for about eight hours, and apply a thin coat of shellac. Leave to dry (about three hours) in warm dry conditions and brush on the same filler as for the silver-grey finish above. Leave to dry for twenty-four hours and then brush on varnish of the same shade as the stain used at the outset.

Varnish-stain

This finish virtually conceals the grain of the wood and is suitable if the grain pattern is unattractive or if a plain surface is desired.

Clean down to the natural wood, and then sponge over with turpentine to get rid of any grease or chemicals. Leave till thoroughly dry, then brush on varnish-stain. Several types are available, including those which are waterproof and unaffected by a considerable amount of heat. The only likely disappointment in giving a piece this finish is through using a coarse brush or applying the varnish too thickly. Two or even three coats, the previous coating rubbed down when dry, give an even colour and are less likely to wear away.

The gloss of varnish-stain, when new, is rather too marked for most tastes. It can be reduced to a pleasant sheen by going over the surface with a pumice stone dipped in linseed oil, and dusted when dry.

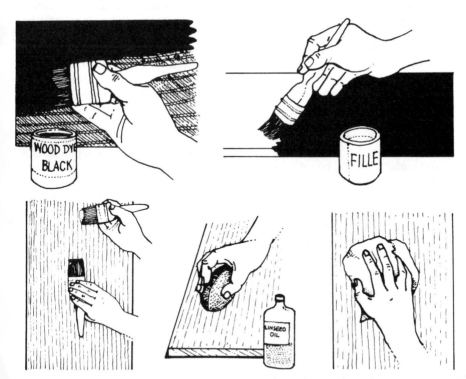

The silver-grey finish to be seen on antique oak can be produced on new timber with careful work, carried out in stages

123

Painted furniture

Probably the most attractive – and easiest – major change to make to the appearance of existing furniture is to paint it. Obviously it would be wrong to cover beautifully grained and fashioned wood of high quality. But many modern pieces, such as fitted wardrobes and dressing tables, cabinets, cupboards and chairs in bathrooms, and all wooden items in the kitchen, lend themselves to a colour scheme which can be extended to the fixed wooden items: doors, window frames, skirting boards, pelmets, etc.

The first objective is to prepare the surface thoroughly. Any existing varnish or paint must be removed with a stripper. Every vestige of the stripper and any remaining polish and grime should be dealt with by wiping with a rag soaked in white spirit, and then washed with warm water containing an ammonia-based detergent or liquid household ammonia.

The surface should be left until it is really dry and then gone over with fine glasspaper to deal with any traces of an earlier finish, roughened areas and swollen grain. The surface need not be glass smooth as it is essential to leave a key for the paint. But any dents, scratches or minor cracks and splits should be treated with filler (see page 112) and rubbed down. Finally, wipe with a lint-free duster to get rid of all debris.

Whatever some paint manufacturers may say all wood needs a primer. This is different from an undercoat. A primer produces the proper surface for the subsequent paint. An under-coat is to conceal a previous colour so that it does not show through the new colour. For softwoods the primer should be that for wood; for hard-woods it is better to use the more expensive aluminium wood primer. If you are not certain of the wood you are treating some manufacturers make all-surface primers which are an acceptable compromise.

When the primer is dry rub down lightly. If you have missed any scratches, old nail holes, etc, or if there are small spots caused by dust and grit, rub down once more and touch up with primer.

The work is now ready for the first of two undercoats. This should be of the shade advised by the manufacturers for the topcoat you have selected. If you have applied the undercoat properly and there are no runs (caused by charging the brush with too much paint and not brushing out evenly) there is no need to rub the undercoat with glasspaper.

Advertising makes much of the fact that only one coat of gloss topcoat is needed, and this is true enough on most items and with some paints. But if they are likely to be subjected to hard wear, as for instance in the kitchen or a children's playroom, a second coat applied now is better than having to deal with ugly blemishes and chips a few months later. When a second coat is applied the first one should be very lightly rubbed down.

As regards the actual painting technique you will, of course, have removed all handles and knobs. Use at least three brushes – 2cm, ($\frac{3}{4}$in) 3cm (1$\frac{1}{4}$in) and 5cm (2in) wide – the narrowest for tricky spots round key-holes, hinges, etc, the medium size for mouldings and narrow edges, and the large brush to cover flat areas.

In portable items such as chairs paint the underside first, then work from the top downwards. On large flat, vertical areas work from the top in an area not larger than 20cm (8in) square. Charge the large brush fairly generously and brush from right to left with vertical strokes, then (without replenishing the brush) with horizontal strokes. Finally brush lightly both vertically and horizontally until the brush slides over the surface and brush marks become invisible.

Do not work for an even line to the side and bottom against the areas still to be painted, and check that the paint has not ridged at the end of these brushings.

Repeat to the left of the painted area (if the job is so wide that the first painting has not gone from one side to the other) and then continue with 20cm (8in) square areas below. After the first area make the first series of vertical strokes upwards, decreasing the pressure as the brush reaches the edge of the painted area; then there is no risk of making a thick double coat at the join.

Incidentally, the non-drip jelly (thixotropic) paints, which are the principal ones for which one-coat use is advised, should be more generously loaded on the brush than with ordinary paints, and the third phase of brushing out should be kept to a minimum, or the coating will be pulled out too far and there may be patchiness, with no chance of remedying it with rubbing down for a second coat.

The second coat with fluid paints is applied in the same way, but the size of the rectangles should be slightly varied so that there is no risk of thickening at the edges, when a chessboard effect results.

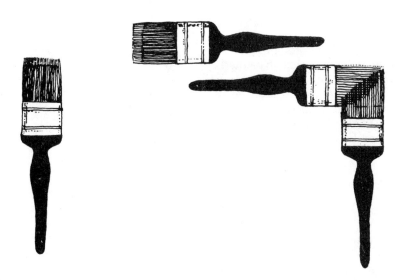

When painting large vertical areas, work from the top from right to left using vertical strokes, then horizontal, finally in both directions until brush marks are no longer visible

Stencil and transfer decoration

The question of decorating furniture with a contrasting colour or colours needs to be carefully considered. Generally speaking, it would be regrettable to spoil the immaculate appearance of good quality natural wood with even minor touches of colour.

But wood which has been painted because it has little character, as in the case of whitewood pieces in bathroom, bedroom or kitchen, can be given a stamp of individuality provided the coloured pattern is restrained. A pretty border around doors and drawers on white painted items in the bedroom, for example, will minimise the suggestion of almost clinical austerity. In a child's bedroom or playroom appropriate designs will be attractive both to child and parents.

Generally speaking, coloured decoration should only appear on painted furniture. Apart from a white background, there are possibilities in a black background with vivid reds and golds. Just how effective this scheme can be may be seen in examples of old Russian and Eastern European furniture and, of course, in Chinese and Japanese work.

Two methods are available : stencils or transfers. Both are easier to use than might be envisaged. Stencil plates can be purchased in a great variety of designs and, provided they are cleaned after each application, a plate will last for thirty or more applications, allowing the design to be repeated as a border or on several pieces.

Stencils

Stencilling enthusiasts like to cut their own stencils, and anyone with some artistic talent – or the ability to copy a design accurately – can make perfectly acceptable stencils, cut from the specially prepared paper sold in art shops. If the stencil is to be used many times it is advisable to coat each side with shellac after the design has been cut out.

The materials required for stencilling on wood are oil colours in tubes, a small sheet of glass on which to mix the colour, a round short-bristled brush, white spirit, and cleaning cloths.

The surface to be decorated must be placed horizontally. In the case of chairs, small cabinets and cupboards they can be laid on a table. Doors of wardrobes, etc, will have to be removed.

A stencil applied to a chair

Make sure the area to be stencilled is dust-free. Squeeze out the oil colour on to the sheet of glass and work with a sliver of wood to a creamy, even consistency. If the colour is not precisely that desired and you are mixing colours prepare a generous amount so that there is no risk of having to make a second mix which will almost certainly not turn out to be exactly the same.

Measure the position for the stencil with extreme care, making very light guide marks with a soft pencil. Place the stencil in position and fix with cellulose tape, making sure that there is no bulge in the centre away from the edges.

First charge the brush quite generously with paint and then dab it on a cloth to get rid of any surplus; apply the colour while holding the brush vertically, dabbing rather than brushing. It does not matter how much paint you get on the upper surface of the stencil and going a little beyond the edges of the design will ensure that the result does not have a ragged outline. Peel away the cellulose tape while holding the stencil firmly and then lift it off quickly. Immediately clean the stencil with white spirit and wipe as dry as possible before repeating the process. Leave for twelve hours and then brush on a clear varnish.

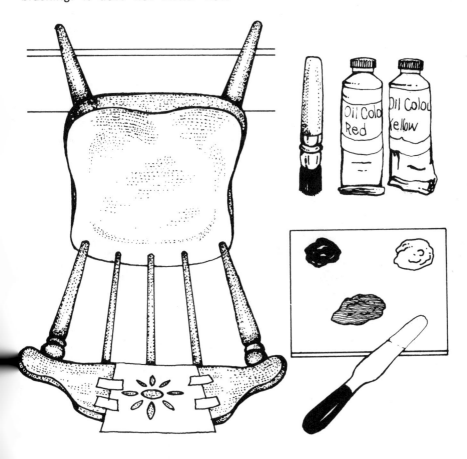

Materials necessary for applying a stencil. The area being decorated should be kept horizontal

127

Stencil and transfer decoration

Transfers

Transfers are excellent; they adhere firmly and will not peel, even with hard use as on the back rest of a chair.

They are printed in oil colours on specially prepared paper which is fairly thick and opaque, but usually an outline of the design is printed on the back for accurate positioning.

Several forms of fixative are offered by the makers. The established one is to coat the transfer with gold size or colourless oil varnish. This is applied with an artist's brush, not too lavishly and with care to ensure that every part of the design is covered but without going over the edges too much.

Now comes the only difficult part. The coated transfer must be left until the fixative is tacky – it feels sticky but none adheres to a finger lightly pressed on it. With gold size this will

Many transfers suitable for children's furniture are available

take between thirty and sixty minutes. With varnish it will be necessary to check at intervals for anything from two to six hours, depending on the temperature and atmosphere of the room.

Patience is necessary while waiting for this vital moment of the right amount of tackiness. Too dry and the transfer will fail to adhere; too wet and it will wrinkle and possibly tear when the backing paper is removed. As a final check lightly draw the knuckle of your forefinger across the surface. If it does not stick and there is a squeaking noise the tackiness is just right.

Lift the transfer from one end, turn it over and lower it into position. This must be done accurately at the first attempt, as there is not much chance of shifting it about once it touches the wood.

With a soft rag gathered into a ball rub vigorously all over the paper backing, working from the centre outwards to ensure that no air bubbles are trapped.

Next rub over the paper with a soft damp sponge, pressing firmly to help the paper absorb the water. Dampen the sponge frequently until the paper is well soaked. This will take about five minutes. Gently lift one corner to see if the transfer is adhering. If any colour remains on the paper it has not been wetted sufficiently. Smooth the corner down again and continue with the sponging.

With the paper removed, very gently wipe over the design with a sponge dipped in warm water and squeezed out. This will remove the slightly sticky surface with which the transfer was held to the backing paper. Then wipe dry, preferably with a wash leather or, if unavailable, use a soft linen rag.

With the most meticulous application it is almost inevitable that some gold size or varnish has got beyond the edge of the design. Left there, it will remain as a rather dark outline beyond the edge of the design, a defect particularly undesirable on a white background. Rubbing carefully with a rag moistened with white spirit wrapped round the end of the forefinger will remove it.

Leave the transfer to harden for at least twenty-four hours. Then coat with colourless varnish. This protective cost is not always necessary as some transfers come already varnished. They are more expensive but save trouble and obviate the difficulty of varnishing to cover the design completely yet not going beyond the edge where it might show, unless the whole area of the item is varnished.

The above type of transfer is that generally preferred by professional cabinet makers and furniture restorers, and has therefore been described in some detail.

But it should be emphasized that newer and purportedly easier types of transfer are worth considering. Self-fixing transfers, needing no gold size or varnish, are fixed either by heat (not really practical on furniture) or by a preparation already on the face of the transfer. It is first moistened with methylated spirit, allowed to reach the tacky stage, and then pressed down, the backing paper being removed by sponging as in the procedure already outlined. After the backing paper has been removed the transfer is allowed to dry for twenty-four hours and is then varnished or polished.

129

Dowels and tenons

Apart from dovetails, which are difficult for anyone but a trained carpenter to make or replace, the usual way to join one piece of wood to another in a typical piece of furniture is by a dowel or tenon.

A dowel is simply a small cylinder of wood which is inserted into holes in the adjacent pieces to be joined. Oak or beech is usually used, but any hardwood is suitable, the main consideration being that the dowel should not shrink with age.

Dowels are sold in many diameters and lengths. Their surface is smooth, and before use they should be given a serrated surface by pulling them through the jaws of firmly held pliers. This will increase the adhesion of the glue when the dowel is inserted.

In repair work the initial task is to remove the dowel which has snapped, leaving the rest of it in the two holes of the pieces which it used to hold together. This will mean drilling into the holes until all traces of the broken dowel have been removed. To obtain a close fit it may be necessary to increase the diameter of the hole slightly and to buy a dowel a little larger than the original. It will help to get the dowel well seated by very slightly tapering it at each end.

Coat one half of the dowel with glue and push home, hammering gently if necessary. Then coat the

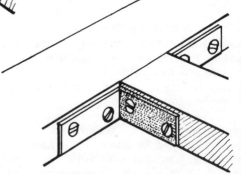

Typical dowelled joints and a tenon joint

Metal angle brackets give a strong joint. Preferably use them in a concealed area

still exposed half and fit the other piece of wood over it, hammering until the edges of each piece meet. Additional strength can be achieved by applying a thin coat of glue to the area of wood around the dowel which will be covered by the end of the second piece of wood.

A tenon consists of a rectangular tongue of wood left in the centre of a length of timber when the rest has been cut away. The tongue fits exactly into a rectangular hole (or mortise) in the wood to be joined. Both tenon and mortise have to be very accurately cut, involving gauges and special tools. The job belongs to manufacture rather than repair.

A joint where a tenon and mortise have been used can become faulty either through loosening because of shrinkage and strain, or because the tenon has broken off.

In the first case all that may be needed is to take the two pieces of wood apart, clean away the old glue, liberally coat both tenon and mortise hole with glue and reassemble, holding together with clamps or several layers of cellulose tape. If shrinkage is clearly visible, a thin layer of plastic wood smeared on the sides of the mortise hole with a thin-bladed knife will help. Leave to dry, smooth away surplus with a file, glue, and reassemble.

When one side of the two pieces of wood held by the faulty tenon is not readily seen when the furniture is in use a small metal angle bracket screwed above or below the tenon will ensure a rigid joint and strengthen the re-glued tenon and mortise.

If the tenon has broken the remains in the mortise will have to be drilled out and the surplus of the tenon on the other side cut away and the surface smoothed. Fill the mortise with a piece of wood cut to fit and glued in. Then use the dowel idea, making the hole above, below or to the side of the removed tenon and mortise. This will not produce as strong a joint as the tenon but should give a reasonably robust joint if the surfaces of the two pieces are also glued. For additional strength add a metal angle bracket.

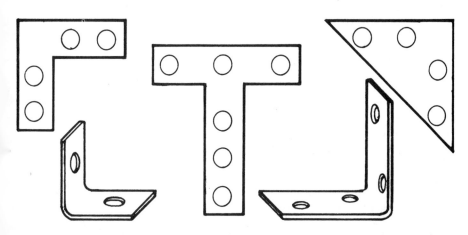

Typical metal angle brackets, all available in different sizes

Dowels and tenons

Makers of modern adhesives claim that their product will produce a bond stronger than the pieces of wood it joins. There is justification for this claim, and if the break of the tenon has not resulted in any slivers of timber falling away, and the broken ends fit like a perfect jigsaw then simply applying one of these strong adhesives may work. But it is essential that the two pieces be held immovable and without any strain for some time after joining, even with the instant contact adhesives. Again, it will do no harm to add additional strength with a metal angle bracket if it can be fixed without spoiling the appearance of the furniture.

In some T and L joints screws may have been used, especially if an earlier attempt has been made to repair or strengthen the joint. It is probable that the screw has been countersunk and the head concealed with filler or painted over. This concealment will have to be scraped away and the head of the screw cleaned in order to give a screwdriver a good grip. Unfortunately it is almost certain that the screw has rusted.

It may even have been unwisely given a coating of glue with the object of making a secure fix. A few drops of rust removing fluid or sewing machine oil rubbed around the screw head may help to loosen it if left for an hour to soak in.

Always use the correct size of screwdriver for the screw head when using strong pressure to turn it. Too narrow or thin a driver will almost certainly widen the slot or actually break it off.

If all attempts fail to move the screw with a screwdriver there is the heat method. Heat an old screwdriver until the metal is dull red and press the point against the screw, holding it there until the metal cools. The heat will have spread to the screw and caused it to expand. When it cools and contracts it should be looser.

A last resort is carefully to chisel away around the screw to make enough room to use narrow pliers held vertically. Here again, if the body of the screw is tightly embedded in the wood the head may break off. Then it will be necessary to drill down with a narrow gauge drill around the screw until it is freed. The hole will have to be filled with a piece of glued dowel and the surface finished off with plastic wood.

A dowel is the best method of restoring the joint. But if a screw is to be used it should be in a slightly different position from that of the previous screw, or failing that, of a larger gauge. Use brass or chromium-finished screws to ensure that there will be no difficulty in the future in removing them through rusting.

Light machine oil will usually loosen an obstinate screw if left to soak in

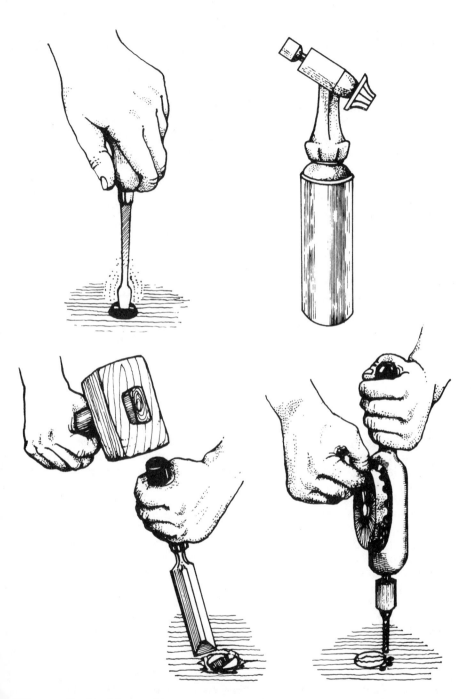

Other methods of loosening screws

133

Drawers

In very few homes do all the wooden drawers move inwards and outwards perfectly. There really is no need to put up with the jammed drawer, the one which slides past the surrounding edge, or gets askew if not adjusted as it is closed.

One may well regret that mass production, unseasoned wood, and other inefficiencies of modern manufacture seem inevitably to cause these defects. It is all the more exasperating when watching a TV programme on antiques or the work of famous cabinet-makers of the past to see how perfectly every drawer fits and moves. But in fairness to the modern maker, it must be remembered that these antique pieces were the work of masters of their craft. Probably the usual run of furniture in the past, now long since worn out and destroyed, was just as liable to faults.

But still there is no need to put up with this sort of annoyance. If a drawer is really stuck when closed heaving on it violently will merely make things worse and probably distort the rest of the construction. It is usually quite easy to remove the back and push the drawer outwards when there will be less stress and strain.

Before making any major repair try rubbing the runners with french chalk, and if that does not work, apply some silicone furniture polish, well rubbed in. Polish is far better than soap which quickly hardens and breaks up.

A common cause of a jammed drawer is damp. The wood swells because the moisture easily penetrates the untreated wood of the interior of the furniture. Aside from the obvious solution of seeing that the cabinet or chest of drawers is not subject to moist air from a nearby open window, steam in bathroom or kitchen and so on, it may be necessary to remove a slight amount of the surface at the top and bottom of the sides of the drawer or the runners.

Empty the drawer of its contents and find out at which point it is jamming. In the worst cases it may be necessary to plane away a little wood but in the majority of instances rubbing with glasspaper wrapped round a block of wood will do the job. The merest fraction needs to be removed to make all the difference.

Quite often the understandable belief that the drawer fits too tightly and therefore jams is in fact wrong. Indeed, wear and shrinkage may mean that there is a certain amount of play so that the drawer does not slide on a true parallel with the runners.

Remove the drawer and check the dovetails which join the sides to the front. If they have loosened then the sides will have moved outwards, thus scraping against the runners.

Unless the dovetails are really loose – in which case the best remedy is to take the drawer to pieces and re-glue it – a little adhesive can be worked into the gaps in the dovetails. As soon as it is tacky take a block of wood, hold it over the dovetails and tap with a hammer, first with the drawer on its end and then on its side.

Another cause of a drawer jamming is that the bottom edges of the sides have become worn. The drawer then drops and scrapes against the stops on the rail. The only solution is to cut away the sides at the bottom of the drawer, glasspaper to smoothness,

Faults needing repair include loose dovetails, worn runners and a warped, broken base—all common causes of jamming or sticking

and glue on new strips of wood to restore the correct depth of the sides. This job is not so difficult as it may sound. The essential is absolute accuracy of measurement.

Yet another source of jamming is that heavy and tightly-packed items have caused the bottom of the drawer to bend downwards or become loose. Usually there is a small overlap of wood at the back to allow for shrinkage and this can be tapped forward. If the sides have shrunk or a gap has appeared through warping the easiest way to remedy the trouble, short of replacing the base with plywood (which does not shrink) is to glue a thin strip of softwood across the underside.

Lastly, when a drawer closes too far inwards and ends up askew, the reason is invariably that the stop at the back has broken or become badly worn. Cut a piece of wood to the same size as an undamaged stop, remove the defective one, and fix the replacement with glue and panel pins.

Doors, chairs and tables

Doors

On all but very large and cheaply made doors on cabinets, wardrobes and cupboards it is unlikely that the wood of a sagging door itself has become distorted. The usual trouble is that the hinges were badly fixed at the outset or have become loose.

Unscrew the door at the hinges and remove them altogether. Check that the recess for the hinge plates is, in all instances, smooth and level, and takes the hinge so that its surface exactly matches the level of the surrounding wood. If it extends above that level, chisel or glasspaper the surface until the right depth is obtained. If the hinge is below the wood surface fix a piece of veneer or thin plywood in the recess.

Whichever is the fault fill all the old screw holes with plastic wood, allow to dry and replace the hinges, first on the door furniture, and then on the frame. Be sure to get the hinges absolutely level in the recess. When fixing on the door have assistance to hold it in position. Do not screw the hinges completely tight until the top and bottom of the door are parallel with the aperture.

Chairs

Uneven chair legs are a familiar fault. The end of one or two legs may have worn down, or the tenon joint at the top of the leg and the seat frame may have become loose.

The usual height for the seat of an upright chair is 44–46cm (17–18in), so a shortening of the legs by 1cm ($\frac{1}{2}$in) will not affect a comfortable seat. To check the length of all four

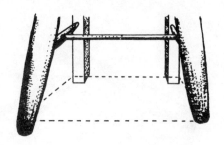

Check the lengths of the legs of a wobbly chair

legs place the chair on an absolutely flat table and rock it to ascertain which leg is too short. Its length determines the amount of wood to be cut from the other legs, checking first that any ferrule or glide fixed to the foot of the legs is not responsible for the discrepancy. The trouble is often caused by these fixtures becoming loose. They are either screwed in or have a press fit; in either case it is easy to remove them. Fill the screw or press hole with plastic wood, allow it to dry, and replace the ferrules, tapping them to the wood leg with a block of wood between ferrule and hammer.

Sometimes, however, one leg is clearly too short. Measure the gap when the other three legs are touching the table and mark this length on each leg. Saw away below the line and then glasspaper away the surplus, checking that all three legs are being rubbed down equally.

If the trouble is at the top of a shortened leg, remove any tie rails by twisting and pulling, and then do the same to pull the leg away. Clean off the old glue and put some plastic wood or a sliver of plywood into the base of the aperture, pushing it well

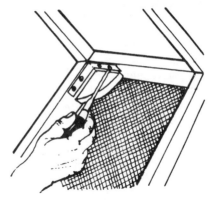

An unsteady chair can be repaired by dealing with the corner braces

down. Put the leg back temporarily to check that the length is now correct. Smear the top of the leg and the hole with glue and press home firmly, at the same time re-glueing the tie rails.

When a leg is actually broken it is best to replace all four legs with new ones, available in a huge variety of sizes and styles. The repair of a broken leg is rarely satisfactory. The stresses to which it is put in use are so great that any but an expert repair will result in another fracture.

A chair which becomes unsteady through loosening of the seat frame or back will usually be found to be faulty because the braces used to support the seat and keep the joints rigid have loosened. These braces will be seen by turning the chair upside down. They are against the seat frame at each corner. Invariably they are pieces of wood fixed with a couple of screws. Remove them, clean off any glue, fill the screw holes with plastic wood, allow it to dry and then re-glue and insert new screws, preferably of one size larger (but not longer) than the original screws. For extra strength screw on a small metal angle bracket below the brace.

Chair backs of the Windsor type often have loose rails and back rest. Repair is a simple matter of carefully removing the back rest and then the rails, cleaning off the old glue, re-glueing and reassembling. If a rail has broken, usually at either end, it will be necessary to drill out the stumps, making sure you remove all surplus wood. New rails are readily available, but may not be of the precise length. Buy a rail rather longer than required, match against a rail which is undamaged and cut to fit. Make a test assembly, then glue the end holes and rail ends and tap them all together.

Tables

A wobbling occasional table or coffee table rarely needs to have its legs cut. The trouble usually is that the glue in the hole fixing the legs to the top, or the tenons, or the braces have become loose. Remove the legs and clean up any screw holes or joints, in the latter case sticking thin ply to the surfaces if the wood is rough and needs glasspapering to a harder surface. Fill screw holes with plastic wood and reassemble, taking care to align all the legs correctly.

Mouldings

Decorative beading and moulding along edges and at corners can be damaged though wear or breakage. Minor damage can easily be repaired with plastic wood. Roughen the edges around the broken area a little to provide good adhesion for the plastic wood which should be moulded between the fingers and applied a little at a time and pressed well in. Make the shape slightly larger and leave till completely dry, then rub down, first with a coarse glass-paper, finishing off with the finest grade available. Apply matching stain (if the plastic wood is not already coloured appropriately), rub with sandpaper again, check colour, apply more stain if necessary, and polish.

If the broken section is more than 4cm or 5cm ($1\frac{1}{2}$ or 2in) long it may be possible to buy a piece for replacement, for many mouldings and beadings are virtually standardized. If not, and the shape is not intricate, it is a comparatively easy job to make a replacement from softwood.

Cut a piece to the correct length but with the depth and width slightly larger. Stick this partly fabricated wood in position with a strong adhesive and leave till thoroughly dry.

By working from each side the silhouette can be followed with a chisel; be careful to leave the shaping overall larger than the adjacent moulding. With rounded file and glasspaper wrapped round a cylindrical piece of wood (eg, a section of broom handle) the exact shape of the moulding can, with patience, be achieved. Stain and again smooth with fine glasspaper, finishing off

with a polish.

If the pattern of the moulding is intricate, or the broken area is extensive, it is simpler to remove it entirely and replace with a new piece. It may be rather difficult to remove the old piece, and care must be taken not to damage the adjacent wood. Clean away all vestiges of adhesive and remove any pins, nails or screws which may have been used to fix it. If an epoxy adhesive is used on the new moulding there will be no need to use panel pins or screws to ensure it is firmly fixed.

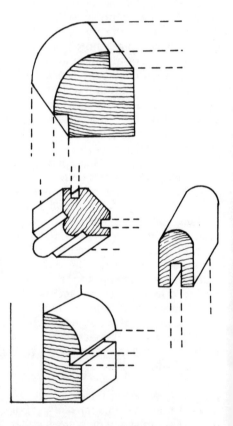

Mouldings are widely available in several sizes and shapes

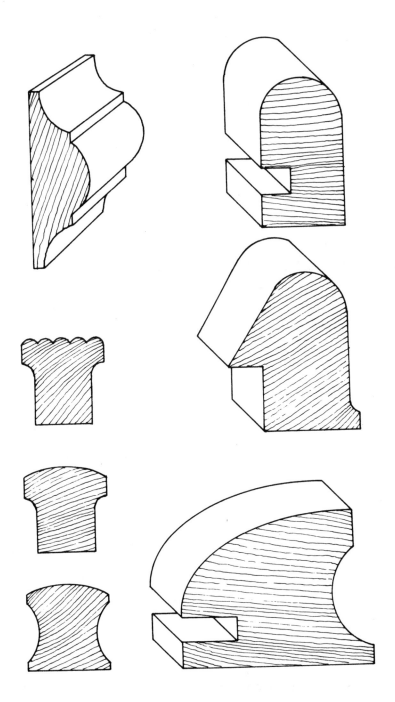

Veneers

A lot of modern furniture is finished with a veneer, allowing finishes to be in virtually any kind of attractive wood over a less expensive wood used in the basic construction of the piece.

There are various types of veneer. Face veneers are thin and mainly give a decorative finish. Constructional veneers are produced in various thicknesses in the same way as plywood, though not cross-laminated as plywood is; these veneers are widely used in the furniture industry. Because of their thickness they are not so likely to peel or chip. Pliable veneers, which are not true veneers, are available under a variety of trade names and are mainly for the amateur, since they are easy to cut. They are produced in a great variety of finishes. In buying a piece of veneer for a repair not only the colour, grain pattern and type of wood should be checked against a specimen from the damaged item, but also the thickness.

Modern adhesives are so efficient that only misuse, prolonged damp, or actual abrasions are likely to damage a veneer sufficiently for the basic wood to be exposed.

The most usual blemish is a bubble caused by trapped air underneath, usually the result of something hot being placed on the surface or, in older pieces, inefficient glueing. Attempting to press the bubble down with a piece of timber hit with a hammer or with a hot iron is futile, as the trapped air cannot escape. A small bubble may sometimes be dealt with by piercing the centre with a fine needle, warming the area with a hair dryer and then gently tapping

with a hammer over several sheets of newspaper placed over the bubble to prevent denting.

More usually the air gap below the bubble means that the glue has long since dried to a skin and can no longer provide good adhesion. It is therefore necessary to introduce fresh glue. Cut into the bubble along a grain mark with the corner of a razor blade or a very thin sharp knife.

Lift each side of the slit by inserting a matchstick so as to provide just enough space to insert adhesive on the tip of a knife blade. Using a transparent adhesive, apply it beneath the veneer sparingly and evenly and immediately wipe away any that may have crept beyond the edge.

Press the veneer back, working from the edge of the bubble area and leaving the edges of the cut to the last so as to ensure that no air is trapped.

Finally, with two or three pieces of paper covering the area to avoid damaging the surface, tap lightly but repeatedly all over the area. So long as the original cut followed the line of grain and a thin blade was used the cut should be invisible.

Loose veneer

This invariably occurs at the edge of a surface. With care it can be lifted beyond the loosened area by inserting a flat, round-ended knife, and gently moving it from side to side; then you can penetrate a little further into the still attached area. The aim is to raise the veneer sufficiently to clean away the original glue on both the underside of the veneer and the surface of the wood base. This can be done with a sharp penknife if the veneer is bent upwards and kept up with a few slivers of wood. Ideally they should be tapered so that there is no risk of cracking the veneer in the area between the raised portion and the main part still stuck down.

When you are satisfied that the glue has been removed (any tenacious pieces can be smoothed down with fine glasspaper) smear PVA adhesive on both sides and press down.

It is essential that the treated area be cramped, with blocks of wood between the cramps both above and below the treated area to avoid damage; as an extra precaution place a sheet of polythene on the upper surface to ensure that any surplus or exuded adhesive does not bond the block to the veneered surface.

If cramps are not available or if the area does not lend itself to their use strap with tightly drawn cellulose tape and fix a weight above the area. Do not remove cramps or weight and tapes for at least six hours.

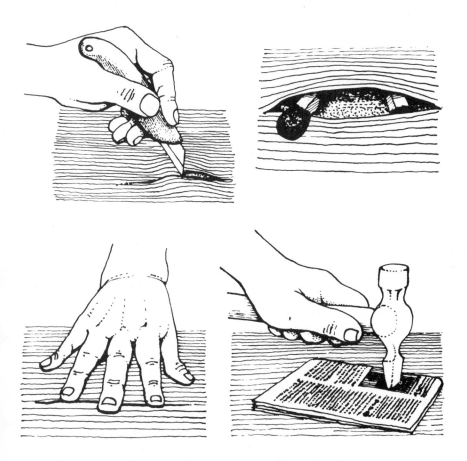

To remove a bubble from a veneered surface: cut along the grain, insert matchsticks each end of the slit, apply adhesive, remove matches and press down. Cover area with newspaper and tap lightly with a hammer

Veneers

Chipped veneer

A more difficult repair is where some veneer has been chipped or broken off completely. Very rarely will the broken part leave a neat break, so the first thing to do is to cut a little farther in, whenever possible following the marking of the grain. If this is impossible it is better to cut away at an acute angle rather than at a right angle.

Check that the undamaged veneer is still adhering; if a slight gap is evident stick down with adhesive, being careful to wipe away any surplus on the exposed wood.

The replacement veneer must obviously be of the same finish and colour, and with a grain pattern as close as possible to the original. Good DIY shops stock a great variety of veneers. Ideally you should take a scrap of your veneer with you to make a good match. In any event you must know what type of wood your veneer is. The type is really more important than exact colour, for it will be possible to change the colour with a dye. The dye must be generously applied at least three times so as to ensure that it soaks in and will not be removed by glasspapering. As you will have to buy a larger piece of veneer than you need you can experiment on spare pieces to find the appropriate hue from dyeing.

Clean up the edges of the undamaged veneer and then fix a sheet of tracing paper with cellulose tape over the area to be filled. Carefully trace the shape. Stick the tracing to the underside of the replacement veneer and go over the tracing with a sharp, hard pencil. With a sharp knife cut out the shape, making the cut on the outside of the line rather than through it. The small surplus will ensure a tight fit and any real excess can be removed with glasspaper.

After checking that the patch is an exact fit, that the graining makes a good match, and the thickness of the veneer is correct, go over the base wood with a piece of cotton wool soaked in methylated spirit to remove dust and any remaining glue. Apply contact adhesive thinly to both the veneer and the wood base. When touch-dry press down, starting from the centre and working to the edges. Leave to dry with a weight evenly covering the whole area. Then lightly glasspaper if the edges are not quite level. Remove all dust with methylated spirit and polish.

Laying veneer

When a veneer on the top of a small table, the face of a drawer or a shelf is very badly chipped and damaged, a completely new veneered surface can be the only feasible repair. A veneer can also be used to cover plain wood provided it is perfectly smooth and more than 2cm ($\frac{3}{4}$in) thick.

After buying the desired kind and size of veneer place it on the area to be covered and mark out the shape with a surplus of about 2cm ($\frac{3}{4}$in) all round. If more than one piece of veneer is being used allow this extra piece 2cm ($\frac{3}{4}$in) extra width at the joint.

Generously dampen the sheet of veneer with cold water and place between two heavy, perfectly clean boards. If more than one sheet is to be used dampen them all and stack them together. They should be left for three or four hours by which time the moisture will have rendered them pliable.

Meantime score the surface to be veneered in order to provide a key. Brush over with Scotch glue and leave to dry. Whatever some dealers may claim, there is nothing better than Scotch glue for veneering, as it is water soluble.

When the veneer sheets are pliable apply another coat of Scotch glue to the wood surface and place the veneer in position. A veneer hammer is available in DIY stores, but a light wooden mallet or a hammer with its head protected in felt will serve.

Tap from the centre towards the edges to get rid of air bubbles, and use a slightly sideways motion rather than tapping vertically. Rub over with the fist as you proceed. This will enable you to check that there is no unevenness and the whole area of veneer is adhering strongly.

When laying more than one piece of veneer lay the subsequent leaf about 2cm ($\frac{3}{4}$in) over the one already stuck down. As soon as it has been firmly bonded cut away the surplus and then rub down with the mallet on each side to close the joint. Satisfied that the joint is almost invisible, cover it with a strip of strong brown paper adhesive tape, then a piece of clean paper and lastly a weight. Leave for an hour or so. Remove the tape and clean away any surplus glue at the joint with warm water.

Finally cut away the surplus round the edges, glasspapering to get a neat finish flush with the edge of the base.

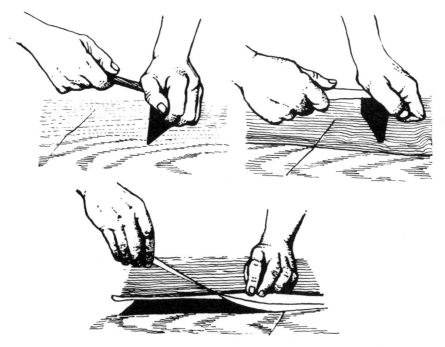

Laying veneer using a veneer hammer

Upholstered furniture

Repairing and replacing upholstery is a project only incidentally connected with work on the wood of furniture. As regards pieces such as easy chairs and sofas, where wood is merely a framework to support, renovation of the upholstery is a specialized craft and, on the whole, better left to an expert.

However, there are instances where upholstery is a minor part of the piece. Chairs with a loose seat and a padded back rest are an example.

In renovating such items the upholstered parts must usually be removed before any work is undertaken on the wooden frame. If the seat is padded remove the material carefully and keep it as the pattern for cutting out a new piece.

Check the exposed wooden frame for loose joints and woodworm, and deal with any defects.

If new padding is required it is easier to buy foam rubber (the high density kind) than to renew the horsehair or wadding. Replace the webbing no matter how good the original webbing appears to be. It is bound to have slackened. Cover the whole of the underside by tacking and sticking a piece of hessian on to it. This keeps out damp and dirt.

For the back of the chair follow the pattern of the original material, tack down on a thin coating of adhesive on the frame, and cover the tacks with braid. Precautions should be taken to pull the material as tight as one's strength allows so as to avoid slackening and creases in use. Four hands are better than two in getting the material tight on all sides.

Many chairs are upholstered in leather or a synthetic version of leather. In this case it is better not to remove the leather unless it is going to be replaced – a difficult and rather expensive job.

Greasy marks can be removed or at least lightened by gently rubbing in some fuller's earth, leaving for a time and then brushing away. If the stain is deep it may be worthwhile rubbing cautiously with a pad of cotton wool just slightly dampened with methylated spirit or a dry cleaning fluid. But do not soak the leather as it will make a ring round the stain.

General griminess and discoloration are best cleaned with a proprietary hide food or saddle soap. When treating the adjacent wood with stain, varnish or polish, beware of applying any of these liquids or substances close to the leather. It will discolour the edge. Stick a length of cellulose tape just over the edge of the leather, pressing it down securely.

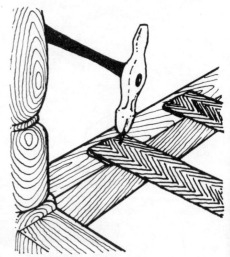

Always replace old webbing on upholstered seating, pulling each length tight

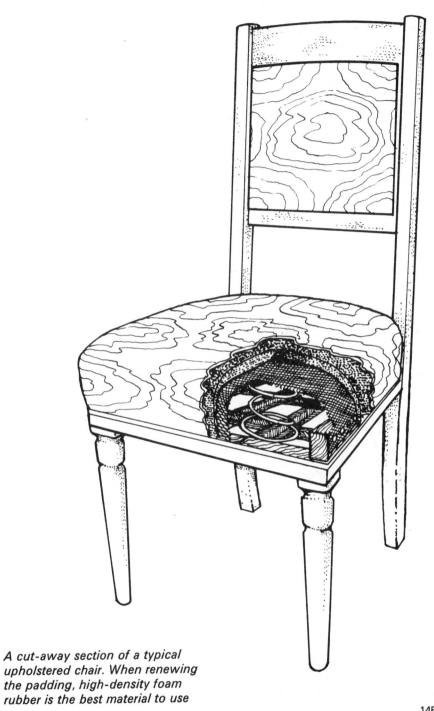

*A cut-away section of a typical
upholstered chair. When renewing
the padding, high-density foam
rubber is the best material to use*

145

Bamboo repairs and cleaning

Chairs, stools and such small items as house plant stands made of bamboo are increasingly popular, especially for use in sun lounges and temporarily in the garden. If well made, as it usually is when imported from Asia, bamboo furniture lasts well despite the degree of flexibility of construction and the absence of connections in joints.

The usual reason for deterioration is a failure to keep out damp, for instance, leaving it unprotected on an open verandah during the winter, allowing dust and grease to collect between the lengths of cane and, paradoxically, causing the bamboo to become brittle if placed too near radiators and fires.

Bamboo furniture deserves regular dusting with a dry paint brush to reach between the canes. Better still is to vacuum clean with a brush attachment. Afterwards, application of a wax polish, used sparingly so that all the polish is thoroughly rubbed to a patina, will protect the surface and inhibit mould and rot.

In an annual spring clean it is worthwhile, on a sunny day, to wash bamboo pieces with tepid water containing washing up liquid and rinsing well to get rid of any trace of detergent. If the water seems to be repelled in some areas it indicates that earlier wax polish has created an over-thick skin. In this case go over the whole piece with a rag just dampened with methylated spirit. This will remove the grease. A glance at the rag will show that a lot of dirt has been removed as well.

If some lengths of bamboo have split or broken it is possible to replace them with a modicum of skill. A length of the right thickness can usually be obtained by searching around supplies in a garden shop if a local craft shop does not stock bamboo. After cutting to the required length let the cane soak in very hot water for thirty minutes when it will be quite easy to bend it to the desired shape. If possible use the original binding as it is difficult to buy — or for that matter to slice away a strip from a bamboo cane — to make a good match. Plastic imitations are available but they rarely have a real bamboo look.

Bear in mind that bamboo can be painted or varnished. This may wear away in places because of friction in what is basically a flexible construction, but an annual touch-up will remedy imperfections. The best method of getting an even, thin cover of paint reaching between the lengths of cane is to use an aerosol paint. Those sold for touching up car bodies are ideal. Give the piece at least two coats, allowing the first one to dry for an hour before spraying again.

There are no nails or screws in the joints of bamboo furniture. When binding is broken, it is best to remove and rewind, following a similar joint, and fixing the end with adhesive

147

Woodworm

The woodworm or furniture beetle is one of the worst menaces affecting furniture; unfortunately the older the item and the better the wood the more vulnerable it is.

Evidence of the presence of woodworm is all too familiar: minute holes in the surface and a fine powder on the floor, with more powder dropping out if the affected area is tapped.

Most woods can be affected, the only exceptions being solid mahogany and teak.

Eradicating woodworm must be tackled over a long period, because its life cycle is at least three years. Eggs are laid in crevices in spring and early summer. The grubs, almost invisible to the naked eye, burrow into the wood and remain concealed for about two years, then they change into winged beetles and gnaw their way to the surface, producing the dust and the visible worm holes. The beetles immediately mate, and the cycle begins all over again. As the beetles can fly, previously unattacked pieces of furniture in the same room or house may be selected for the next batch of eggs.

The object of any treatment must be to kill the grubs hatched in early summer as they start to make their holes, and to wage prolonged war on those which are living well below the surface for month after month.

Insecticides sold to treat woodworm are completely effective when properly used. The newly hatched grubs on the surface will be killed if the liquid is sprayed or rubbed over the surface and into crevices and joints. Those already in their burrows will succumb only if the insecticide reaches them. This means using an aerosol or plastic container with an injector so that the liquid can be forced well into the holes. Merely putting a film of liquid over the hole will not be effective, and even accurate injection into the hole may not reach the grub through a screen of dust. Complete eradication is only certain if the treatment is repeated regularly, say every three months, and especially in March and April when the newly fledged beetles are moving outwards.

Some precautions in using an insecticide are advisable. Beware of applying it to the surface of light coloured wood without making a test on an area where possible staining will not matter. Be careful not to get the liquid on the skin; wear rubber gloves and burn any duster which has become impregnated. Avoid breathing the fumes, especially with an aerosol. Apply the liquid at arm's length with the windows open. Keep children and pets out of the room and cover any house plants with sheets of newspaper.

The marks of woodworm are clearly visible in this table leg

148

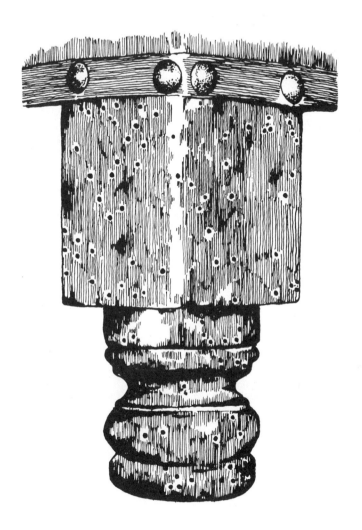

Pottery and Porcelain

Maurice and Barbara Grover

Illustrated by Evelyn Bartlett

Introduction

Over the last decade or two, interest in collecting old pottery and porcelain has become more widespread, possibly due to programmes on television about our national heritage and press reports of fortunes found in attics. Whatever the reason, be it mercenary or love of artistic things, more people are coming to appreciate the beauty and quality of our forefathers' work.

The restoration of ceramics is no new idea: at an early date makers camouflaged cracks and chips with ornamental inlay, and repaired damaged rims with metals. Some factories rescued pieces damaged in the firing by painting over the cracks, others even made wooden bases. Because modern technology has produced new durable adhesives and glazes, restoration of pottery and porcelain has only recently become a craft acceptable to the antique trade who have been exporting vast quantities of undamaged ceramics over the years and now find difficulty in replacing their stock. So you will now find restored pieces in the shops thus giving the collector a wider choice.

Thanks to the early collectors who treasured their possessions and kept their fine china under lock and key in a cabinet, we can today visit their stately homes and have the pleasure of admiring their collections. In the nineteenth century it became fashionable for members of the upper middle class to collect porcelain – imports from China and the Far East were much sought after. Generally, the lower middle class (aping their betters!) collected the cheaper European ceramics. All were proud of their possessions and took great care of them. However, fashions changed and the next generation collected something more modern and consigned their parents' treasures to the rubbish heap, where today many people are digging to find them.

Many of us would love to go to an auction and buy a magnificent, undamaged piece of pottery or porcelain but unfortunately the prices are usually beyond our means, and so we have to make do with damaged pieces which, while retaining their character, will have to have their blemishes facing the wall.

Restoration of pottery and porcelain is not difficult but is time-consuming which is why it seems expensive. The antique dealer knows this and so you may find badly damaged pieces in his shop at reasonable prices. If you have seen these pieces and wondered whether it would be possible to restore them yourself in a professional way, the answer is yes, if you have patience and concentration.

This book is a simple guide to the arts of restoration. However, it must be emphasized that it takes years to become proficient in this craft, and although the basic technique is simple to learn, it is the hard work and practice afterwards that get results. Many things are best left well alone until confidence has been gained; if you start by obtaining some damaged domestic china and a good supply of Staffordshire or similar coloured figures, you will quickly gain skill and get passable results.

Finally, we cannot emphasize too strongly the fact that you get out of the craft exactly what you put into it. Never say 'that will do' – only give up when you know you can do no better.

153

Types of pottery and porcelain

It is as well to make a study of the types and forms of the pottery and porcelain that may come your way.

The Greek word for pottery is *ceramic* and this is the best collective word for describing all types of china and earthenware. When you first pick up a piece you should be able to ascertain whether it is pottery or porcelain, and if porcelain, whether it is hard-paste or soft-paste.

Hard-paste porcelain

Briefly, hard-paste porcelain was first made in China in the ninth century AD by mixing equal quantities of china clay (kaolin) with china stone (petuntse). This was first fired at 900°C (1650°F), then glazed and refired at 1300°C (2570°F) which vitrified the whole thing, that is, gave it the consistency of glass. China exported these wares to Europe in large quantities during the sixteenth century. Hard-paste porcelain is translucent and has pits in it, probably caused by the bursting of bubbles during firing. The Meissen factory discovered the secret in 1710, and in 1750 William Cookworthy found china clay in Cornwall so enabling the factories of Plymouth, Bristol, New Hall and Coalport to produce the hard-paste porcelain which is in general use today.

Soft-paste porcelain

Soft-paste porcelain was first produced in Europe from 1575 and in England from 1745 at Chelsea, Derby and Worcester, and also at Bow and Lowestoft in a slightly different form. The differences between soft- and

154

(above) *New Hall teapot;*
(right) *Types of porcelain*

hard-paste are to be found in the ingredients and firing procedure used. For soft-paste a glassy mixture of sand and flint was combined with white clays to produce a creamy porcelain; this was first fired at 1100°C (2012°F), then dipped in glaze and refired at 900°C (1650°F) – almost the opposite of hard-paste. As its name implies, soft-paste porcelain can easily be damaged and in restoration should never be subjected to harsh abrasives which could scratch the glaze. Never be tempted to soak the article in bleach as this could get under the glaze and cause permanent staining.

Pottery

Pottery is much more coarse and opaque than porcelain. There are many different types and earthenware has been made from the earliest times. The first pots made by our forefathers were simply for domestic and practical use; gradually decoration was added, perhaps by scratching the wet clay and later by painting crude designs with natural pigments. Glaze was applied to make the pottery waterproof. After this, crude ornaments were made and as techniques improved, more ornamental

Meissen coffee pot

Worcester sauce boat

Bow

Lowestoft

Worcester

Bow figure

wares were produced. In the eighteenth and nineteenth centuries there was mass-production of figures and ornamental pottery at the Staffordshire factories where much of the painting was done by children. Apart from this pottery there is salt-glazed stoneware and terra cotta. Elers produced smooth-surfaced red stoneware which was fired at a very high temperature rendering it very hard and non-porous.

John Astbury and Thomas Whieldon produced figures of salt-glazed stoneware. Later came creamware which was produced by many well known factories; this frequently comes into the restorer's hands, and with practice restores extremely well. Wedgwood produced various forms of coloured stoneware in the late eighteenth century; most notable are his black basaltware, jasperware and caneware. All are difficult to paint and should not be attempted by the beginner. Mason's Ironstone is a type of very tough stoneware, varieties of which were produced by several factories in the nineteenth century. Henry Doulton also turned out large quantities of stoneware at his Lambeth factory—the Art Pottery decorated notably by the Barlow family is particularly well known.

Delft, majolica and faience are all tin-glazed earthenwares from different European factories and require special treatment when being restored. They are easily identified as the glaze when chipped will reveal an earthenware body underneath.

This short outline will give you a rough idea of the diversity of ceramics, and we hope that it will encourage you to obtain books from the library and study the subject at your leisure.

155

Choice of articles for the beginner

Choosing suitable articles for restoration is extremely important; the selection of something too complicated could make the beginner feel unequal to the job before giving himself a fair chance. Pupils tend to come to us bearing large boxes of broken 'goodies' which they hope to repair in two or three weeks, and on sorting these out we usually recommend about six simple items to start with.

First take a look at your domestic china. You probably have a cup or two with missing or broken handles; perhaps there is a teapot with a chipped spout and a knob damaged or missing. Casserole and vegetable-dish lids are well worth doing as they are either irreplaceable or, as in the case of Denbyware, very expensive. Similarly, it will also pay you to repair cracked and chipped plates from your favourite (or only) dinner service.

This may sound most uninteresting but each of the items mentioned will provide some useful practice in various aspects of mending and modelling before you embark on anything more valuable or ornamental. You certainly cannot make your things any worse and at least they will be usable again. We have many articles around the house that, had we not known how to repair them, would have been consigned to the dustbin years ago; instead they have been in constant use without disintegrating or losing their glaze.

As already mentioned, a supply of Victorian Staffordshire figures would be the best thing on which to practise ornamental restoration for a month or two. Damaged Staffordshire figures and animals can still be bought at auctions or antique fairs at moderate prices; both the modelling and painting are so crude that even a beginner can be confident of producing a reasonable restoration if all the rules are followed and no short cuts are taken. Apart from Staffordshire figures there are other rather crude Victorian figurines to be had. Many of these are German and come from a group of factories at Thuringia; although mass-produced, they provide a little more scope for modelling hands and arms, and the painting is more demanding.

Moving on from these, Doulton Lambeth wares repair well but avoid any with breaks in the high relief for the time being. The highly coloured Imari plates from all factories are a wonderful exercise in painting provided that you have made a good join. Whenever replacing missing or broken parts, always bear in mind that the overpainting can spoil a good repair just as surely as a bad repair can never be painted properly.

Things to avoid

Certain restoration jobs should not be attempted until you have gained experience, and others should always be left to the expert. For example, any pieces with underglaze and the very popular flo blue are best left well alone for the time being, as are comports on fixed bases, since these have a nasty habit of splitting. All matt wares such as biscuit, Parian, Wedgwood and terra cotta are too difficult until the basics have been mastered.

There are some articles which look like china but on closer inspection turn out to be slag glass, plaster, alabaster or even some other com-

Some Staffordshire figures

position, so be very careful. If you are not sure seek advice before you start, especially if the article is supposedly valuable, since the wrong treatment could cause disintegration, cracking or discoloration. Avoid plates and bowls with large areas of plain colour as they really need an air brush. Modern lace work cannot be repaired satisfactorily. Old figures with ruffs and frills can only be tackled by experts. Silver, gold and bronze lustre should be treated with caution as it is not possible to reglaze to the original brilliance. Sticking only might be the answer.

The secret of successful restoration is to go at your own pace, paying attention to detail; we could tell you many tales of tears and frustrations experienced by some of our pupils who try to run before they can walk. A valuable article badly restored and then taken to an expert can be an awful problem, since there are usually hours of work involved in taking the piece apart and cleaning it before a proper restoration can be done. This is the greatest fear we have concerning amateurs and we do beg you to proceed slowly and then we shall all be happy.

Setting up a workbench

One of the minor blessings of this craft is that it does not require a large number of expensive tools. A quite modest outlay will buy everything the beginner needs and many articles will be found in the home.

All trades require good working conditions and ceramic restoration is no exception; a room with a good natural light is desirable, preferably with a north-facing window which will make it easier when mixing colours for painting. The room should also have ventilation. The first essential is a solid table or bench – this is a dusty and dirty craft so don't use your best antique. Cover the top with old newspaper to give it some protection.

Materials (1)
Araldite 100 HV and 100 AV, obtainable from any hardware shop, is a very good adhesive for ceramic repairs because it will stand the heat during the restoration process and forms a good tough base for filing, sticking and modelling. There are many other manufactured epoxy glues which are just as good and which the beginner may wish to use, but for the purpose of this book we will refer to Araldite. These resins and hardeners are generally quite harmless to handle but people with particularly sensitive skin should use barrier creams or thin rubber gloves, although we find that this craft relies on a sense of touch and gloves are impracticable. It is advisable to wash your hands regularly, otherwise you will put dirty fingerprints all over the piece you are working on and it will be extremely difficult to wash the

158

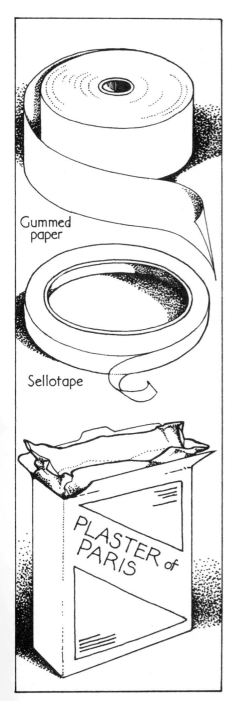

Gummed
paper

Sellotape

PLASTER of PARIS

Araldite off your fingers once it has cured.

Titanium Dioxide can be obtained from the chemist in powder form and can be mixed with Araldite or any other resin and hardener to provide a colouring to the adhesive and a key for the glaze. You should add just enough powder to produce a white paste which is used for sticking parts together.

French Chalk, again obtainable from the chemist, forms the basis of our filling medium when mixed with titanium dioxide powder at a ratio of 1:1. After the resin and hardener have been mixed, the powder is added in small quantities until a putty-like paste is formed. This is used for filling holes and modelling. It is easily workable, tough when dry and leaves a good surface to receive the first coat of glaze.

Industrial Methylated Spirit has a lot of uses in restoration work. It is a clear wood alcohol which evaporates and leaves no harmful deposit on your work, unlike the domestic spirit which leaves a blue colouring. A licence from the Customs and Excise is necessary before it can be purchased from the chemist.

Gum Strip Paper and Sellotape are required for strapping the pieces being mended and covering filled holes before baking.

Sandpaper in several grades will enable you to rub down the surplus Araldite on the new mends. Grades M2, 0 and flour paper are the most useful. Other grades can be used and no doubt the beginner will try various sandpapers until he finds those which suit him best. We have noted that some of our pupils get on better with different grades.

Setting up a workbench

Materials (2)

Files – flats, half rounds and rounds – are a great aid for rubbing down and you can't have too many of them. When starting, you will use far too much Araldite which is not a bad thing but it means you will have to spend a lot of time rubbing down. A file is much quicker than sandpaper, but you must take care not to file the original glaze off your ceramic. The largest file you should need is about 15cm (6in) long. Small needle files are essential for all the small corners you will come up against. All can be obtained at an ironmongers.

Scalpels are probably the most used tool in the workshop. The most useful are : a no 3 handle fitted with a no 15 blade to enable you to work in the small crevices and for cutting back the paint; and a no 4 handle with either a no 20 or no 22 blade for normal work such as cutting off excess Araldite.

A Stanley Knife is a more robust type of cutting tool and is especially useful for levering out rivets.

Plasticine is a great aid to the restorer. It can be used for supporting an arm or leg until the adhesive has set; press moulds are made with it; and a retaining wall for vinyl rubber compound moulding can be built with it. Use only white plasticine as Araldite tends to absorb the colour.

A Tin of Dry Sand is used for standing newly joined parts in, allowing them to balance so that gravity will help to pull them together.

Melamine covered board, about 15 × 30cm (6 × 12in), will make a good mixing board. It is easily cleaned

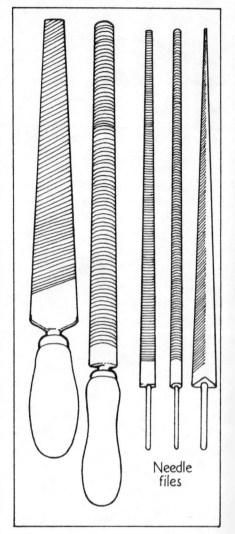

Needle files

after use and does not absorb the Araldite.

An Apron is essential. Restoration is a mucky job and you will probably find it easier to work the pieces in your lap, so your clothes will need protection.

An Old Plastic Bowl is the best thing to use for cleaning the ceramics.

160

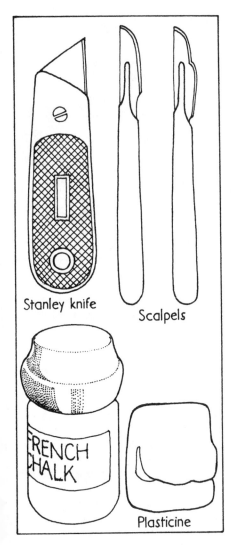

Stanley knife

Scalpels

FRENCH CHALK

Plasticine

The only other piece of equipment the beginner will require is to be found in the kitchen and that is a domestic oven, hopefully large enough to take the piece to be baked. If the piece is too large try making a false oven by leaving the door open and covering the gap with tinfoil. Both gas and electric ovens will do an excellent job. The electric oven is safer as the heating elements around the sides are guarded by a covering so that if the broken piece inadvertently touches a side no harm will be done. A gas oven usually has a naked flame which could damage the piece badly if allowed to come in contact with it.

Set the oven at 100°C (220°F) for all the restoration processes; Araldite will break down if this temperature is greatly exceeded and will either damage the ceramic irreparably or the low-temperature glaze will yellow and spoil all your hard work. Many oven thermostats are not very accurate at this low temperature so it is advisable to get the Electricity or Gas Board to check yours. Alternatively, check it yourself with an oven thermometer which can be purchased from an ironmongers — make sure the thermometer is hung in the centre of the oven as there will be a temperature differential between the top and bottom.

For the trade generally there are some mechanical tools such as flexible drives and grinders which reduce the time taken rubbing down, and a special paint spray known as an air brush. But for the home worker doing his own repairs the items mentioned will be sufficient. More information about mechanical aids, and details of the materials needed for painting, will be found under separate headings.

You can use your kitchen sink but some of the resins you will find in old mends will stain it and yet others do not have the nicest of odours.

Paint Stripper such as Polystrippa or Nitromors will remove paint and stubborn resins from old repairs.

Flash will clean off all the grease from old ceramics.

Cleaning

Examine the damaged piece carefully for previous repairs and cracks, which may not show up at a glance. Start by removing all detachable objects such as ormolu and candle holders on candelabra. There are a number of vases made in two pieces and held together with a bolt and wingnut; these are sometimes difficult to undo and a little oil will help. Put all the parts to one side and keep them safe.

If after close examination you find no previous repairs, soak the piece (or the broken parts) in boiling water to which Flash cleaner has been added. Wearing rubber gloves to protect your hands from the heat, take a long-haired brush (an old shaving-brush will do) and clean off the dirt. A toothbrush is especially useful for cleaning dirt from bocage and difficult corners. When clean, rinse and dry in a warm oven to draw out any water that has been absorbed into the body of the ceramic. The temperature must not exceed 100°C (220°F).

Where you find previous repairs, examine for plaster of Paris replacements and check these with the number of broken parts, or you may find yourself minus several parts when you start mending as plaster of Paris dissolves in water. Look also for resin bonds and rivets.

Most resins will become pliable in boiling water and the old mend will be easy to pull apart. Others may need a little more persuasion and it may be necessary to ease the pieces apart with a Stanley knife or scalpel. It is essential to work in very hot water

162

as a small temperature drop will cause some resins to start hardening again and you will do more damage if you try to force the process. When you have separated the pieces, scrub off the old resin with a stiff brush or scrape it off with a sharp knife. Be sure the edges are clean and that there are no tiny pieces of glue still adhering otherwise you will have problems later when you start mending.

There may be cases where the old mend will not come apart using this method. If it fails, try boiling the piece in an old saucepan until the parts separate. For the really stubborn resins the best thing to use, on hard-paste porcelain only, is a proprietary brand of paint stripper such as Polystrippa or Nitromors. Just paint a thick band over the join and leave until it has had time to destroy the resin. Two or three treatments may be needed. Wash thoroughly afterwards to remove all traces of the stripper, for any left on the porcelain will start to break down the new mend.

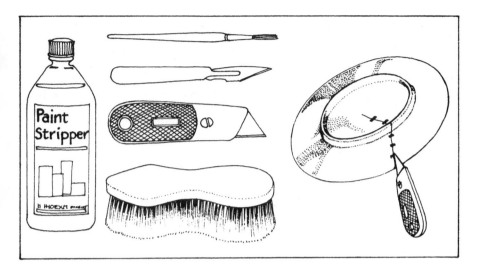

Paint stripper can also be used to remove paint on old hard-paste repairs – it will also remove original gold leaf and colours on some porcelain, so before using it make sure the colours are covered with a hard glaze. If in doubt try a tiny corner, otherwise you could end up with a white piece of what was once a colourful porcelain. Stripper should never be used on soft-paste porcelain or pottery as it will soak into the body and stain indelibly; it will also break down the new adhesive.

Before the advent of modern glues much valuable porcelain and pottery was repaired with staples or rivets. When done by a craftsman these repairs were hardly noticeable as the rivets were hidden from view, and even today it is difficult to see the mends from a distance. In these circumstances we try to dissuade our customers from having their pieces restored. However, if dirt has got into the crack there is no alternative but to take the article to pieces and restore it the modern way.

Normally rivets have been bonded with plaster of Paris which can be removed by soaking the piece in boiling water. When the plaster is soft, ease out the rivets with a Stanley knife; do this gently or you may chip the edge of the hole. Some rivets – those holding handles for instance – are pushed right through the body of the piece and soldered on one side; to remove these you will have to file off the solder and fiddle about until the rivet can be pushed back. It is a most tedious job which cannot be hurried.

When satisfied that all the parts are clean and dry, try fitting them together. If they do not fit perfectly then you have not done the cleaning properly and if you look carefully you will find a tiny piece of glue or dirt on an edge. Some glues are the same colour as the body and are difficult to see – a magnifying glass is a great help. As soon as the fit is perfect you are ready to carry out the next stage of restoration which is sticking.

Joining domestic china

The first result is not going to be perfect — remember it has taken the professional restorer years of practice to reach his high standard — and it is for this reason that we urge the beginner to mend only cheap and domestic china until he becomes proficient.

Take the cleaned parts to be joined and put them into the oven — set at 100°C (220°F) — to warm. While they are heating, mix the two components of the Araldite (resin and hardener) into a syrupy liquid which will rapidly change into a transparent paste. Mix in an appropriate quantity of titanium dioxide powder until the paste is the required colour. A box-wood stick is an admirable tool to use for mixing. Cut the gum strip paper into suitable lengths — 25mm × 3mm (1in × $\frac{1}{8}$in) is adequate for most jobs.

Using oven gloves take the parts out of the oven, scrape a thin quantity of Araldite over one edge, then press the parts firmly together so that any surplus will be squeezed out at the side. Test for a close and even join by running the blade of a scalpel over the edges. When satisfied that the join is perfect, strap it on both sides with gum strip paper, and after checking that the join has not moved, put the article into the oven. Apart from keeping the join intact during the move to the oven, gum strip paper will shrink while drying and pull the mend together.

After half an hour remove the piece from the oven, let it cool, then immerse it in warm water to remove the gum strip paper and all traces of

the gum. When the piece is dry remove the excess Araldite from the edges of the mend with sandpaper, taking care not to damage the existing glaze — a little trial and error will be needed in finding which grade to use. The sticking process will be complete when you can rub your finger lightly over the join without feeling any ridges.

Sometimes holes and chips will be left on the line of the join; these can be filled with an Araldite putty mixture (described under 'Setting up a Workbench' page 158). After mixing leave for about an hour to allow the Araldite to saturate the powder. The actual time will depend on the room temperature: the hotter the room, the faster the mixture will mature. If the body of the pottery or porcelain is coloured, a little powder paint can be added to match.

Smear a little Araldite round the edges of the hole and press the putty home with a finger dipped in industrial methylated spirit, expelling all the air to leave a solid mass. Strap over with either gum strip paper or sellotape and leave for 12 hours, after which the strapping can be removed and the piece baked in the oven for half an hour. After cooling it can be rubbed down.

When you are completely satisfied with the repair, clean the piece all over with flour paper — there are bound to be lots of fingermarks from handling however careful you are. Flour paper will not harm the original glaze if used carefully.

There are several things to remember about the restoration of domestic ware such as cups, saucers, casseroles etc. In any household these are of necessity washed and heated continually. The use of detergents and

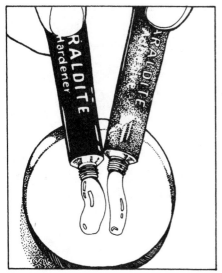

Mix Araldite resin and hardener

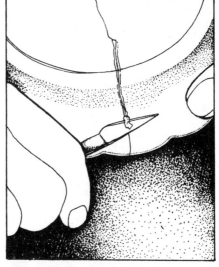

Clean off surplus Araldite

Dampen gum strip paper

Strap the join with gummed paper

dish-cloths breaks down the low-temperature glazes causing them to peel off. However, there is no reason why a mend should not last for years if care is taken when washing. High temperatures will also gradually break down the epoxy resin adhesives. It is inadvisable to put repaired domestic china into a dishwasher. The strength of a joint once bonded becomes less as the temperature is raised, so it is not recommended that you repair the base of a casserole if you are going to use it at high tempertures.

Normally we would not recommend having everyday china restored unless it is part of a service which cannot be matched.

Joining ornamental ceramics

Having practised on domestic ware, the beginner should now have enough confidence to tackle the more demanding ornamental pieces. Ceramics can be classed in three main groups. Hard-paste porcelain has an extremely hard body and glaze. The restorer should handle it with respect because of the razor-sharp edges where it has been broken; these should fit together well as hard-paste breaks cleanly and very little difficulty should be experienced when sticking. The glaze will not scratch when abrasives are being used for the rubbing down. Soft-paste porcelain is more delicate and can be damaged by scalpels and abrasives; it does not break so cleanly and will have minute chips missing at the edges. Pottery is the softest of all and needs especially gentle treatment – the body could be accidentally cut away with a sharp scalpel.

Having made sure that the parts are quite clean, examine the decorations and look for gilding. As you will have discovered when practising on domestic china, the article being repaired is handled all the time; gold leaf will not stand up to the wear and will rub off easily. It can be protected by a covering of wet tissue paper.

Prepare the Araldite and gum strip paper while the parts to be joined are heating in the oven; add colouring to the resin to match the body of the ceramic.

Scrape a thin layer of cement on to one edge and press the parts firmly together. When a good join has been obtained stick the gum strip paper at right angles to the fracture, then

(left, above and centre) *Repairing an ornamental piece*

(below) *A locked-out piece*

stand the piece in a tin of sand at the appropriate angle so that the join does not fall apart while the glue sets. To hasten the curing time, bake it in the oven, in the tin of sand, for half an hour at the usual temperature; as well as a much quicker setting, this will also give a slightly stronger joint.

If the part being bonded is a peculiar shape and you cannot be sure that the corresponding surfaces are fitting properly, it will be best to set the article aside and allow the Araldite to harden naturally. At a room temperature of 16°C (60°F) it will set in about 12 hours. This will allow you to examine the mend the next day and if not satisfactory, it will be possible to take the join apart with boiling water and start again.

Fill in any small holes along the join with a putty mixture of Araldite, titanium dioxide and French chalk, coloured if necessary, then strap and leave for 12 hours until ready for baking. When cool, rub down in the usual way.

Delft or tin-glazed ware has a very hard glaze over a soft, coloured body and when this breaks, large pieces of glaze inevitably flake off, leaving the restorer with holes to fill. To simulate this glaze, mix Chintex glaze into the Araldite until a very thin emulsion has been obtained. Apply this with a brush until the hole is filled and there is a smooth surface. Leave for 12 hours when a very light rubbing down is all that should be necessary.

Difficulties will arise when a piece has been shattered. Then you are faced with a number of parts to be stuck and they could lock out.

Before a piece is broken it is one solid mass, therefore when adhesives are introduced more bulk is put into the original space. On one or two pieces it does not matter because it cannot be discerned with the naked eye. However, the more broken parts there are, the thicker the adhesive layers, and this becomes apparent when the last part will not fit. It is advisable therefore, to stick all the broken parts together in one go. If it is a valuable piece it is best left to the professional restorer.

On a great number of figures the protruding parts such as arms and legs are the most vulnerable to damage and probably the most difficult to stick. It may not be possible to stand the figure at the correct angle in a tin of sand, so you will have to prop the broken part in place with plasticine, examining it from time to time to see that is has not moved.

Rubbing down can be awkward and this is where you will find the use of the small needle files invaluable to rub away the surplus adhesive; you will have to experiment with either a flat, half-round or round file to find the best type for the job in hand. Always file across the join so that you do not file away too much, and do not scratch the glaze. When filing fingers and other delicate parts, be very careful – just one wrong twist and off they will come.

Rubbing down correctly is extremely important as you will discover when you start painting: faults in the mending can never be covered up with paint.

Mending cracks and chips

We have all seen a dealer in an auction room or shop, balance a plate or bowl on one hand and flick it with his fingernail. This is a good way to find any cracks which are difficult to see with the naked eye. If the piece gives a nice ring then you know that it is perfect; but if it makes a dull sound you can be certain there is a crack somewhere.

It is possible to get the nice ring back by buttering in Araldite adhesive. Heat the article in an oven at a temperature not exceeding 100°C (220°F) and when really hot, insert a razor blade into the end of the crack to open it up. Butter some Araldite (which will become very runny on contact) into it; repeat the process on both sides and when full, pull out the razor blade. You will know if you have a good bond by the amount of surplus Araldite which squeezes out. Strap with gum strip paper and bake in the usual way. This process must be done very quickly for there is only a short time when the Araldite is thin enough to run into the open crack and before it begins to cure. Rub down with sandpaper in the usual way until the surface is smooth.

Dirt and grease will accumulate in old cracks and become difficult to remove. You should wash the piece in boiling water and Flash, again opening out the crack with a razor blade to allow the dirt to float out. This process will take some time and it may be advisable to leave the piece to soak, occasionally washing off the dirt as it oozes out of the crack. Another method, to be used on hard-paste porcelain only, is to lay cotton-wool

soaked in domestic bleach along the crack to draw out the dirt. This could take two or three days and the piece should be thoroughly washed afterwards to get rid of all traces of the bleach. Be careful as the fumes are very potent, and do test a section first as the bleach may lift the colours from the porcelain – especially gold leaf, as we discovered to our great cost when trying to clean up someone's plate. We had to regild the whole plate with 22-carat gold. A most expensive mistake!

Do not use bleach on soft-paste porcelain or pottery as it will penetrate under the glaze and into the body, staining indelibly. We were once asked to restore a soft-paste comport which the owner had bleached and which had looked beautifully white until it was placed by a window in the full sun. Within hours the bleach showed up a dirty yellow about one inch either side of the crack.

When an article has a large crack almost the whole width across, it would be better to break it out and mend in the usual way. There is very little one can do to mend star cracks at the bottom of cups and bowls as it is impossible to peon them up. All you can do is to get as much dirt out as possible by washing, and then apply some Araldite to the hot surface – some will go in, enough to strengthen it. Where a crack has sprung, that is, has warped through being broken for some time, the two edges will be out of alignment when pulled together. This can be overcome by using a G-clamp to push the edges into place for sticking. Put paper between the clamp and the body of the ceramic to prevent them sticking together.

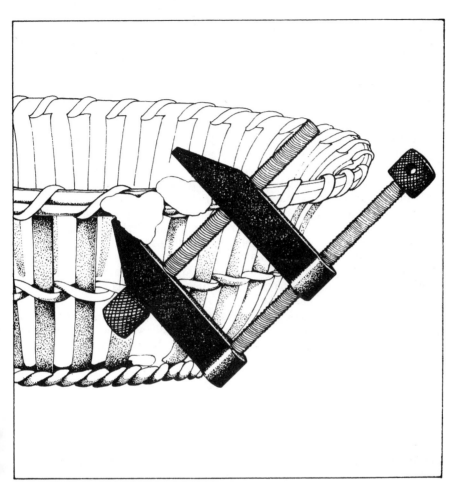

Using a G-clamp

Chips can be filled with an Araldite putty mixture as described previously (page 164). Make sure it has been thoroughly mixed, roll it into a ball and leave for about an hour so that the Araldite will penetrate all the powder. During the waiting time ensure that the chip is clean and dry, then apply a little adhesive to the rough surface. Take the putty and press it into the chip, making sure there are no air bubbles and that it is adhering to the edges. Strap with sellotape and leave for 12 hours at normal room temperature, then take off the strapping and rub down. Care should be taken to mould in the edges and flow with the curves.

If you have too much putty mixture roll out the surplus into long sticks which when dry can be used as cores for modelling arms and legs; alternatively, it can be flattened and dried for other purposes which will be described in the next section.

169

Modelling

Ceramic figures are very vulnerable to damage, especially their heads, arms and legs; many broken parts have been lost and the restorer has to build replacements.

Although we prefer to use Araldite putty, and in certain cases Sylmasta, there are various compositions available in the shops and all are equally good for making missing parts. Nearly all putty mixtures will sag and have to be held in place until they have set. It will be best for the beginner to practise modelling on an easily accessible piece such as a plate with a section missing. Follow the first method described under 'Press Moulding', page 174.

Making an arm or a leg sounds difficult but with practice you will become proficient. Since there must be something solid to stop the putty mixture sagging, now is the time to use the cores you have previously made from excess putty. Look at the figure you are about to mend and decide at what angle the arm or leg should be. If by chance you have an illustration this should be easy; if not look for any rough spot where the original limb has been resting, giving you a clue to the angle. Failing any signs, try a rough model with plasticine to give you the idea.

Having decided on the flow of the limb, take the Araldite sticks, which must be thinner than the limb to be made, and cut them to appropriate lengths — from shoulder to elbow, and from elbow to wrist for an arm. Each end should be cut at the correct angle to give a good join. Now stick them to the figure with Araldite and prop into position with plasticine. Allow to dry for 12 hours, then the props can be taken away. If the angle is satisfactory bake in the oven for half an hour to give good strong joints to the core to enable it to withstand the pressure you exert in the next stage.

Cover the core with Araldite putty, smoothing it over to the required shape with a finger or stick dipped in industrial methylated spirit. We find a most useful guide to getting the correct shape is to look at the contours of your own limbs; this is especially helpful when making a hand. Having modelled the arm and wrist to your satisfaction, leave for a further 12 hours, then put the final touches to it with sandpaper and files. Get it as smooth as possible and if anything fractionally smaller than required because the various coats of paint you will use later will make the limb larger. The same process applies to legs and feet.

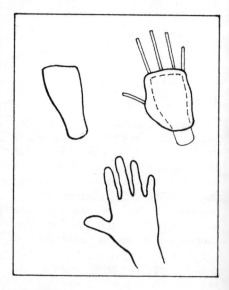

Making a hand

170

Making a hand is not difficult if you think about it. Decide first what the hand is supposed to be doing — perhaps holding a bunch of flowers — look at your own hand in a similar pose and make a flat core of the wrist and palm. The core should be long enough to allow you to hold it comfortably. Flatten out the palm of the hand to the required angle. When dry, cover with putty and model the wrist and palm until you are satisfied with the result, then pierce holes with a cocktail stick where the fingers should be. Allow the wrist and palm to dry for the usual 12 hours.

The next stage is to put on the fingers and thumb. Allow some putty mixture to cure for at least 3 hours by which time it should stay where you mould it without support. Roll it out to the finger thickness and cut to the required lengths. Scrape Araldite adhesive on to the holes to give a strong bond, push in the fingers with a sharp stick and smooth off around the knuckles. You will now be able to bend the fingers to the required angles and roughly model them to shape. Leave to harden, supporting them with plasticine if necessary. When dry, shorten the hand to match the wrist, stick with Araldite and allow to set. Finish off with sandpaper to leave a good surface ready for painting.

Unless you are skilled in the art of sculpture modelling, heads should be left to the professional. However, if you wish to have a go, you can make a block of Araldite putty and after purchasing the appropriate tools, make a start from scratch.

On many Staffordshire figures there is a little blob of grass usually painted in bright colours; this is called bocage and is easily damaged. To replace it, take a metal tea-strainer and press putty through the holes; it is then possible to cut the resulting bocage off the metal with a sharp scalpel. Carry this new bocage to the damaged portion, which should have been covered with adhesive, and slide it into place.

To simulate wool on sheep, cover the relevant area with putty to the appropriate depth, and then tease out with a pointed stick until you have matched the original pattern.

Lace on figures can be simulated with a thin layer of Araldite but this is extremely difficult and should be left to the professional restorer. Ribbons can be made by rolling and flattening the mixture to the desired thickness and length, then sticking it in the right place propped up with plasticine where necessary.

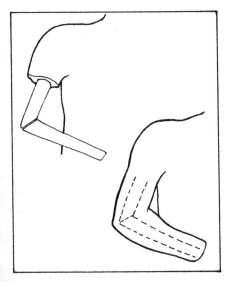

Making an arm

Modelling

Those flattened pieces of surplus putty that you have been keeping can be used to fill large holes in the bases of figures. Smear Araldite round the inside of the hole. Insert a hardened piece of flattened putty (a little larger than the hole) and leave to set; this will give you something solid on which to build up the base.

Flowers and leaves are easily damaged and no doubt you will find these missing on many old ceramics. Some people do not mind and consider such damage fair wear and tear – unless it is too obvious and spoils the beauty of the piece, in which case they will instruct their restorer to put an odd petal here or flower there. It is really up to the owner to decide how much restoration is required.

When modelling petals and leaves, use a putty mixture that has been curing for at least 3 hours at a room temperature of 16°C (60°F). Roll it out on your mixing board to the correct thickness and with a scalpel dipped in industrial methylated spirit, cut out the shape of the leaf or petal. This can then be stuck on to the figure with Araldite and propped in position with plasticine until hard. If it has been made properly there should be very little rubbing down to do.

On Staffordshire figures and similar pottery and porcelain, you will find crude flowers with a stem and five or six petals; these can be made freehand by using the same well-cured putty. Take a piece the correct size and roll it into a conical shape. Hold the pointed end, which will become

172

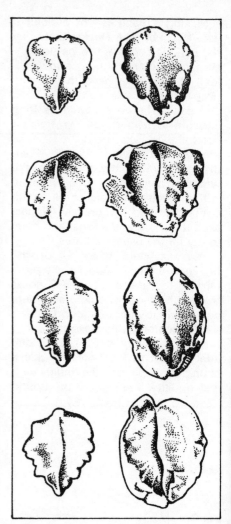

Plaster of Paris moulds

the stalk, between thumb and finger, and flatten down the top of the cone which will become the flower. With a sharp stick dipped in industrial methylated spirit, model out the shape of the petals and when satisfied with your effort, leave to harden. File and rub down where necessary, and attach with Araldite.

Many times we have been given a

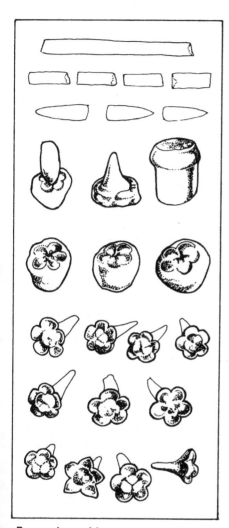

Pressed moulds

the two stub ends of the cup or mug at the side of the board and draw what you think the handle should look like. When you are satisfied with the flow of the handle, roll out your putty mixture and make a core by placing it on your drawing; leave this to set. Next day you can stick the core to the mug and when the adhesive is hard enough, add more putty and model any intricacies you think the handle should have. Leave it to harden, then rub down as usual.

Making a new knob for a lid is done in a similar way. First make the rough core, and when the putty is dry, stick the core to the lid. Allow the adhesive to set, then add more putty until you have the shape you want. Knobs may prove more difficult than they look because they must be centred and straight from all angles. What looks like an easy job to start with could turn out to be the most frustrating.

Finally, teapots are probably the most common ceramic we are asked to restore. The usual fault is a small piece missing on the spout, which is easy to mend. But over the years nearly all our pupils have experienced great difficulty getting the lines to flow with the original curve. The problem wasn't solved until we explained that in the restorer's craft you are trying to simulate other people's work, and to do that you must try to visualize the original artist and think like him; this is difficult, but our pupils took the point and their work improved. Spouts can be made by wrapping the putty mixture around a coil of plasticine which has been shaped to the correct inside curve. When the putty is dry, the plasticine can be poked out with a stick leaving a nice round hole and a base on which the outside can be modelled.

cup or mug and asked to put a handle on it. Usually after a lot of research we have found a photograph of the identical piece, only to find that the handle is facing away from the camera. In cases where the original shape is not known the restorer has to use his imagination. The easiest way we have found is to draw the handle on the mixing board. Place

Press moulding

The most suitable medium for press moulding is plasticine because it can be used over and over again. Unfortunately an individual plasticine mould can be used only once, and the image will sometimes get damaged or distorted during the separation from the pattern.

To make a press mould of the rim of an open-work plate, take a lump of plasticine, roll it in your hands until it is warm and pliable, then roll it out on a board with a rolling pin or glass jar until it forms a slab about 13mm ($\frac{1}{2}$in) thick. The thickness depends on the size of the job. Trim it until you have a piece the size of the missing part plus an all round margin of about 25mm (1in). This will be pressed on to one side of an undamaged section of the piece to obtain an impression of the missing part.

Before doing this, moisten the piece with water in the area that the plasticine is going to be applied to prevent it from sticking. You may then press the plasticine against it with an even pressure; be sure that it overlaps the rim of the ceramic and is clearly indented. Remove the plasticine gently, taking great care not to smudge the image. The resulting mould should have a smooth surface where it has been against the ceramic, otherwise air bubbles and other imperfections will be reproduced on the new work.

Place the mould over or under the missing section. If the ceramic has a corrugated edge you will find that the mould will fit naturally into place. Bend the overlap of the plasticine mould over the top edge of the plate to hold the mould in place, and secure it at the bottom with sellotape. The missing part can now be filled with putty mixture. First smear the broken edges with Araldite adhesive, then press the putty in gently so that you do not distort the mould. Finish off by smoothing over with your finger dipped in industrial methylated spirit. Leave to cure for 12 hours after which time you can take off the plasticine and rub down in the usual way. Since you can only get the imprint of one side with this type of mould, the other will need more

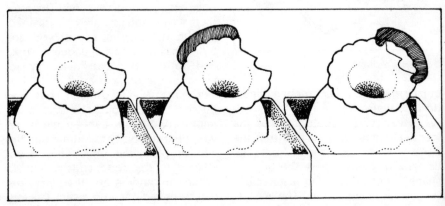

Plasticine moulds

rubbing down than usual in order to remove the surplus putty.

Press moulding can also be used when reproducing high relief on ceramics, but the pattern should be studied carefully to see if there is any undercut. If there is, a hot vinyl would have to be used instead since the plasticine mould would be distorted when removed.

Assuming there is no undercut, take the impression by pressing the plasticine on to the area you wish to reproduce. Put some putty mixture on to the broken part, modelling as accurately as possible by hand first. Take the mould off the image and wet it with industrial methylated spirit, then press it gently over the putty. The surplus putty will be squeezed out at the bottom of the mould and must be cut away. This procedure may have to be carried out several times until you have the required moulding. The plasticine should be moistened with industrial methylated spirit each time.

Handles can be moulded with plasticine but an impression has to be taken from each side. Press the plasticine halfway over the handle from one side and then insert at least two keyways (matchsticks will do) into the plasticine on either side of the handle, leaving them protruding sufficiently to secure the other half of the mould. Smear a little oil over the plasticine to stop the two halves sticking together, then take the impression from the other side. When the two sides are taken apart, you will be left with two half moulds which can be filled with putty mixture. Place the two halves together and the keyways in the plasticine will ensure that the two sides are matched perfectly.

When you wish to make several casts of the same part, it is better to use plaster of Paris to make the mould. Make a wall of plasticine around the part to be moulded and pour a runny plaster mixture over it to cover the part by about 25mm (1in). When hard it should lift off easily. Before it is filled, the mould should be smeared with grease (petroleum jelly) to prevent the Araldite putty from bonding to it. The mould can be used several times.

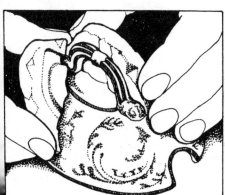 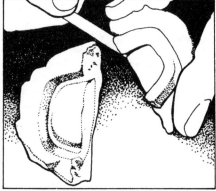

Moulding a cup handle

175

Liquid rubber moulding

Plasticine and plaster of Paris are good mediums for moulding simple items, but they leave imperfections that will need filling before the job is ready for painting. Also, they cannot be used to reproduce any area with undercut.

Hot melted vinyl compound is especially useful for making moulds of intricate missing parts. This is a rubber-like substance which is easily cut up into small pieces for melting in a saucepan (see list of addresses for suppliers). It will melt at a temperature of 120–150°C (250–300°F), and will cause a burn if allowed to come in contact with the skin. The heat will not damage ceramics but warm the piece first to avoid crazing – a network of fine cracks that may appear on the surface of the glaze.

To make the mould, build up a retaining wall of plasticine around the part to be reproduced; leave enough room for the liquid rubber to flow all around and make it high enough to give at least 6mm ($\frac{1}{4}$in) clearance at the top. Make sure there are no holes from which the rubber could flow out.

Place an old saucepan on the stove and add the cut-up pieces of vinyl rubber gradually until the compound is completely melted, stirring all the time. Do not allow the heat to rise above the recommended temperature. Remove from the heat and allow to stand while air bubbles seep out. Pour slowly and to one side to allow the liquid to flow around the part and at the same time expel the air. Fill to the top of the retaining wall, and allow the compound to cool thoroughly for

some hours before removal.

Fill the resulting mould with Araldite putty; make sure there are no air bubbles by pressing the putty into the mould with a stick. Leave for 12 hours, when the casting should be hard enough to remove from the mould and offer to the repair site. Cut away any surplus putty with a scalpel, and file until it fits, then fix with Araldite and support with plasticine if necessary. Leave for a further 12 hours, after which it can be baked and rubbed down.

These moulds are excellent for flowers and complex patterns but there can be problems when trying to remove such a mould from say, a handle. It can be cut and eased off but the casting that is produced will need a lot of rubbing down. The best way to make a rubber mould of a handle is to lay the piece on its side and make a retaining wall of plasticine around, but not touching, the handle. Pour in the vinyl rubber until the handle is half covered, leave to cool for an hour or so and then fill the mould completely. Provided that the first pouring has had time to cool sufficiently, the rubber will not stick to itself and will part cleanly. No keyways are necessary because the two pieces can easily be lined up for filling. Two strips which will need the minimum of rubbing down.

The position of the piece is most important when you are using this method of moulding. We have sometimes spent hours thinking out the best way to tackle a job in hand and have many times been frustrated by air locks appearing where they are least expected. On our second try, by moving the piece perhaps a degree or two either way, we have succeeded in getting a perfect mould.

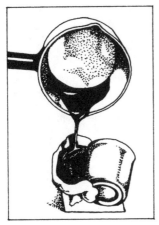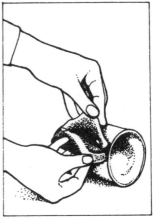

Making a rubber mould

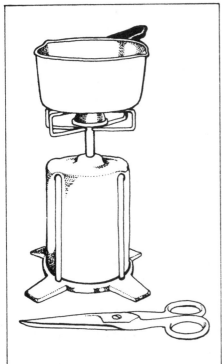

Saucepan for heating rubber moulding

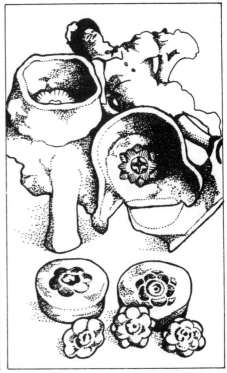

Rubber moulds for flowers

Painting materials

A completely clean, dust-free atmosphere is essential, so it is advisable not to mend and paint at the same time; dust and hairs adhere so easily to wet glaze and are very difficult to remove. Clean up the workbench and spread it with plenty of newspaper. Try to do all painting by daylight. Light is very important when matching colours; as already mentioned, this is best done in a natural light, if possible by a north-facing window. Most materials can be obtained at your local hardware and art shops.

Brushes

These need to be sable hair; they can be bought in different series and at varying prices. Settle for three or four basic brushes to start with – the cheapest will do, but take good care of them as you will find that even these are very expensive. When buying round brushes, do ask to test them in water as they must form good points. You can obtain Windsor and Newton or Rowney brushes from most good art shops: the numbers quoted here are Windsor and Newton. We would suggest a 6mm ($\frac{1}{4}$in) short-handled flat brush W.N. series 608 which is a good basic brush, and a selection of W.N. series 33 – say an 0, 2 and 5. A long-handled flat brush is useful for using inside tall vases, but it is better to collect as you go along. Keep all your brushes absolutely clean with brush cleaner. Do not leave them standing in cleaner, and wash them from time to time in warm soapy water. Stand them upright in a jar so that the hairs are not misshapen.

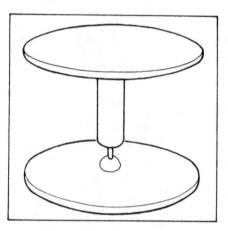

Banding wheel

Brush cleaner

The various glazes and varnish mediums require different solvents and these are usually named on the products by the manufacturers. Polyclens Plus brush cleaner and restorer is the one we use most, although turpentine substitute or methylated spirit is needed when using cold finishes. Chintex supply their own brush cleaner which can be obtained when buying the glaze.

a yellow tinge which can affect the finished appearance. Propol Clear Glaze is an almost completely clear, cold medium and is based on Araldite. Mixed by weight with equal parts of resin and hardener, and diluted with thinner, it makes a good medium for mixing with oil colours. After it has been mixed, it has a usable life of 5 to 6 hours depending on temperature, and is dry in 4 to 6 hours. When ordered, it comes complete with an explanatory leaflet.

Glazes

There are several different glazes on the market, all of which have their relative merits. We always prefer to use a hot glaze as we find that baking gives a harder and more suitable finish. Chintex supply an excellent clear glaze (and thinner) which has a shelf life of about a year. It should be very liquid when it arrives and is best kept in a dark, cool cupboard. Chintex clear glaze is an acrylic glaze; they also make a clear glossy stoving lacquer which has a yellow tinge not too welcome to most restorers, although it is still prefered by some. Unless you actually stipulate that you want the tinted glaze, you will be sent the clear acrylic one. The Sylglas Company also do a hot glaze.

When baking is not possible for various reasons, there are several cold glazes that can be used. Polyurethane clear varnish mixed well with oil paints can be used in exactly the same manner as a hot glaze but must be left to dry in its own time. Unfortunately, nearly all cold glazes have

Sundry requirements

You will need to acquire one or two white ceramic tiles from your local do-it-yourself shop – these are excellent for mixing and matching colours. You will also need a plentiful supply of cotton rags; toilet or kitchen roll can be used but both are expensive and messy. A few words to your friends and they will probably be only too glad to offload all their old rags on you. A piece or two of old silk is invaluable for dusting off excess gold powder and for cleaning those precious pieces before the final glazing – it is so soft it picks up the smallest speck of dust. Johnson's baby powder or any unwanted talcum powder is also a must for filling small cracks. Save any small pots and jars for brush cleaner. You will also need a no 3 scalpel, some flour paper, a magnifying glass, preferably on a stand, and perhaps a banding wheel, although as these are expensive, you may prefer to wait until you are more proficient before deciding to buy one.

The final and most important requirement is of course your paint; as there is quite a lot to be explained, the next section is devoted to colours and colour mixing.

Paints and mixing colours

When it comes to painting we always use oil paints, and choose Artist's rather than Student's as they are more permanent – they are also slightly more expensive but in the long run it pays to buy the best. Alternatively, powder pigments can be used but we find that oil colours mix better with all the glaze mediums. There are many different colours and to buy them all would be a costly business. However, the ones given below should provide a basis on which to work and with careful mixing, you should be able to obtain the correct shades. When buying paints, purchase small tubes, except in the case of titanium white. Quantities used are very small and the tubes tend to get very messy with constant use.

There are five basic colours needed to obtain a white background. As there is no such colour as pure white, a combination of these will help you to arrive at the right shade. They are: titanium white, Payne's grey, raw umber, oxide of chromium green and Naples yellow. Even the most white-looking background will need the addition of one or more of the latter four to the white.

Other colours that you will need are – *Blues:* French ultramarine, cobalt and cerulean; *Browns:* burnt sienna, burnt umber, vandyke and madder; *Yellows:* Windsor aurora, yellow ochre and raw sienna; *Reds:* crimson and scarlet lake, rose madder, cadmium red, Alazarin crimson, Indian and light red; *Greens:* viridian, cobalt, deep green, permanent green, olive

180

and light green; *Blacks:* lamp and ivory.

This selection of colours is only meant as a guide; more can be added to it and others left out as experience is gained. Do not worry if one colour is unobtainable, try something else instead. Titanium white is the only essential shade; titanium is the whitest substance obtainable, so do not be talked into buying anything else as it will inevitably discolour and ruin your restoration.

Although there are so many colours available, very rarely can one be used direct from the tube. It is nearly always necessary to add small quantities of some other colour until the desired shade is arrived at. This recognizing of colours only comes with constant practice and is almost like learning to read, using colours instead of words.

Whites can nearly always be matched by mixing the background colours listed above, but close scrutiny of your piece may reveal a hint of blue or even red. Black may sometimes be better than Payne's grey. Experiment on your tile until you are satisfied.

Blues are very tricky; for instance, dark blue Worcester needs French ultramarine mixed with a little crimson, and a little black will help make an even darker colour. Cobalt blue and black make dark navy. Some of the reds mixed with the blues tend to change colour in artificial light, so care must be taken in selecting the right shade and testing before starting. Chinese blue is often not blue at all but almost green; viridian green may help mixed with white and Naples yellow. If this still appears too green try a little Payne's grey or, for a bluer effect, a dash of cerulean blue.

Later you will use washes of a darker shade without the opaque white to produce a transparent finish.

Yellows are very variable. Use lemon when there is a tendency to green, and more brilliant shades when mixing orange and Staffordshire reds. Aurora with a touch of burnt sienna is excellent for flowers, and very pale yellow can be obtained by combining aurora yellow and white, with just a touch of Payne's grey.

Reds are never used in excess in their pure form, but are most necessary for blending with other colours. Earth reds – Indian red and light red – are most used, and with various yellows make up the colours found so frequently on Chinese porcelain and also on Staffordshire figures; additions of burnt sienna will give subtle varieties of tone. Purples and lilacs are all derived from reds and blues – more white, Naples yellow and Payne's grey are used for lilacs and mauves. Flesh colours need careful mixing and this will be described under a separate heading.

Greens can be bought in a large variety of shades and can of course be mixed by combining various shades of blue and yellow. Burnt sienna mixed in to a green gives an olive shade which, if a little white is added, will match the soft colour of many china leaves.

Blacks and Browns are the final group of colours and are found in varying degrees and shades when restoring. Grey has many variations. Black often needs toning down with the addition of a little brown. Raw umber provides a useful substitute for a faded gold especially on old Coalport.

We hope that this will give you some idea of the complexities involved in obtaining the exact shade. It is a good idea to experiment before starting to paint the pieces you have mended. Try mixing colours and painting them on to a tile. Bake the result and keep a note of the colours for reference later on.

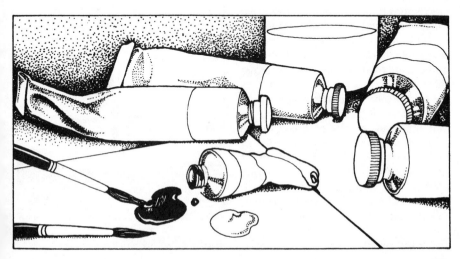

Starting to paint

Before you apply the first coat of paint, make sure that your repaired article is absolutely clean and free from dust and hairs. Try to avoid painting where there are animals shedding their coats. If there are any fingermarks or bits of Araldite left anywhere on the piece, remove them by rubbing all over with flour paper. Where Araldite is particularly stubborn on a rough or matt surface, do not rub but take an old brush and apply a little Polycel paint stripper to the offending places. Leave until the resin lifts, then wash well with warm soapy water and dry thoroughly. Any Polystrippa left on the piece could cause the paint to peel at a later stage.

Once you are satisfied that your work is clean, take a flat sable brush and paint Chintex clear glaze thinly with one straight stroke along the joins. If there is a completely new section paint this all over. The glaze seals the repair and gives you a chance to spot any tiny holes and cracks that may have been missed. We must stress that even the most expert of painters will be unable to make a good job if the repair is bad and no amount of overpainting can improve this; in fact the opposite is true as the more coats of paint you apply to it, the worse will be the fault.

If there are cracks or holes in the joins, shake some baby powder or talc on to a tile, mix with a little glaze and paint the mixture over the faults so that they are filled in. Keep a brush especially for painting on this powder mixture and clean it thoroughly after use.

Put the piece in the oven and bake

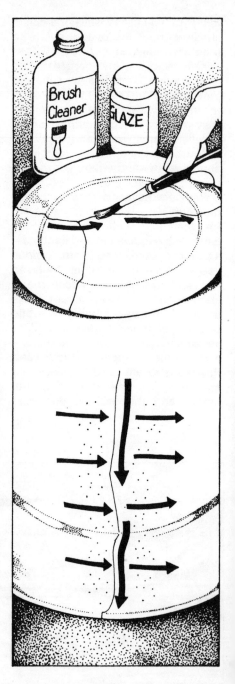

Applying white paint and glaze

for half an hour at 100°C (220°F) – remember to check the accuracy of your oven thermostat from time to time. Remove the piece from the oven and when quite cold, carefully rub down with flour paper, just enough to provide a matt surface as a key for the next coat. Again ensure that the surface is free from dust and hairs.

Squeeze a small amount of titanium white on to your tile and with a 6mm ($\frac{1}{4}$in) flat brush, mix paint and glaze, being careful to add sufficient glaze or the mixture will become 'stringy'. Paint this on to just cover the repair, overlapping no more than is necessary to cover the joins. Clean the brush and with clear glaze try to soften out the hard line with stippling and feathering movements all round the painted edge; do not pull the paint off the join. If there is a lot of pattern on the piece, use a little ingenuity and attempt to edge out around the design as far as possible. Bake again for half an hour, then leave to get quite cold. Rub down very gently as before, again trying to obtain a smooth

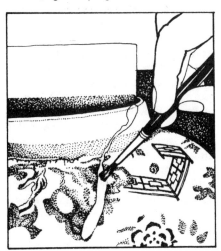

Applying clear glaze

flat finish with no humps and bumps. In between coats always make sure there is no dust or dirt adhering to the paint.

If the joins still show too plainly you should apply another coat of white paint. Never start to apply the true background colour until you have a matt white base to work on as all colours are built up from white. Apply the second coat in exactly the same way, but this time set the article aside for 2 to 3 minutes before edging out with clear glaze, and finish by pulling your brush over the join with horizontal strokes to produce a tight skin over it all. Bake as before.

This business of fading out the paint so that it blends into the surrounding area without leaving a hard line or ridge is tricky; it is perhaps the hardest part of painting and will therefore require quite a lot of practice. Confining your painting to the smallest area possible is also difficult; overpainting large areas is very easy but is not the mark of a good restorer. Most repairs are detectable under an ultraviolet lamp. A mend will show up as an opaque line, but the overpainting very often obscures the original nature of the break, making a repair seem more extensive than it really is. A broken hand will look like a complete new arm if the whole forearm is painted in an attempt to cover the cracked wrist; even the extension of clear glaze can have this effect, which makes you realize how careful the restorer must be.

If your join is very good, it is always worth considering whether to overpaint at all; sometimes, on a very valuable piece, it is better just to touch in where the white join shows.

Background painting

Having obtained a white base to work on, now is the time to start mixing the background colours.

White backgrounds

As already outlined, start by adding small quantities of basic background colours to the white paint. Glaze medium does not remain workable for very long once it has been mixed with paint, so do not mix too much at a time. If for some reason the paint does go off or there is not enough to finish, it is a good idea to take a note of the colours used so that you are able to obtain the same shade again.

Squeeze a little of each colour down the right-hand side of the mixing tile so that they are readily available. Add small quantities of them to the white with a cocktail stick, mixing well after each addition. Continue adding and mixing until you are satisfied with the shade. Apply this to the repair as before, leaving and edging out, then pulling the glaze across with horizontal strokes to form a thin skin. Bake for half an hour and when cold, rub down.

Mix a fresh amount of background colour, making sure that the shade is absolutely right; if necessary add minute quantities of some other colour as described in 'Paints and Mixing Colours', page 180. You will be surprised at the diversity of colours needed to make up an almost white background. When you are satisfied that you can do no better, paint one stroke vertically down the join, and with clear glaze, use criss-cross strokes all down and over the repair. These strokes should cancel each

other out so that there will not be any brush marks. Bake and rub down as before. If there is no pattern to be applied, dust, making sure there are no bits adhering to the paint, and give one or two final coats of clear glaze, blending out with thinner at the edges. Bake the final coat for three-quarters of an hour to obtain a good hard finish.

Coloured backgrounds

As mentioned before, you must always start with white when building up any background colour. Look carefully at the article and try to decide how the original colours were built up. Many ceramics were glazed with one colour and then dipped into others to get a multi-coloured effect. As we cannot do this we have to experiment and, by trial and error, try to produce a finish that matches the original. All this requires a lot of ingenuity as it is much more difficult to copy someone else's work than it is to devise your own style – you have to identify with an unknown artist who probably got the effect by accident anyway! If the background, for example, is dark blue, you must start with white and build up from pale blue to a darker blue, finishing with an overall translucent glaze of pure dark blue with no white in it.

Some brown earthenware needs a background colour of yellow ochre with brown on top; many gold finishes, especially on Oriental porcelain, have light red beneath the gilding. It is well worth while trying to copy these to get the right effect. Matt backgrounds such as those to be found on Wedgwood, Parian, terra cotta and biscuit wares need very different treatment and should be left well alone as even the expert is not always successful. Royal Worcester porcelain, Belleek and Worcester Scaleware are also difficult so play safe and leave them to someone else.

If your piece of pottery or porcelain has now to be decorated, do not apply the final clear coats of glaze as you will be working straight on to the rubbed-down surface. There are of course exceptions to every rule but these will be quite obvious when you have been painting for a while and have seen how the decorations are applied.

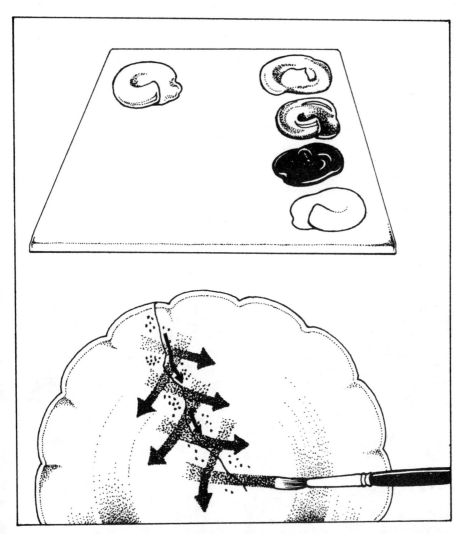

Applying background colour using basic shades

Pattern and detail painting

Most people enjoy painting in the missing decorations and details on their restored pieces as this is when you really begin to see results. Try not to overpaint more than is absolutely necessary. If you have to paint a large area with background colour, it is inevitable that you will sometimes have to cover areas of pattern; remember to take a sketch or tracing of what you will be covering or you could find yourself with a large blank area and no idea what was there.

We have already mentioned the need to edge out round designs as far as possible. If, however, you still find that you have covered more than is necessary, take a no 3 scalpel fitted with a no 15 blade and uncover the pattern using sloping cuts to avoid a hard edge. If the pattern is repetitive, find a similar spot and trace it, then transfer the design to the blank area, taking care to ensure that it matches. A volatile pencil can be used for this as it will not rub off as easily as ordinary pencil, but will disappear when heated at a later stage. If you decide to paint freehand, great care should be taken with geometric designs; measure the distance between spots and circles etc, used as edgings since few things look worse than an uneven design.

As mixing the right colours is quite an art, experiment on your tile until you are satisfied; keep the colours subdued. Never use a colour on a piece you are restoring that is not already there; this is particularly tempting when replacing a missing ribbon, fan or flower. Use a thin round sable brush with a good point, a no 5 or even less for very fine detail. A magnifying glass on a stand is a great help when painting small designs and intricate details. These range in price considerably, but it is worth getting the best you can afford. Once you get used to using one, it can save your eyes from strain.

Painting in the pattern

When you are painting, thinner can be mixed with the glaze to make your paint flow more easily; Chintex glaze tends to go sticky very quickly. Various simple tools can often help you to obtain the required effect. Cocktail sticks drawn through the paint will form a thin line or pattern; the applied paint must be at just the right consistency and you will need to dip your stick in clear glaze to stop it from pulling the paint off, but you will soon learn with practice. Veins of leaves can also be done in this way, provided the background is the same colour as the veins. Hairs on ornamental figures are often done like this, or they can be drawn in with a thinned glaze medium and a no 0 brush.

Raised colours can be achieved by building up the paint in thick layers, or by mixing talc with white paint to form blobs and raised lines, which can then be baked and later glazed and coloured. Some old Chinese and Korean ceramics have black specks in the glaze – a little cigarette ash mixed with the final glaze gives a very realistic finish.

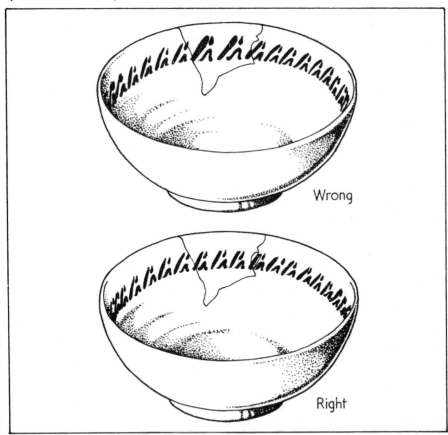

Correct matching of the pattern is important

Flesh, crazing and pot lids

Flesh

The painting of limbs and faces needs careful study. Naturally the new parts must match the originals. Many arms and hands look almost white, but when put to the test they are far from this. You can buy a flesh colour in Artist's oils but we would advise against this as it can look very flat even when applied with other colours. Flesh colour is made up of five basic shades: white, black, Payne's grey or blue, red or crimson, and perhaps a dash of burnt umber. As skin has a translucent deep look, these colours should be mixed and built up from white in layers, finishing with a transparent overglaze to which a little red or crimson and/or brown has been added.

When tinting cheeks, fingers, toes and knees, dry powder pigment applied to the tacky glaze in minute quantities with a dry brush will, with practice, produce an excellent effect. Eyes and lips should be added before the final glaze. Black or brown Indian inks applied with a fine brush are sometimes easier to use for fine lines such as eyelashes and eyebrows; the right colour and texture for lips can only be obtained by making up a thinned glaze and paint mixture. Remember to bake the ceramic in the oven before the final glazing or the colours may run.

A finish that is too shiny can often be subdued if it is dusted with talc immediately on removal from the oven.

Crazing

Crazing of one sort or another is a very common feature on many sorts of ceramics. Crackle ware and forms of early mock crazing must certainly be simulated as a plain area of paint would look very strange indeed. The difficulties in imitating the very fine crazing are obvious; however, a very sharp, hard lead pencil can be used to lightly draw in the lines, then glaze can be carefully applied over the top. Although the brush will remove some of the lines, the effect is usually quite good and certainly gives a realistic hint of crazing. The lines on crackle-ware were made by a deliberate, unknown process and are easily copied with the correct colour of paint or waterproof ink. There is usually a continuity of pattern so make sure you get this right. Unfortunately, it can be a very tedious and time-consuming business but is necessary for a good finish.

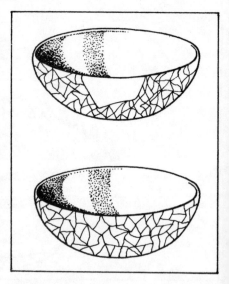

Pencil in the crazing pattern before inking it in

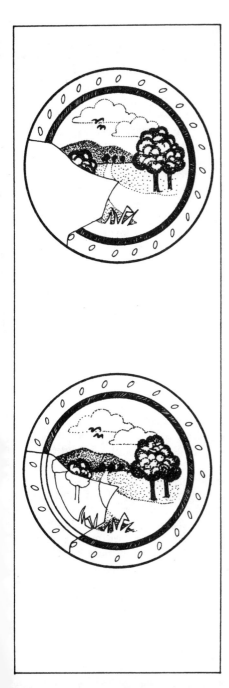

Ink in the design before painting

Pot lids

Pot lids are very popular collectors' items and are easy to repair. However, the pictures on top are very often damaged and this calls for a certain amount of repainting. Illustrations of most pot lids are reproduced in the comprehensive books available on the subject, so there will be no trouble in finding a copy for any missing sections. But since the actual picture is a transfer, the difficulty lies in achieving such a flat smooth finish – as is the case with any other ceramic with applied pictures. Those of you who like intricate painting will enjoy doing these and the method suggested here can, with care, be excellent.

Apply your glaze and white paint as described in 'Starting to Paint', being careful not to overpaint the original picture more than you can help, and rub down. Using Indian ink and a very fine brush, paint in the outlines and then paint in the picture with ordinary water-colours, shading where necessary. Allow it to dry thoroughly, cover very carefully with clear glaze and bake as before. The glazing has to be done carefully to ensure that the water-paints are sealed as they are not very durable. Rub down gently and apply another coat of glaze, edging out with thinner. Bake again. A coat of car polish over the whole picture gives a lasting and almost undetectable finish.

As every piece of restoration differs in some way or other, it is virtually impossible to compile a complete guide to painting – the beginner will have to learn by his own mistakes. But if things really look wrong, it is usually better to put the piece away for a while; it may not look so bad after a day or two!

Gilding

Most pieces have gold of one sort or another on them. The very shiny modern gold can never be simulated and should not be attempted. Other golds vary enormously in shade and texture so that it is very difficult to achieve a perfect match or finish.

Gold powder
Gold powders can be purchased and a blend of different shades can usually produce something very near the original.

To paint with gold powder, put a little on your tile and mix with glaze. The addition of a little raw umber paint can sometimes help produce an old gold effect; used alone, as already mentioned, raw umber is a fine substitute for faded gold especially on old Coalport, and is also invaluable in shading. After painting, bake the piece in the oven for half an hour at 100°C (220°F), then let it cool and coat the painted area with clear glaze. Do not rub down gold work. If you do not wish to bake the work, lacquer can be mixed with the gold powder and allowed to dry naturally. There are brands of lacquer on the market which come complete with gold powder but as this is usually rather coarse and not the right colour, it is better to buy and blend your own.

Silver and bronze powders are also available and should be applied in the same way. Silver very often looks better with the addition of a small amount of black paint, but as with high-fired gold, the brilliant finish on silver lustre is impossible to obtain and painting on this and bronze lustre should be kept to a minimum.

Gold leaf
The best results are of course obtained with gold leaf. Gilding by this method takes a lot of practice, but when well done produces a much softer and smoother finish. To start with it is as well to practise on a tile. Paint a pattern on the tile with George Whiley writing size – the addition of a small amount of black paint to the size will enable you to see what you are doing. Keep the lines thin unless you are planning a band of gold. When finished, put the tile aside for at least 2 hours, when the medium should be just tacky. Clean your brushes with pure turpentine. If the size is too dry the gold leaf will not stick and if it is too wet, the size will come through. While it is drying, remove a leaf from the booklet in which it is supplied and cut it to the shape or size of pattern to be covered.

Lay the leaf on the pattern with tweezers and smooth it very gently with a finger. Again using tweezers, carefully peel off the tissue-paper backing and if pieces are missing, apply another piece of gold leaf on top. When all is covered, lay a piece of tissue (from the booklet) wax side down over the gold leaf and gently smooth and rub with your little finger. To level the edges, brush with a dry sable brush or use a modelling tool. Repeat the whole process the next day if necessary.

Objects gilded by this method are not baked and it is only used on valuable pieces that are not washed too often. If the piece is going to be washed, a coat of polyurethane varnish should be applied as a final protective coat. Ceramics that are not so valuable and will be washed more frequently can be gilded in exactly

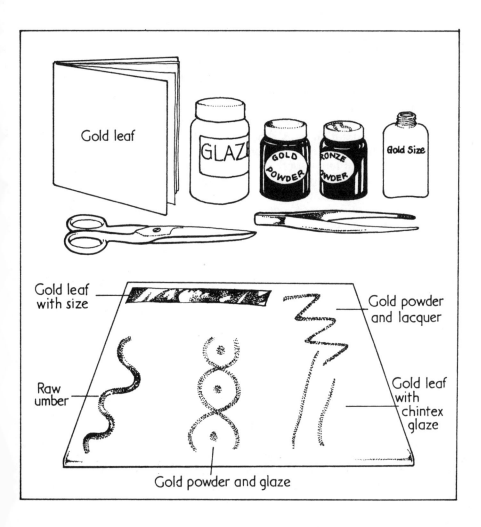

Gold leaf

GLAZE

GOLD POWDER

BRONZE POWDER

Gold Size

Gold leaf with size

Gold powder and lacquer

Raw umber

Gold leaf with chintex glaze

Gold powder and glaze

the same manner using Chintex glaze instead of size as the medium. Apply the glaze and leave for 10 to 15 minutes before laying on the gold leaf. Bake at about 66°C (150°F) in a domestic oven for 20 minutes. When cold, apply a coat of clear glaze and bake again for half an hour.

When applying gold leaf on indentations, use an india rubber cut in a wedge shape for pressing on the gold leaf; and when painting size on a dark background, add a little white paint.

Gold leaf can be obtained in a variety of colours and unless you have a great deal of work to do, it is perhaps better left to an expert who will hold larger stocks. It is very fragile and must be handled with great care.

Mechanical aids

This book would not be complete without a more detailed mention of the mechanical aids that can be employed for restoration work. They are really only useful in the more advanced stages of repair work or to anyone who is envisaging a professional career in this craft.

There are of course very expensive tools to be had, but an ordinary two-speed power drill of the type found at do-it-yourself shops or ironmongers will do almost as well. It should be mounted on the workbench and with the addition of various drills and grinding tools, can be a great help at times. You should be very careful when using this tool as it is essential not to damage the glaze of the original piece. Grinding down ceramics to make a good join should be avoided except when all else fails – this is usually when a piece has 'sprung', that is, has warped through being broken for some time. At all other times the piece should be taken apart and restuck. There is no excuse for a faulty join: this is the sign of bad workmanship and is to be deplored.

If at any time you acquire a large pot or vase that is broken round the top, a very passable lamp base can be made by grinding the damaged top off. If you are doing this for someone else, do make sure that it is done at the owner's risk, in case the whole thing disintegrates.

Sometimes it is difficult to clean the inside of a large vase or pot – a flexible drive attached to your drill can get where perhaps your hand cannot, and can be bought at a small

cost. Drills of various dimensions are useful, as quite a few new parts need holes drilled in them, but remember to use them with great caution as at no time should you damage the original article by heavy handedness.

The other mechanical aid much used by the professional is the paint spray or air brush. Again, this is to be used with caution as it is easy to overspray an article. Contrary to the general impression, using an air brush properly needs a great deal of skill. Because of the spread, it is really only suitable for use on plain subjects with very little decoration. On plates and bowls with no decoration the spray is really the only answer for satisfactory edging out. As a spray is in no way a complete substitute for the brush method and as it is rather expensive, its use is possibly not advisable for the beginner.

The air brush itself is a small pen-like tool with a reservoir to hold the paint, and is used with a compressor which will produce a pressure of about 32lb psi. Chintex glaze and thinner – in a proportion of 2:1 – are mixed with paint to the right shade; this mixture is put into the reservoir and sprayed on to the surface of the ceramic, keeping the brush moving all the time. If any pattern is obscured, the paint can be removed with a brush dipped in clear glaze before baking, or with a scalpel after baking. As thinner is used the finish is much softer and, unless finished off properly by brushing on a coat of clear glaze, can scratch or peel very easily. The air brush must be thoroughly cleaned directly after use or it will seize up and become very hard to get working again properly – it may become blocked with small particles of dried

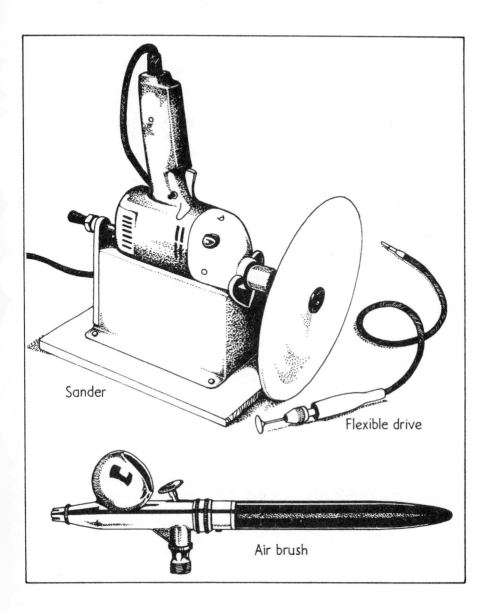

Sander

Flexible drive

Air brush

paint. A mask should always be used and spraying should only be done where there is proper ventilation.

An air brush is seldom used for applying patterns but can be used for special finishes on ceramics, and very effective gradual shading can be achieved as well as speckling and spots. All these effects need much practice and it depends a great deal on the object whether an air brush will produce the best result.

193

Research

This is a very important part of restoration. Most pieces with any value and age attached to them have identifying features that it is important to reproduce when replacing missing parts. Modern limited editions should also be correctly restored, although this is fairly easy as most good china shops carry illustrated catalogues of these, and no doubt the actual factory would be only too willing to help you. Sometimes we are brought figures with the most fantastic and funny additions which say much for the restorer's imagination and ingenuity, but are a complete give-away in terms of accuracy.

As many pieces are well known, the reference section of your local library should be the first port of call. Most of the larger libraries have a good selection of illustrated books that you can browse through; if they haven't got the particular book that you need, they will usually try and obtain it for you. If the library has a photocopier, make use of it so that you have a picture to refer to when you get home. If relevant, make a note of the colours you need as the photocopy will be in black and white.

Museums are always helpful; some specialize but if you can't get to the museum concerned, many of them have photographs and booklets that you can purchase. It is always better to see the whole article as very often a picture shows the wrong aspect and the part you need to see is not visible, which is most frustrating. For real life models of birds and animals you may need the help of a good bird or animal book, or, as once happened

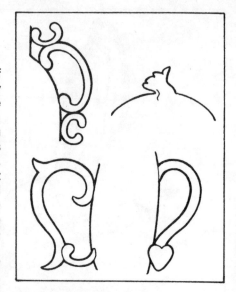

Characteristic shapes

in our case, the natural history section of your local museum may come up with the answer.

Handles and knobs are very distinctive features of the older, well known factories and many pieces can be identified by them. You can obtain books which give you drawings of the knobs, handles and other appendages attributed to various factories. Bow, Worcester, Caughley and Lowestoft (to name a few examples) all have typical handles – Old Worcester for instance, has a flower instead of a knob on some lids. These must be right: accuracy is essential. Some factories have their own museums and the curators are usually able to help with any problems you may have.

It is quite a good idea to make a scrap book from any pictures or cuttings you get hold of; in this way you can build up a very useful reference library of your own. Keep your eyes open when you are out visiting:

194

Examples needing research before repairing

a friend or acquaintance may have a similar piece to one you have to repair and be willing to lend it to you to take a mould!

Many figures, bowls and plates have writing on them which is partly missing – here again it is important not to guess. Sunderland jugs and bowls have many different rhymes and dates on them. If too much guess-work is used on the Wearmouth Bridge design, a piece could well be attributed to a different period as the transfer alters significantly over the years – this shows how careful you must be. The style of writing and the words on Victorian China Fairings also vary considerably and should always be checked. Never cover a maker's mark on a piece of china.

Colours are important and again are often associated with certain factories and artists. The identification of missing colours is usually relatively easy as there is nearly always some

part left which will give a clue to the missing section. However, handles can be tricky since those on items such as old Staffordshire Toby jugs were painted in many different ways. If nothing is visible, it is best to use some colour that is already on the piece; never get 'carried away' and use paint of an entirely different shade. Cup handles very often have a gold decoration on them; if they are part of a set, try to get this right.

The list of details to research is almost endless, but you can see how important all this is especially if you want to be satisfied with your finished repair. If you really cannot discover what a missing part should be like, it is better to leave well alone and just tidy the thing up. Lastly, if you feel that anything is really beyond your present capabilities, put it away until you are more experienced, or have it repaired properly if it is something you treasure.

Conclusion

To conclude it is perhaps a good idea to point out some of the snags and pitfalls that can arise when handling old and damaged ceramics. A bad repair can be very damaging to a valuable piece. The method described here does not recommend the grinding down of surfaces, except under exceptional circumstances. Every piece of rare pottery or porcelain is precious and mutilating it in this way tends to give the restorer a bad name. Aim at doing as little as possible, especially when painting.

If you are unfortunate enough to have an extensively restored piece to work on, proceed carefully as the materials used could be of a non-durable nature especially when baked. If the whole article is not to be done again, use the cold method of sticking and painting on the part that you are restoring.

Some old pottery, such as Toby jugs and cider jugs which have been exposed to smoky and greasy atmospheres, will sometimes exude brown grease when baked; old cheese dish bases behave in a similar way. This will wipe off, but usually reappears on subsequent bakings, so again you should use the cold method as Chintex glaze will not adhere to a greasy surface.

Bubbling can occur in the glaze during baking, especially between fingers and in cracks and crevices where paint tends to pool. You can usually prevent this by applying the paint while the article is warm.

Cheap wares, such as Victorian and Edwardian toilet jugs and basins, and mass-produced vases will often craze all over in an alarming fashion even when baked at a low heat; experience will soon tell you which pieces are likely to do this and whether it matters. As has been previously mentioned, comports should never be heated unless they have been dismantled; the tops are made under stress and as they cool more quickly than the bases they can split, leaving a gap that cannot be pulled together.

When large parts are replaced in vases or plates, shrinkage may occur during baking especially if you are using Araldite putty. Sylmasta putty is better, but if the part persists in shrinking, cold glazing may again be the best method to use.

If any white paint starts to brown in the oven, no covering coat will obliterate this, it will keep coming

Type of comport liable to split if heated

through. The only solution is to take it all off with Polycell paint stripper, wash and dry well and start again, making sure that your oven is at the correct temperature. Similarly, there are occasions when the paint starts to peel – we have yet to discover the cause for this, but in any case the easiest method of dealing with it is to start again, making sure that everything is clean and dry.

These are just a few of the problems facing the restorer. Frustrating they may be, incurable they are not.

Many restorers refuse to divulge the secrets of their trade, no doubt fearing that there will be too many competitors in the field. During our years in the business we have found this to be far from true. The professional has nothing to fear and much to gain. Many would-be restorers find that they are unable to apply themselves to the craft with the patience and dedication that is needed to succeed, and soon fall by the wayside; however, they are able to appreciate the skill of the craftsman and thus recommend and encourage his work. Those who become really interested and accomplished are welcome as there is plenty of work for all and the load increases with the passing years.

We hope that this book will help you to embark on this absorbing business or hobby. As you become more confident, you will soon develop your own ideas. This is the fascination of the job; there is no 'right way', only the way that produces the best and most reliable finish.

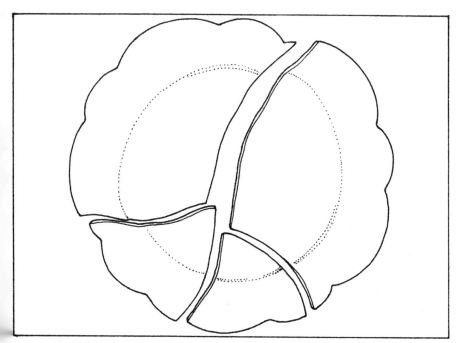

Plain plate best left to the expert to repair

Prints, Paintings and Frames

Ian Cook

Illustrated by the author

Introduction

The renovation of old paintings is a subject in which more and more people are becoming interested. This is especially so with the do-it-yourself trend of recent years, and whereas not everyone may wish to be an expert restorer, anyone who owns a painting or print, either purchased or inherited, will profit from an understanding of the basic mechanics of 'picture science'. As expertise becomes more expensive and preservation and conservation of existing raw materials becomes more necessary, then renovation by the amateur is made increasingly relevant. In the case of frames, always expensive items, renovation is certainly worthwhile, not only to save cost, but also to preserve the aesthetic, period look of the complete picture.

Due to the lack of skilled restorers, most renovation work done on watercolours and prints until fairly recently was in fact undertaken by the collectors themselves — sometimes, admittedly, to the picture's detriment. The advice contained in this book should help the would-be renovator by explaining some of the techniques available to the experts, and also some of the inherent dangers to be avoided. Of course where valuable works of art are concerned, one has to be careful that, by trying to be a penny-pincher, one does not in fact become a pound-loser. Amongst the less important art auction sales of the major salerooms appear many works damaged to a greater or lesser degree, sometimes merely dirty, but often scarred due to over-zealous or unskilled restoration work. In these cases of course, the eventual prices realised are far below what they would have reached if in better condition.

Since old paintings and prints are becoming more sought after, even lesser items can be of much greater value than was expected. So if you are fortunate enough to own a painting or print of value, or even if you only think you may own one, by all means learn the techniques contained in this book but before embarking on an extensive renovation, obtain an expert's advice and if necessary leave the restoration work to him. On the other hand, if all you want is an improvement in the appearance of a favourite picture by Aunt Matilda and the picture or frame is due to be thrown away, then you have nothing to lose at all in any experimental renovation work.

Remember that, despite attentions from would-be restorers, wars, riots, pollution and other hazards, innumerable seemingly fragile paintings and prints have survived as reminders of previous ages and as such are not only furnishings but can be viewed as parts of each one's own inheritance, to be lived with and enjoyed now and in the future.

Some examples of different types of paintings

Oil paintings

Dark surfaces

Rows of dark oil paintings set in baronial halls have led many people to believe that the majority of old paintings are boring and dull. However one must bear in mind that sometimes these paintings are presenting themselves to us with the accretions of not just a few years but perhaps the dust and grime of three hundred years or more. Any housewife knows how dust accumulates in even the most inaccessible and protected of places, and whereas electric light and central heating are relative newcomers, the wax candle and open fire which produce their own brand of dust, dirt and discoloration have been leaving slight deposits on a room's furnishings for many years. The windows, glass, furniture, floors and cutlery have all been cleaned many times over, but how does one clean that old picture over the fireplace? Through quite rightly not wishing to cause damage, people leave these relics – sometimes survivors of the cavalier or puritan age – to look darker and darker.

A further complication in this darkening process is due to the fact that almost all old paintings have been coated with a varnish made from a mastic resin. This varnish looked fine when first brushed on, but it gradually turns yellow and after many years it becomes completely brown. Added to this, heavy cigarette or tobacco smoking in a room over many years adds a further brown layer of nicotine deposits, so it is not surprising that a good many paintings originally executed in quite brilliant colours now appear as dull,

Features of the darkening process: a. the sky appears yellow; b. the distance appears dark green; c. the foreground appears dark brown

202

unattractive shadows of their former selves. Typical changes in appearance are that the browns, greens and reds appear almost black, whites show as dirty, brownish yellow and blues appear as dull greens.

However, it must also be stated that sometimes owners think that their paintings are dirtier than they actually are. For example, many painters of the eighteenth and early nineteenth centuries had a great fondness for brown, such that their landscapes often have a great deal of brown detail in the foreground. When originally painted and varnished, this would have contrasted nicely with the landscape vista in the distance and was accepted as part of the recognised formula for successfully constructing a presentable painting. Most portrait painters gave a dark background to the sitter, and in still-life paintings too a dark background was used as a contrast against the details of flowers or fruit. It is in these cases that one can sometimes come

to the wrong conclusion and think that the painting is dirty, when in fact the picture was originally intended that way. Any attempt at cleaning such a painting would give very little result, with the temptation to try and clean in a harder, more vigorous way finally resulting in a badly damaged painting with a rubbed paint surface.

Sometimes earlier attempts at cleaning or renovation only reveal themselves in the years that follow. For example, many old oil paintings have had linseed oil or other oils rubbed on them. These oils discolour and leave a sticky surface for more dust and dirt to settle on.

All these factors contribute to the appearance of your pictures. While this may make the thought of successful cleaning daunting for the amateur, it is wise to know the mechanics of picture darkening and not to be too hasty in pronouncing a picture 'dirty'.

Examples of dark backgrounds in a portrait and a still-life

Oil paintings

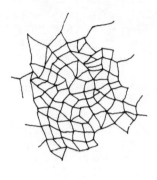
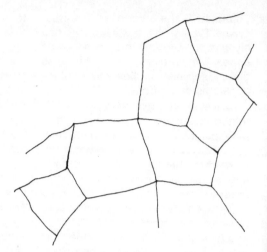

The appearance of the craquelure often enables an expert to place a date on a painting

Surface cracks

Cracks in paint, known as the 'craquelure', are to pictures what a patina is to old bronze – in fact, they are becoming considered a hallmark of antiquity. Oil paint hardens with time so that a hundred-year-old oil painting painted on canvas, shows cracks over its surface approximately 1–1½in apart. As the age increases more cracks appear such that a seventeenth-century painting appears covered in a fine cobweb pattern of cracks sometimes only ¼in apart. The appearance of the craquelure allows an expert to place a date on the painting, often, after considering other factors, to within a few years.

However, various other factors can influence the degree of cracking. Often the stretcher (the wooden frame which has the canvas tacked over it) shows through in the pattern of the cracks. On some eighteenth- and nineteenth-century paintings there appear rings of cracks which,

some have reasoned, may arise from the artist's habit of resting a painting-stick against the canvas during the painting. Cracks which are dispersed evenly throughout the paint film are not to be worried about, but are a feature to be proud of. In fact, the time to worry about the cracks is when they are not in evidence; the art-dealing experts viewing a picture sale are looking specifically for areas in a painting where no cracks appear. This is because if an old painting has been restored (ie repainted over a damaged area), cracks in new paint cannot be easily manufactured and the restoration becomes obvious to a trained eye. Of course this is not the complete guide to spotting restored areas, as some skilful restorers can complete the repair with a finely painted network of cracks, to pre-serve the uniformity of appearance.

On rare occasions, wide cracks may occur in the painting, due to shrinkage, and can be very distract-ing. In these cases the cracks can be

The outline of the stretcher showing through in the pattern of the cracks

repainted in colour to match, but often this only camouflages the defect and in some opinions they are best left, leaving the picture, as the experts say, in an 'honest' condition.

It may come as a surprise to the amateur art enthusiast to realise that very many signed paintings do not in fact bear a signature which was put on by the artist or is even contemporary with the painting. Here craquelure helps establish the authenticity or lack of it of the signature. Obviously if the signature is of the same date as the painting, the cracks will go through the paint of the signature as well as that of the background. When this is not the case, it may reasonably be assumed that the signature has been added later. In art-saleroom parlance, when a painting 'bears signature', it is implied that it bears false signature.

However, armed with this knowledge of craquelure to date a painting, do not be too hasty in labelling the Dutch seventeenth-century painting in the local museum a modern fake because it exhibits no cracks at all. Some paintings on wooden panels or copper show no cracks at all even though they may be three to four hundred years old. On the other hand, occasionally one may see a more recent painting where all the brown pigments show multitudinous, unsightly cracks. This disfiguring feature is due to a bitumen constitutent in brown paint which in fact never dries properly and takes on this unsightly thickening cracking which is hard to describe but can be seen in many of the portrait paintings by the famous painter Sir Joshua Reynolds. It cannot be remedied.

Oil paintings

Flaking paint

Sometimes, unfortunately, the paint on a picture has flaked away. This may be due to various causes, such as defects in the preparation of the canvas or panel, or scratches or accidents happening over the years. The most important aspect of flaking paint is to try to find or keep the pieces of paint which have flaked away. This may sound an improbable task, but in a good many cases of extensive flaking in nineteenth-century paintings, where they have been framed behind glass, the pieces of flaked paint are to be found contained within the space between the canvas and the glass. That this is important can be seen from the prices sometimes realised at auction by paintings in this condition, when the picture has never been taken out of its frame, and all the missing pieces can be seen. A skilled restorer is able to piece all the flaked areas back into place like in a jigsaw puzzle, adhering each piece using a beeswax and hot spatula-tip technique. Beeswax has a fairly low melting point and by placing each piece into its respective position after coating with a thin wax layer, gentle touching with the hot spatula is sufficient to melt the wax. When the heat is removed the wax re-solidifies, leaving the flaked piece held firmly in position, usually providing a perfect repair.

Should you therefore have a valuable oil painting where some flaking has occurred, it would be important to get it and the pieces to a skilled restorer as soon as possible. If the picture is not of that importance, a quick adhesion, using the beeswax technique and a spoon handle instead of a spatula, heated in near boiling water, may suffice. Alternatively you may even be able to glue the pieces back with a good adhesive.

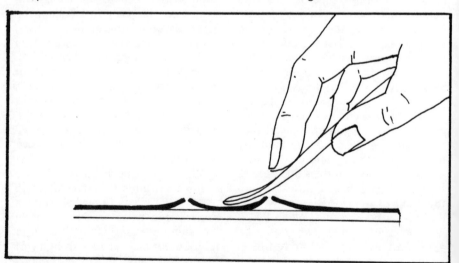

Re-adhering flaking paint using a heated spatula

Often, however, the flaked-off pieces are long gone, and pieces of the white 'ground' (preparation) now show, proving to be very distracting. If a quick improvement in the appearance of the picture is required, it is enough just to repaint these missing areas with either oil paint, acrylic paint or watercolour, using a colour which matches the surroundings. This technique will only stand up to casual observation, for, if viewed from the side, the depression left as a result of the thickness of paint having been lost, will show, and shadow formation and the uneven texture will reveal the damaged area. This is why a skilled painting restorer will not only repaint a flaked area but will use a filling medium on the missing area to ensure that a continuation of surface is made, and only then repaint.

For simplicity, if a repair of this type is to be made by the amateur, ordinary putty, even acrylic paint, or some other filler could be applied, with the aid of a palette knife carefully handled. It also helps if a little paint of the approximate colour of the surroundings is mixed with the filler, because if, after completing the filling and leaving it to dry, a purely white-filled area is left, then several coats of thin paint on top would be needed to cover over the glaring white. If the filler is approximately the right colour then this added complication can be avoided.

If the amateur, following these instructions, just repaints the lost area, or uses a putty filler, no permanent alteration to the picture has been done. If at a later stage a skilled restorer wishes to obtain a perfect finish, both these repair techniques could easily be reversed by him, with no damage to the painting having been done.

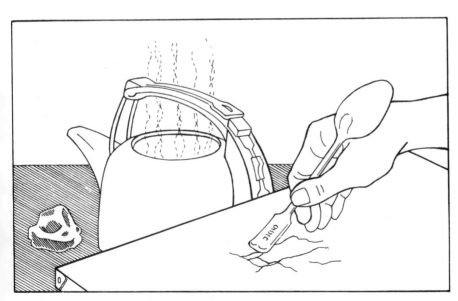

A quick adhesion using beeswax and a hot spoon handle

Oil paintings

Repainting a missing portion using a stippling technique

Repainting

To enable one to properly ascertain the colours of a painting, it is often necessary first to give the painting a very diluted coat of varnish so that the true colours can be seen.

Some restorers keep to 'in-painting' only, so that if a piece of blue sky is being restored, blue paint will be applied to the missing portion only, using a stippling technique, and not to any surrounding areas. This practice has the advantage of keeping the adulteration of the painting down to the minimum; however it will usually be observable if examined carefully.

On the other hand, restorers who have a good knowledge of what paintings should look like, when restoring for example a small area of sky, may find it necessary to build up a cloud or add another branch to a tree or something similar, so that the final repair will be completely undetectable to the naked eye. The obvious disadvantage is that one does need to have a great deal of skill and also that it does increase the amount of repainted area in the picture.

It might come as a surprise to most people to see some gallery pictures, which superficially appear in perfect condition, illuminated using an ultra-violet picture inspection lamp. Under these conditions, paint which is old takes on a ghostly and translucent appearance, whereas the repainted areas stand out boldly in black. If you have just invested in an expensive painting it is probably not advisable to inspect it through such a lamp as it may cause disappointment! However, it is now widely recognised that many, if not most, good paintings have had certain small restorations completed on them and it becomes of serious concern only when restoration exceeds 25 per cent of the picture surface.

Cleaning surface grime

It must be admitted that the cleaning of an old, yellowed, oil painting is a fascinating experience, as the original colours and quality of painting are gradually revealed. However, holding to the old adage that 'an ounce of prevention is worth a pound of cure', it might be advisable first to state that the best way to ensure no surface

Surface grime should be carefully removed using cotton wool soaked in white spirit

grime builds up is to dust the painting regularly and carefully with a feather duster or something similar. Do not rub with a rag as this might cause a piece of paint to flake away.

If the painting has an old coat of varnish and is covered in dust and grime, a piece of cotton wool soaked in white spirit and carefully wiped over the surface will take off the surface dirt. It will also reveal, to a degree, the brightness of the picture underneath, as it will make the picture appear semi-varnished until it evaporates, whereupon the picture will once more resume its duller appearance. As long as the painting is in oil paint and older than five years, white spirit will not harm it at all. In fact, the older it is, the safer. Only if the painting has been recently varnished would the white spirit be inadvisable, as it would tend to dissolve the new varnish. Old varnish or paint will be completely unaffected.

Sometimes a white bloom will be seen over the surface of the picture. This is quite a common feature and if, when wiped over with white spirit, it is seen to disappear but return when the white spirit has evaporated, it will only be necessary to revarnish the oil painting with a good varnish

to ensure the disappearance of this unsightly bloom (see page 212).

On rare occasions, usually with paintings of little value which were probably not varnished on completion, surface grime can become quite ingrained. *If you are sure the painting is of little value*, then to achieve an improvement, wipe the surface gently using cotton wool buds soaked in an ammonia solution (10 per cent Scrubbs cloudy ammonia solution diluted with an equal amount of water) but be careful not to rub hard, and only work on a small area at a time, with the picture lying flat, and after cleaning a small area, dry it using clean swabs.

The danger of this technique is that it will remove paint as well as dirt and so should only be tried on oil paintings of very little value, or by someone with good experience of oil paintings. Hot soapy water is never to be recommended for cleaning old oil paint as it will only partially remove grime and will loosen the paint from the ground of the canvas, leaving a rubbed, semi-clean painting as a result.

After removal of surface grime, the next stage involves removal of the old varnish.

Oil paintings

When removing old varnish, work carefully on very small areas at a time

Removing old varnish

If the varnish is very new, white spirit might suffice, especially as modern varnishes should not become progressively more insoluble as the older varnishes have. However, the problem now encountered is that the solvents available for old varnishes may also attack or dissolve the underlying paint. Thus any removal of old varnish must be done in a very careful manner, using cotton wool swabs on a very small area at a time. Typical solvents are acetone, methyl alchohol and ethyl alchohol. These organic solvents can be diluted using white spirit. Acetone is probably one of the most commonly used solvents but

it has its disadvantages. Diluted ammonia solution can also be used.

However, it is also interesting to note that most people would start to clean a painting by beginning on the sky; here lies the reason for many a disaster over cleaning a painting. Sky colours – white, greys and blues – are the safest colours to clean with solvents and as he sees a crisp clean sky revealed, the amateur may fall into the trap of thinking that the cleaning is going well and easily. In the hurry to complete it, it is easy to forget caution and, using the same concentration of solvent on the foreground of the picture, disaster occurs because colours such as greens, reds and

Sky colours are the easiest to clean. Exercise great caution especially when cleaning the foreground of a painting

especially browns are much more easily removed. The danger lies in possible over-cleaning of the detail of these colours which leaves a picture devoid of the detail which the artist originally laboured over. This sad story has occurred many times even with some important paintings in public collections, resulting in the very 'thin' appearance of these 'earth' colours in many of them.

If in doubt on the removal of old varnish in dark detailed areas, be over-cautious, even if necessary leaving the old varnish on and relying on a new coat of varnish to brighten it. It is better to leave it like this than continue and lose the detail of the painting. Most professional restorers recognise that complete varnish removal, even with the greatest of care, does often remove a little paint. They, however, will be more able to replace and strengthen weak areas than will the average person.

Sometimes, after cleaning, a white bloom will be seen on some parts of the painting, leaving the would-be renovator concerned that the painting is ruined.

This blanching is commonly met with and will disappear on revarnishing, but when seen it does show that caution to avoid overcleaning must be taken.

Oil paintings

Revarnishing

The varnishing of a painting is a most important operation as not only does it give the colours of the painting a glowing appearance, but also provides the painting with its future protection. However, a thick glossy coat of varnish, while allowing all the original colours to shine brilliantly and also offering good protection, does look rather glossy and brassy. A more matt finish on the other hand is difficult to apply and as matt varnishes involve the addition of wax as a matting agent, they offer less protection but give a much more pleasing appearance to the eye.

A suitable compromise can be achieved by various means. In preparing the oil painting for varnishing, ensure that the picture is absolutely clean and free from anything like fluff or dirt; it is also advisable to work in a warm room with the picture also warm. Dilute the varnish down to 2 parts varnish, 1 part white spirit, and, using a wide brush with the painting lying flat, apply the varnish with criss-cross strokes, until all the paint has been covered in a varnish film. A second coat may be considered advisable after the first has dried. A certain degree of reduction of gloss may be achieved by continuing to brush even whilst the varnish is tacky and, by using a stippling technique, a certain rendering down can be achieved, at the same time ensuring thorough impregnation with varnish. If a more matt effect is desired, a wax matt varnish can be mixed with the gloss, depending on the degree of mattness required. However, this method will

Applying varnish with a brush, using criss-cross strokes

require the varnish and brush being heated slightly to dissolve the matt wax varnish.

Sometimes an attractive finish can be achieved by applying one of the commercial soft wax picture varnishes, after the brushed varnish has dried hard. The wax paste is applied using a soft cloth and gently polished when dry.

Nowadays the use of spraying techniques has introduced new scope into the realm of picture appearance. Small spray units can be purchased or varnish can be purchased in spray cans. The advantage of spraying is that it applies a very even coating of varnish and also, using the spray bottle warmed, matt varnishes can be applied, giving acceptable 'eggshell' finishes. However, unless used carefully, spray units only impart a very thin film of varnish which may offer slightly less protection for the future.

The picture should be sprayed from a distance of 10–15in, with the picture positioned vertically, using a very light side-to-side technique, being careful not to allow varnish to become saturated in any one part of the picture. To prevent the varnish running, varnish lightly three or four times rather than trying to complete the spraying in one operation.

Whichever way of applying the varnish is chosen, remember always to take the greatest care over cleanliness and the removal of fluff and dirt. In this connection, do not wear woollen clothing while brushing, or a few hair fibres will adhere to the picture surface, which will irritate the perfectionist ever after! One famous restorer chose to complete his varnishing in a greenhouse, where the air had been previously damped down by a water spray to remove dust particles.

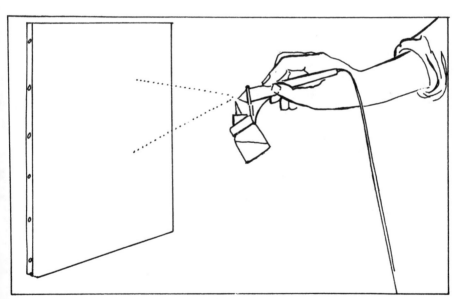

Spray varnishing

Oil paintings

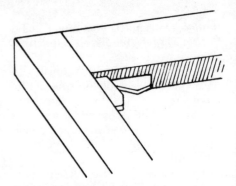

Tightening canvas

Occasionally the canvas of a painting may become slack and the painting sags or shows bumps. The support of the canvas, called the stretcher, enables this condition to be remedied. Canvas is usually attached to the stretcher by means of tacks and it might appear that the only way to treat the condition would be to re-tack all around, but fortunately this is seldom necessary. Viewed from the back it will be seen that each corner of the stretcher is joined by means of tongue and groove, with small pieces of wood known as wedges left inserted. If these wedges are given a careful tap they will open the wooden stretcher very slightly and so tauten the canvas. However, care is neces-

Reverse of a canvas showing wedges

sary here so that the wedges are only tapped gently and in the direction needed, to overcome the sagging. In some very old paintings the wedges may not still be in existence but usually the stretcher will show slots at the corners where pieces of wood may be fitted in as wedges. Some long established bumps may need the assistance of a warm iron applied from the back.

Re-lining a canvas

Repairing canvas

Very many paintings have suffered rips or holes during their existence. An important portrait I once owned had been used previously by a descendant of the subject as a fencing partner and had consequently received minor 'wounds'. Cromwell's troops are reported to have taken delight in shooting at family portraits of Royalist families, a special trick being shooting out the eyes.

Of course most rips, tears and holes have not been made in such spectacular ways and are much more likely to have been caused by leaning the picture against a chair, forgetting about it and an accident ensuing when the dog comes running in !

In the case of extensive rips, re-lining is often called for. Re-lining involves cutting the picture around the edge so that it is freed from its old stretcher. The ripped or holed painting is then adhered on to a new canvas and cleaned as necessary. Finally the new canvas is tacked on to the old stretcher, tightened, re-stored and revarnished.

Modern restoration techniques have developed what are known as 'vacuum hot-tables' for re-lining canvases, using a hot wax medium as an adhesive and a partial vacuum to press the two canvases together. Obviously this method of re-lining will be beyond the scope of the average renovator and should only be performed by a skilled restorer. Nowadays some restorers prefer canvases to be re-lined using other adhesives, even water soluble pastes, which are more easily removable in the future. To re-line a non-important painting, a flour paste and some thymol crystals (acting as a fungicide) would suffice to perform a

Repairing a small tear from the back of the canvas

fairly simple re-lining operation well within the abilities of a reasonably careful operator.

A small rip where the edges meet can be repaired in the following way. Working from the back, apply a contact glue to the torn edges. Lay the painting flat, position the torn edges together, apply a piece of brown paper over the repair and, using a weighted book as a press, leave until dry. After the glue has hardened, peel off the paper. This method has the advantage of being almost invisible from behind and one does not have to use a patch, which, with the passage of time, may make its shape visible on the front surface of the painting.

After joining a rip it will usually be necessary to fill in carefully any missing areas, thus providing a uniform texture to the surface of the painting, making it ready for any repainting that is necessary. Sometimes it is helpful to impart a slight weave texture to any filling, to emulate surface texture of the canvas. This effect can be achieved by gently pressing a piece of similar canvas on to the filler while it is still soft.

Oil paintings

Paintings on wood

Many paintings have been painted on materials other than canvas; wood prepared for painting on has been known from the earliest times. The important fourteenth and fifteenth-century paintings are mainly executed on well prepared wooden boards. The correct way to refer to paintings on wood is 'on panel.' Sometimes the paint is directly applied on to the wood, revealing the texture of the grain in the completed picture, but usually panels are prepared by being rubbed down well and then covered with a smooth preparation or 'ground' made from plaster of Paris (gesso).

The main renovation necessary results from the rather distressing and distracting fact that panels are prone to crack apart. This was brought to public attention rather spectacu-larly some years ago, when Rubens's famous masterpiece 'The Chateau de Steen', in the National Gallery, suddenly developed an horrific split, accompanied by a loud crack. The only available course is simply to glue the panel back together with a good wood glue. It is important that this be done as soon as possible so that the internal stresses and strains of the wood do not further warp the panel and allow it to become accommodated permanently to its new cracked appearance. The re-glueing can be done using standard woodworkers' tools and clamps, being careful not to leave any glue on the surface. Occasionally, to combat warping and to hold a panel together, a supporting framework known as a 'cradle' is built on to the back of the panel; this operation is best left to a professional.

Treatment for woodworm can be undertaken from the back of the panel and any surface holes filled and re-painted.

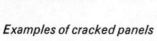
Examples of cracked panels

Paintings on board

As a convenient, lighter means of providing a paintable surface, millboard, or sometimes even cardboard, has been used. The problem of cracking is rarely met with but sometimes a bump or lump may be in evidence, due to some accident or other misfortune. This is a rather difficult problem to deal with because, by virtue of its stiffness, millboard or cardboard will not usually allow itself to be easily pressed back flat. The only way to alleviate the unsightly lump or depression is to very carefully cut or scrape away at the back of the board beneath the bump, until one is nearly at the paint layer — at which point great care must be taken. It will now be found possible to either flatten the bump or push out the dent. Lay the painting flat, fill the hollowed-out area with a hard-setting glue, then lay a piece of paper over the glue to seal it in. Place a book over the top and leave to set hard. This will alleviate what would otherwise be an unrestorable defect.

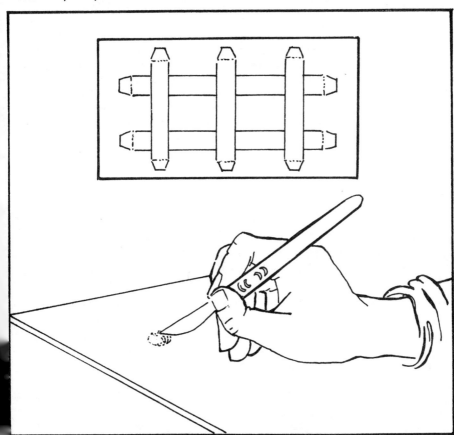

(above) *A supporting 'cradle' on the back of a painting;* (below) *Scraping away the back of a bump*

Watercolours

A definition

Painting in watercolours has been known for many centuries and developed long before the use of oil paint. Interestingly it has been especially an English pursuit for the past two centuries, competence in its use being considered at one time an essential part of education. Consequently, as a legacy of the Victorian era, there are many skilful paintings executed in this medium.

Some of the terms may need explanation. 'Watercolour wash' is the term used to describe watercolour diluted with water only, painted across a sheet of paper. 'Pen, ink and watercolour' implies a pen and ink outline, with watercoloured areas. 'Gouache' is the term given to watercolour mixed with the thick pigment, Chinese white, which gives guache an almost oil-paint opaqueness rather than the transparent delicate effect of a watercolour wash. Gouache may also be referred to as 'bodycolour' or 'watercolour heightened with white'.

The most common defect occurring with watercolours is that of 'foxing' (brown-spot staining).

Foxing

The unsightly brown spots seen on watercolours and pages of old books have long been the subject of debate as to cause and origin. However, you can understand foxing only too well if you observe what happens to uncovered jam, soup or even an old pair of leather shoes left in a warm damp place. They all develop spots of mould and this is what foxing actually is, occurring on and in the paper. Many a person having a foxed watercolour has taken it out of its frame and been dismayed to see that the brown spots are not just on the glass of the picture but are actually in the paper, sometimes in evidence on both front and back of the paper or card used for the painting. Usually the discoloration is brown but it may also occur as black spotting.

An important point to realise is that by correct chemical treatment the discoloration can be completely removed and the mould killed, leaving the watercolour quite unblemished. If the brown spots have been either scratched out, painted over, locally bleached white or in any other way tampered with, then the watercolour will have been to a greater or lesser degree permanently damaged. Any repainting necessary with water-

How foxing often appears

colours is a much more difficult operation to complete successfully and cannot easily be reversed or tried again.

The correct way to treat foxing in watercolours so that no retouching is ever necessary is basically that of treating with a bleaching or oxidising agent, usually whilst the watercolour is wet. Due to the obvious difficulty of handling and other variable factors, *valuable watercolours should always be left to an expert*. So if you know of no one reliable, it is better to leave it foxed and enjoy its appearance of antiquity rather than have to live with a bleached, washed-out, ruined watercolour which will also have a drastically reduced value.

How to stop foxing getting worse

As we have already seen, foxing is due to a mould growth, thus any steps to stop mould formation will be of benefit. The present museum practice is to use a fungicide-impregnated paper either inserted behind the watercolour in the frame or, if the watercolour is kept in a portfolio or drawer, a sheet is kept in with the portfolio.

The preparation of your own fungicide-impregnated paper is, in fact, quite elementary. Obtain a small amount of thymol crystals from the local chemist. Dissolve several crystals in a small amount of warm water, and when they are dissolved, allow this solution to drip on to a clean sheet of white blotting paper. After it has dried, you will have a thymol-impregnated sheet of paper, which has fungicidal properties. It may be necessary to repeat the operation after several years so that the fungicidal properties are renewed.

Interestingly it is now the practice

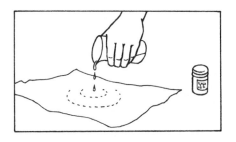

Preparing a fungicide-impregnated paper

of some museums to leave old drawings and watercolours in their foxed state, just ensuring that the mould growth does not get any worse by storing them in portfolios with the thymol-impregnated paper present. This is because, during the bleaching process involved in removing foxing, there may, as a side effect, be a slight deterioration in the cellulose formation of the paper – perhaps shortening its life – no matter how carefully controlled the process is or how well the drawing looks afterwards. However, as well made paper does seem to have an amazingly long life, it is a case of weighing up the short- and long-term aims.

No valuable or well loved watercolour or drawing should be kept in a damp place or left to hang on a damp wall, as this will of course provide all the conditions for mould. On the other hand do not remove the watercolour to a position where sunlight may strike it, as this will cause fading and possible acidification (browning) of the paper. As modern technology and scholarship increases with respect to foxing, it is not as serious as it might appear to be. So, if in evidence on any of your watercolours, drawings or prints, you should not worry too much.

Watercolours

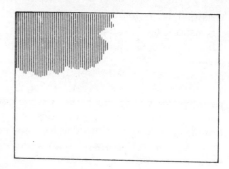

Appearance of damp staining

Damp staining

Damp stains, or water stains as they are sometimes referred to, often occur as a result of a burst water-pipe or a flood or some other partial soaking. After drying, the watercolour or print is seen to bear a stain at the edges of the soaked area. Professional wet-cleaning techniques can usually completely remove such staining, by the same process used to remove foxing. However you can avoid the formation of a water stain if you know how to deal with the watercolour at the time of the accident. For example if you were unfortunate enough to spill a cup of tea or water over an unframed watercolour, the natural tendency might be to dry off the soaked parts of the watercolour with clean blotting paper. As a result of taking this action you would be left with a stain on the picture. Rather you should take what at first might appear to be the most drastic action – that of running a bath of cold water and immediately immersing *all* the watercolour; after leaving it immersed for, say, fifteen minutes, remove it from the bath and allow to dry gently. Although this may sound highly dangerous for a watercolour painting, you will be surprised to note that no running or loss of watercolour will be observed, and as all the watercolour has been immersed and suffused with water, any stain or chemical in the solution will have been diluted and washed away and no blemish will be left. Most watercolours can stand immersion in cold water for several hours; many that are thinly painted in watercolour wash would be un-

affected by immersion for a week or more. The points to remember are (i) immerse *all* – not just part – of the watercolour in cold water (ii); do it immediately, before the stain dries in.

Cleaning surface grime

Surface grime presents a different problem, and what might appear to be only a slight defect is one of the most difficult to remedy.

If the grime, which sometimes occurs on drawings or watercolours kept unframed, is of long standing, then it may well be that it has become fixed into the paper and is impossible to remove chemically. However, if the watercolour or drawing has any value, you will be well advised not to try this yourself.

You can use a wad of cotton wool soaked in a carbon tetrachloride solution (the dry-cleaning agent), or pure acetone or benzine in the event of any grease-based dirt. Care is needed here however to ensure that the cotton wool is changed as it gets dirty, and also that you wipe over *all* the picture, using a very light technique.

When the grime has occurred only recently then a very soft rubber, used in sweeping strokes, *not a round*

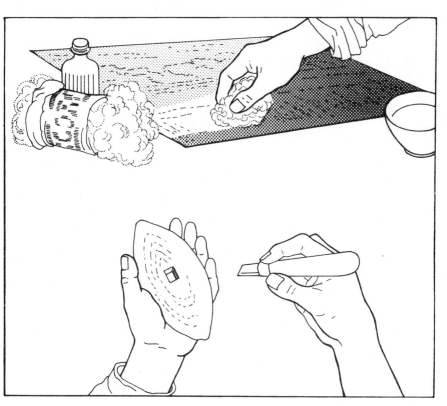

(above) *Take great care when removing surface grime;* (below) *Cutting a piece of cuttlefish bone to use as an abrasive agent*

rubbing technique, should remove the grime. It is important to remove it as soon as possible because if left on for a few years, grime soon becomes fixed into the paper and resists any easy attempt to remove it.

On the rare occasions when in-grained dirt is to be removed and the only way to do so is to abrase it away, it should be remembered that any abrasive action will also remove the paint surface. Thus only on white areas, such as a white cloud or white paper areas, should abrasions be employed. The most effective abrasion agent is in fact white cuttlefish bone as sold for birdcage use. Cut a small

cube from the complete shell and, using it skilfully, you can eventually even shave newsprint from the surface of newspaper without rubbing through the paper itself. However, the use of cuttlefish bone as an abrasive is only a last-ditch method of cleaning and if used on a coloured part of a watercolour painting will of course spoil the appearance.

Thus, again in the case of surface grime, prevention is worth a pound of cure and if it is of long standing, one may just have to live with it. These techniques can also be used for cleaning prints.

Watercolours

Mending rips, tears and scratches

The worst type of rip to repair is a scissor-type cut, as you cannot take advantage of the fibrous shredding effect you get with rag-made papers. In a normal rip or tear, if you examine the torn areas carefully, it will be seen that many small fibres are in evidence at the torn edge, and if the rip is put back in the same way it was torn, these fibres can to a certain extent be re-knitted, and instead of a cross-section as in (a) you have in fact the situation as in (b). Thus in the repair (i) must be glued on to (ii); if glued the wrong way, then (c) will be the result and an unsightly join will be left. It is possible, using great skill and possibly a tool such as a metal spoon, to press the ripped areas back together so well that an almost invisible repair is made. Usually after glueing the torn edges, a piece of tissue is glued over the back to further strengthen the repair. A thick clear wallpaper glue would be the best adhesive for this type of repair and of course, whilst drying, keep the repair under flat pressure.

In the event of scratches and also sometimes with the edges of a tear, it is necessary to repaint the lost area. Here extreme care is necessary in order to retouch the missing area only and not, in carelessness, to repaint over on to the other, un-damaged parts. It is perhaps worth stating that if the scratch is in a blue or very light area of the picture, successfully repainting the area will be very difficult for the amateur, and even for the professional, for that matter; but if in a dark area, with skill one can make the repair completely invisible. However, if in doubt, consult an expert in the field.

These techniques can also be used for mending prints.

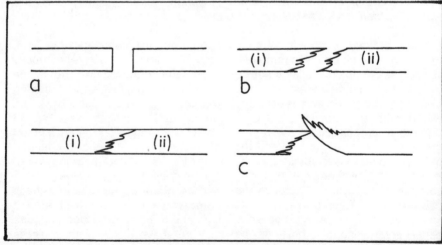

(a) Cross-section of a cut and (b) of a tear; this is easier to repair invisibly if (i) is glued to (ii) and not as in (c)

Straightening buckled watercolours

Watercolour drawing paper, being made from rags, will of course exhibit some of the same qualities as cloth. Consequently the paper will stretch when wet or damp and shrink when dry. Sometimes, after being kept in a damp position, a watercolour is seen to be buckled. If the buckling is not too serious, all that may be necessary to remedy the situation will be to press the watercolour out between two sheets of clean blotting paper and keep it pressed flat for several days. If the buckling is severe it may be necessary to re-stretch the water-colour paper. This principle will be familiar to anyone used to painting in watercolours. The paper is wetted and, in the case of a watercolour, a quick immersion in cold water should suffice. If not wishing to completely immerse the watercolour it is just possible to wet the back of the water-colour with a wad of damp cotton wool. After the paper has partly dried, the edges are taped, using brown-paper gummed tape, to a firm board. When the paper dries, after several days, cut the edges with a sharp knife, and the watercolour should remain in a flat state with all the cockles pulled tight. However, if you own a valuable watercolour or drawing, you would be well advised to leave the re-flattening to an expert as there are many variable factors to consider, such as the condition of the paper. Again, as a very slight propor-tion of the edges of the work has to be taped over, this may not be advisable with an important water-colour where every area is of value, and some other technique might have to be resorted to.

Method of straightening a buckled watercolour

Watercolours

Removing backboard stains

It was an unfortunate practice in the last century to back a frame with thin wooden boards. This seemingly innocent practice has resulted in what are termed 'backboard stains' or 'backboard burns'. Where the boards were joined brown staining appears in the strips down or across the picture, including the mount. If there are knot holes in the boards, these are often reproduced in the picture, the staining having traversed through cardboard $\frac{1}{8}$ in thick.

Successful cleaning of backboard staining will usually be beyond the scope of the average renovator as it involves removing the watercolour from the cardboard to which it is often glued. Further, the staining can attack the fibrous make-up of the paper, and the chemical action necessary to remove the stain makes the whole operation a very delicate manoeuvre, and can leave one with a watercolour in two pieces on one's hands. Although I have managed to clean many hundreds of badly back-board-stained watercolours successfully, prevention is obviously important. If you have any valuable watercolours or drawings in old frames which have old boards, it will certainly be in your interest to invest in a new backing board. Nowadays any reputable framer should stock museum-board backing card which has been designed to help preserve watercolours and drawings. A good plywood or hardboard should complete the framing in order to preserve the work of art for future generations.

Backboard staining: if wooden backboards have been joined vertically, the stains appear as illustrated (right)

If backboards have been joined horizontally, the stains appear as illustrated (right)

224

225

Prints

In almost every home, prints of some description are to be seen hanging on the walls, especially nowadays with the introduction of the limited edition. Possibly each type deserves a special mention.

Modern limited editions

These are usually printed on a modern gloss paper and present no problems in their inherent structure; they will last for an indefinite length of time if framed and preserved correctly. Often the problems come from an exterior source; for example, I once had to clean a modern print which had had a child's boiled sweet stuck to it! If the print has been rolled for a long time or has some bad creases, take it to a reputable framer who will be able to glue it down or otherwise successfully frame it.

If you are framing a limited edition print yourself it is important that you do not, under any circumstances, cut

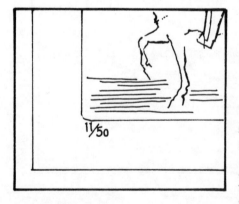

A limited edition print

the white border to the print, known as the margin. Often the margin bears a title, signature, or pencilled numbers. If the print does bear numbers, such as '11/50', this means that the print is number eleven of an edition limited to fifty copies. When framed, these details should all be visible as they are part of the print which entitles it to be called a work of art.

Old prints

These will be etchings, engravings, mezzotints, woodblocks, aquatints or lithographs. They will usually be printed on a handmade rag-based paper and many of the aspects of renovation as applicable to water-colours and drawings are equally relevant to this type of print. In the case of all these types of print, the margins are most important. In the case of etchings, engravings, mezzo-tints and aquatints, that part of the margin which shows the plate mark should always be displayed within the edges of the mount or frame. This plate mark shows itself as a rectangular indentation in the paper surrounding the illustrated subject and is the mark left by the metal plate as the paper was pressed against it to take off the inked details during the print-making process.

Coloured prints of the nineteenth century and beyond are usually of an etched, engraved, aquatinted or litho-graphed base, skilfully hand coloured, and all the points relevant to their renovation are to be found in the section on watercolours, and are really the prerogative of the expert. However, in the case of small black and white engravings and etchings, the following renovations may be successfully resorted to by the amateur.

CROSSING THE RIVER AVON.

An example of an old hunting print

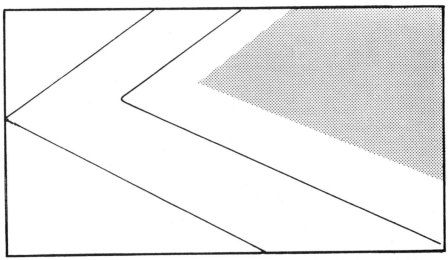

The indented plate mark within the margins of a print should always be displayed

227

Prints

How to remove foxing from small engravings and etchings

This procedure is an easy renovation for anyone who is reasonably careful; if in doubt try it out on an unimportant print or piece of paper first. The difficulty comes when larger prints have to be handled because of the weakness of the paper when wet. So at home, only use this technique on small or unimportant prints and definitely not on any finely coloured print. Small etchings or engravings can often be found in old travel books, and were originally used as illustrations. If cleaned and coloured they can make an attractive and inexpensive decoration.

To clean the foxing, obtain a tray or dish of a suitable size in which to immerse the print. Make a bleaching solution from one part 1 per cent standardised sodium hypochlorite solution (obtainable from any chemist as the babies' utensil sterilizing agent 'Milton'), mixed with three parts cold water. Pour this bleaching solution into the tray. Run an amount of cold water into a bath or sink to act as a rinsing bath. First immerse the print in the cold-water bath, then, handling with care as now the paper is wet and thus weaker, place it in the bleaching solution and leave for approximately 5 to 10 minutes, after which time the discoloration should start to disappear. The marks in the paper where the foxing was present will still show but should take on a more translucent appearance. After this length of time, remove the print from the bleaching solution and

leave it in the water bath for a further 10 minutes in order to dispel the bleaching agent, then remove it and allow it to dry gently. Before the print is completely dry, press it out between two clean, dry sheets of blotting paper. As it dries, so the foxing will be seen to have disappeared. If any foxing does remain after this treatment, repeat the whole operation until the print is clear. The bleaching will also whiten the white-paper margins, and thus brighten the black ink and give an impression of freshness.

This technique will be equally safe with pencil drawings and will even brighten the original pencil strokes.

Small etchings or engravings are often found in old travel books

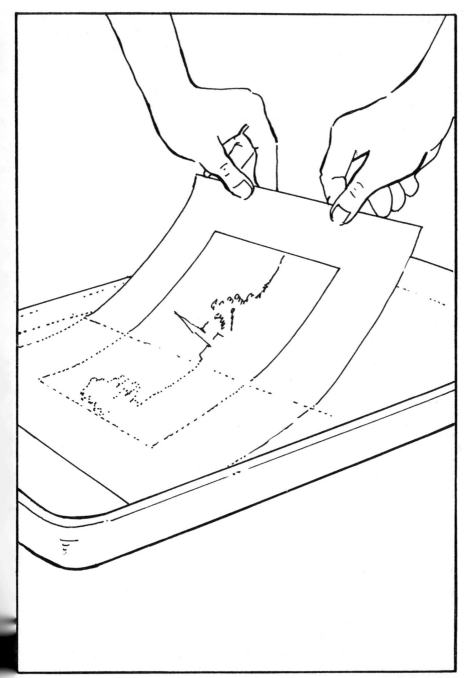

To remove foxing, a print should be immersed first in a cold-water bath, then in bleaching solution, then finally in the water bath again

Prints

Colouring

The colouring of old prints to make them more attractive has always been popular. Many of the old established print publishers of the nineteenth century employed teams of girls or unemployed artists to wash in the various colours, which was sometimes done with exceeding skill. As all the shadows and tones of the picture in most old prints have been included in the final inked version, successful colouring is made much simpler and is purely a technique of applying colour washes to the appropriate areas. Before colouring one's own prints, it might be profitable to look at old coloured prints in the local library, museum or shops and then observe the way the effects are achieved. The most important aspect to remember is at all times to use only a very diluted wash of any colour, then you will avoid garish results.

Use a sable watercolour brush and watercolour paint, and learn to apply an even wash in quick, deft strokes. Often a palette of just six colours is quite sufficient. A typical palette might consist of Naples yellow for light clouds, orange for dark clouds, Prussian blue for sky, rocks or the distance, sap green for trees, yellow ochre for trees and detail and vermilion for red detail. Always remember to work in extremely dilute colour, especially when using Prussian blue. Some colourists prefer to size the prints first, to make the paper less absorbent, facilitating more controllable colouring.

Applying a watercolour wash

Mending rips, tears and holes

Prints can be mended in the same way as watercolours (see page 222); the techniques for cleaning prints are also similar to those for watercolours (see page 220).

It is often useful to keep pieces of old worthless prints so that, if necessary, a piece of etching or engraving of the same type is available if it is found necessary to repair a hole or jagged tear. In the event of a hole it is obviously best to do the repair with a piece of a print of the same texture and thickness. The hole is prepared by chamfering the edges using cuttlefish bone so that the cross-section is as in (a). A piece is then cut out from a similarly etched section of print, slightly larger than the hole to be mended, and chamfered as in (b), then glued into position with a patch of tissue as a backing. Any white areas then remaining can be re-touched after the whole repair has dried, as in (c).

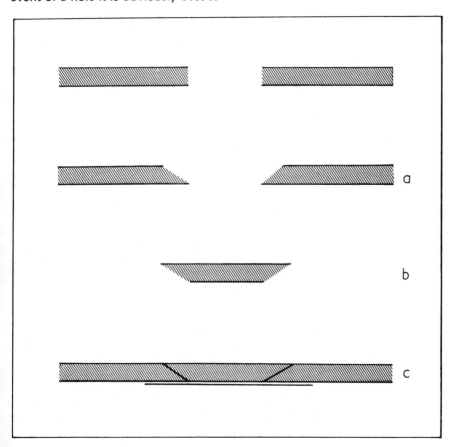

Method of repairing a hole in a print

Other types of picture

Miniatures

The art of miniature painting in England has produced innumerable exquisite works of beauty and great craftsmanship. Often painted on vellum or thin ivory and preserved under glass in narrow frames, they still retain their freshness and charm.

If you have a collection of miniatures, it is wise to find a dry, well aired spot of wall, away from direct sunlight, on which to display them. If stored in drawers or cabinets it is advisable to include in the drawer a sheet of fungicide paper as described previously (see page 219). Occasionally, when a mould may have developed on the glass, it is necessary to take them out of their frames, clean the glass, and when satisfied that the miniature is bone dry, lightly blow and dust it to remove any surface mould. On no account should watercolour miniatures ever be rubbed or wiped with a wet swab, or paint will be instantly removed. As evidenced by the many thousands of miniatures in perfect condition, they would appear to survive the rigours of time exceedingly well, and fortunately the need for restoration is very rare.

Pastels

Unfortunately many pastels have proved themselves to be fertile sites for mould growth. I well remember purchasing an important pastel at one of the London auctions some years ago. It was purchased unseen, surprisingly cheaply. On collection, it was found to be two-thirds covered in mould. However, with time, most pastels become more fixed into the paper and less susceptible to being blown from the surface, and in this case, on removing the pastel from the frame and taking it out from behind the glass, it was found that, with care, using a soft squirrel brush, a good deal of the surface growth could be brushed away without disturbing too much of the original pastel. After slight re-touching this same pastel was re-sold in London at more than twenty times the price of three months previously!

Of course it goes without saying that if you have a pastel, you should use all the means described earlier for inhibiting mould growth so that the need for future restoration can be avoided.

Chinese rice-paper paintings

Produced in Canton and surrounding areas from 1800 to 1880, these abound in salerooms and antique shops around the country. Often of almost incredible fineness, these represent a fairly cheap investment in the fine-art world. Due to being painted on fragile rice paper, they almost invariably develop splits and losses if kept out of the protection of a frame for any length of time. All that can be done then is to glue them down on to a stiff card, positioning them so that the splits are fixed together. On rare occasions with important works, you can insert missing areas using spare rice paper and a filler to fit, but it is not a job recommended if you want to keep an even temper!

Examples of miniatures (above) *and rice-paper paintings*

Other types of picture

Silhouettes

Silhouettes, popular in the nineteenth century, have found a revival of interest. They are usually found in good condition. In rare cases it may be necessary to bleach the surrounding card white, as described previously (see page 228). Often with this cleaning process, the black paper silhouette will need re-adhering, so if you do undertake this job yourself, be prepared to see the black paper silhouette floating freely in the bleaching bath.

Paintings on glass or porcelain

Usually, apart from being very fragile, paintings on glass or porcelain exhibit no special problems, and may be cleaned by any of the methods used for oil paintings. It is rare for them to need any extensive cleaning, but care should be taken in framing and hanging them.

Samplers

These charming mementoes of childhood days of the Victorian era or earlier, are often framed and make admirable 'country-cottage' furnishing pieces. On the rare occasions that one might be found dirty or creased, it can be washed and ironed gently on the reverse, remembering of course that they are usually well over one hundred years old and so require careful handling.

Silhouettes

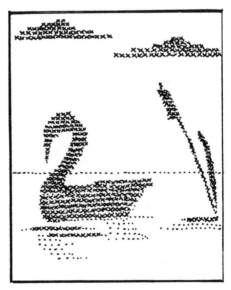

Paintings on porcelain (above) *and glass*

Samplers

Frames

Types

Generally speaking frames for oil paintings are completely different from those used for watercolours and prints. Oil-painting frames need to be much heavier and thicker to complement the picture they surround. The paintings are often well served by the ornamental decoration around the whole frame or in the corners, whereas watercolours and prints generally need a thin frame and a cardboard mount to provide a window for the painting. Watercolours and period prints always need to be framed behind glass whereas nowadays only in the case of very important or small oil paintings is glass found advisable.

Frames surrounding your pictures may be of the following types : carved frames covered in gold leaf ; wooden frames having plaster cast decoration, covered in gold leaf ; wooden frames painted either in a reproduction gold finish or some other colour ; or frames with part plastic finishes, as with some modern ones.

It would appear that a gold finish has been most acceptable to furnishing taste as most frames incorporate it in their decoration. In fact, during the last century all exhibited paintings had to be in gold-leafed frames, often, in the case of watercolours, even having the mount rendered gold.

Of course, framing is always a matter of personal taste, but if you have a painting in its original frame you would be well advised to try to retain the original frame, not only from an aesthetically pleasing point of view, but also to maintain the value and interest of the painting. Picture dealers when viewing any picture sale automatically have their eyes drawn to paintings in their period frames. On many occasions quite important paintings have been overlooked through being disguised by a cheap, modern frame. Also of course, if you can renovate the old frame, a good deal of expense will be saved.

Removal

The removal of a picture's frame has possibly been responsible for more accidents to pictures than any other

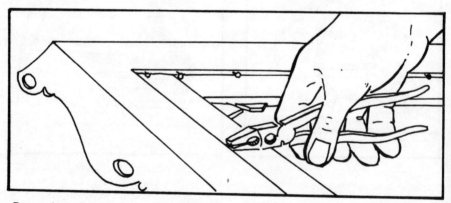

Removing a frame

single event. Even the leaning of the picture against a chair or table corner, as a preliminary to the removal, has caused many a rip or hole. So after carefully taking it down from the wall, lay the picture face down on to a clean flat table or on the floor and then, using a good pair of pliers, take out all the fixing nails or pins from the back. Only when *all* the nails have been removed and any sealing strip or paper around the edges has been removed or cut, then, with care, prise either the canvas stretcher or card out from the frame. Immediately find a safe place to store this so that no harm can come to it while in this unprotected state.

Some different types of frames

Frames

Repairing chipped gilt frames

Often after a piece of gilt has been chipped away or has been lost, its absence is revealed by the white gesso base which is left to irritate the eye. Sometimes it is sufficient to obtain a reproduction gilt paste — stocked in most art shops — and, using a brush and white spirit to dilute the paste, repaint the missing area.

If no glaring patches of white or old wood appear to break up the uniformity of the frame it is quite amazing how repainting alone will improve the appearance of many a 'tatty' frame. If the frame's beading has chipped or flaked away, and you wish to get a little more involved, you can fill the missing areas with a filler such as plastic wood, putty, or barbola paste and then, using a small piece of wood, engrave any detail or pattern of the original pieces into the soft filler. When dry, retouch the area with diluted gilt paste.

However, if faced with a more intricate or valuable frame you may wish to adopt the following professional technique.

Usually, no matter how decrepit the frame has become, there are areas of the frame which retain pieces of the original pattern, whether it be an inner beading pattern or the outer swept finish of the corners. To repair the frame successfully, it is necessary to re-mould some of the pattern to use as repair pieces.

Obtain a ball of Plasticine which will become softer when slightly warmed. Then carefully, so as not to

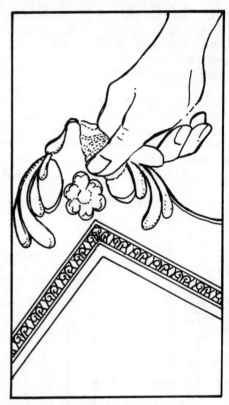

Using barbola paste to re-mould detail on a frame

cause more damage, press the Plasticine around undamaged sections, to take off a mould of the pattern. Using pieces of Plasticine to complete the mould, pour mixed plaster of Paris to the required depth. Allow plenty of time to dry, then remove from the mould and sand or cut the pieces to fit and glue into place. It may be necessary to repeat the mould many times in the event of major repairs, but as the decoration was usually made from a mould in the first place, all the parts should be re-mouldable.

After glueing into place, you may be tempted to purchase gold leaf in small book form and using red gold

238

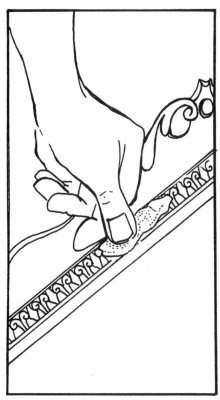

Taking a mould of the beading on a frame

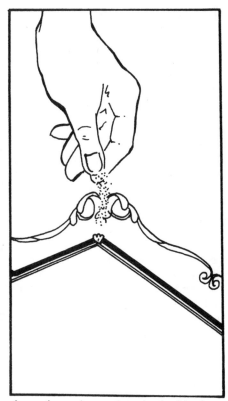

A repair can be made to look older by sprinkling it with dust

size, learn the art of gilding. Speaking from experience, this is often quite unnecessary due to the fact that freshly applied gold leaf, no matter how expertly applied, looks completely out of place on a repair of an old frame, due to its new brightness. After re-gilding repairs I have had a great deal of trouble toning down the bright appearance of the new leaf. It is far simpler to paint the filler over with a red or yellow paint as a ground and then apply the gilt paste. Diluted gilt paste achieves a much closer match to the old gold and is of course much easier to apply and less expensive.

After repainting with gilt, the repair usually looks out of place due to its newness and here the tricks of the professional can complete the repair. Most old frames of any intricacy accumulate a patina of dust in the nooks and crannies of the design. Using a brush, apply some paper gum to these nooks and crannies, and then sprinkle on some dust obtained from a vacuum cleaner bag. After any surplus dust has been blown off, an old toothbrush with some black ink on the bristles, flicked near the frame may complete the restoration by leaving some reproduction fly spots! This will usually finish the repair and deceive even the most experienced eye.

Frames

Brightening gold leaf

Usually if one takes warm water and a brush to a frame with gold leaf on it, some cleaning will occur, but more often the leaf is removed and a very sad rubbed frame is left. I have found that a piece of lemon rubbed lightly over the surface of the frame not only removes some of the dirt, by virtue of the texture of the lemon flesh, but also brightens the original gold leaf.

Unless in a very dirty state, the renovation of gold leaf is best restricted to the lemon treatment by the amateur renovator so that no permanent loss occurs. If it does, you can however resort to the reproduction gilt finishes, which, although coming close, never reach the luxuriance of the original leaf.

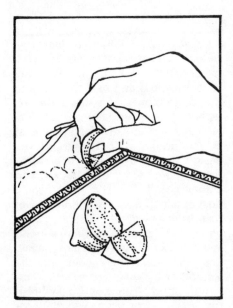

Renovation of other types of frame

Most picture framers have, over the years, accumulated stocks of old frames, often of better quality than that which now surrounds many pictures. Often you can obtain some good old frames fairly inexpensively or, if necessary, completely renovate your old frame. Even if the frame is old and looks completely decrepit, the wood may be of fair quality, and in these days of dwindling resources and high costs it may be better to attempt some 'last-ditch' renovation.

In the case of old plaster and gilt frames, these can be stripped by being immersed in hot water and abraded so that all the old gilt plaster comes away. After the application of a paint stripper, the original wood should be revealed. After drying, sanding, re-staining and waxing, one could be quite pleased with the quality of the finished frame, especially when one remembers that the frame was about to be discarded as a piece of old rubbish! It might surprise some people to know that a good many expensive and sumptuous-looking pine-frames now surrounding mirrors began their lives as gilt frames of nineteenth-century paintings.

If you are fortunate enough to own a set of pictures framed in what is known as maple veneer, then these frames – which were popular in nineteenth-century sporting circles – should always be well looked after. They rarely show any bad signs of wear and apart from the need for an occasional waxing, retain their furnishing charm to this day and are certainly unobtainable from any standard framer nowadays.

Re-mounting prints and watercolours

In the case of watercolours and prints it is often the mount that is of prime concern to the observer. Often the mount becomes discoloured or foxed, or one just gets plain tired of it. As the mount can either make or break the appearance of the water-colour or print, great attention should be paid to its colour, decoration and size ; in fact it should be considered part of the work of art itself. A common mistake made in cutting a new mount is to have an equal border all around the picture. It is now commonly recognised that to achieve a balanced effect, a greater width should be allowed along the bottom, so that the appearance is not as in (a) but as in (b).

When cutting a mount, first decide on the colour of your card, remember-ing that quality watercolours should really be mounted using an off-white/ cream card. Of course taste varies and you may prefer a tinted colour to complement either your own furnish-ings, or a colour in the picture.

Measure the picture and decide the width you require for your mount, remembering the additional width to the bottom edge. By means of a simple addition you should be able to calculate the total size necessary. Cut this size out using a sharp knife and a board or old cardboard slipped underneath so that you do not find yourself cutting your new front-room carpet or table. Remember that the cutting of the mount is an exercise not to be hurried.

Using a ruler as in the illustration, you should be able to find the correct corner point. Using a sharp knife, run the blade along, using a metal ruler as a guiding edge. Either cut the card completely, or lightly score the line with the knife and ruler and then, if you have a steady hand, follow the scored cut freehand, remembering of course to maintain a steady angle of approximately 45° so that a bevelled edge is produced. Completion of the corners may present a little difficulty. It is usually found advisable not to

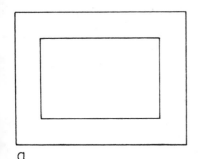
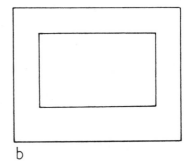

a   b

When cutting a new mount, do not leave an equal margin as in (a) but allow a greater margin at the bottom as in (b)

cut right to the corner, but to press the rectangle out and finish the cut with a new razor blade used carefully. It is best to practise this technique before finishing the corner on your carefully measured, almost completed mount. With a little experience a neat corner can be your reward. If you do not use this technique, you must exercise great care when getting near the corner so that the cut does not extend too far.

After the cutting of the mount has been completed, you may wish to aid the presentation of the finished picture by drawing lines around the cut-out window and adding a wash. This is usually termed as a line and wash and is generally of the type shown in the illustration.

A watercolour wash is chosen to complement the colour scheme of the picture, this wash being always very diluted and not in a strong colour. In order to prevent a hard edge forming in the painted wash when you paint back to the beginning, some framers first put on a wash in clear water. This has the effect of helping to achieve an even wash of colour as you join back to the beginning, when doing the actual watercolour wash.

The lines should be drawn using either a lining pen and watercolour, or a watercolour felt-tip. If you apply the lines after painting the wash the lines follow the edges of the wash, finishing it in a neat fashion. Sometimes a thin strip of gold paper can make the line-finish even more effective.

Another way of achieving an excellent renovation in the event of an old stained mount is to cut another mount with a window just slightly larger than the old mount. This, when placed over the old mount, will achieve an effect of even greater depth and will cover over any staining or discoloration on the face of the old mount.

To facilitate measuring, it is sufficient to draw around the old mount and, whilst keeping it very still, press a pin through where you wish the inner corners of the new mount to be.

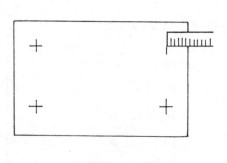

Method of finding the corners

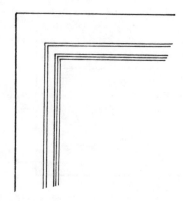

A typical mount decoration

Replacing glass

Old glass often becomes dirty and discoloured by nicotine, fly spots and so on. You can clean it with warm soapy water, but take great care when handling it as it can become more brittle with age. Some old glass, when viewed from the side, gives a wavy appearance due to imperfections in its manufacture, and you may like to get a new piece of glass cut.

When choosing glass, do not forget to tell the glazier that it is for a picture or, better still, give him the frame to cut the glass to size, and then he will be sure to use picture glass which is thinner than standard window glass. A modern introduction into the glazing world has been non-reflective glass. It is occasionally used for framing purposes, but does tend to give a slightly misty appearance to the picture.

To achieve a remarkably clear, clean glass both on the inside and outside, you will find that a rag moistened with methylated spirit will produce a streak-free, grease-free shining surface with no finger prints visible on the glass when the framing is completed, even when viewed from the side.

Finally when replacing glass, whether cutting it yourself or merely transporting it, take great care in handling the edges so as to avoid accidents.

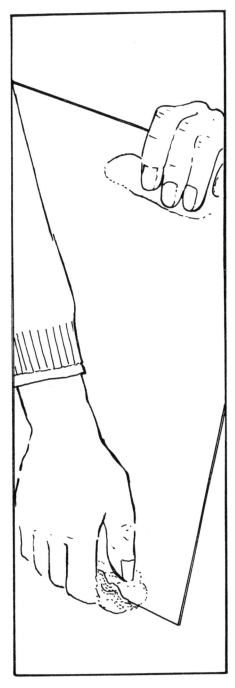

Handle glass with care

Conclusion

Remember that although this book explains many useful techniques, it cannot replace experience and 'the feel' of what looks right or is necessary. Further, to anyone trying a new craft for the first time, remember that practise is one of the greatest of teachers, and if you are considering the renovation of a painting or print of value, do not be afraid to consult an expert in the field. If the restoration is to be carried out by a professional obtain several opinions and estimates.

Of course, prevention is always better than cure — so take every care over choosing where you display or store paintings or prints. They should be kept in a safe and airy place, away from direct sunlight and extremes of temperature. Your paintings and prints will then continue to give pleasure to the present generation and provide modest heirlooms for the future.

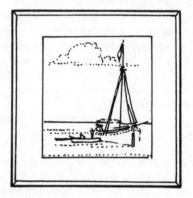

Glossary

Acetone A colourless, organic solvent with a characteristic odour. Dissolves varnish films and some paints. Highly inflammable

Ammonia Valuable cleansing agent, usually obtained as a 10 per cent solution in water

Beeswax Obtainable either in natural yellow-brown, or white fine grade. Melting point is *c* 65°C

Benzene Solvent for oily deposits. Highly inflammable

Bloom A cloudy appearance sometimes seen on the varnish of oil paintings. Probably due to the presence of moisture

Brushes For oil painting, bristle, sable or similar. For watercolour painting, sable

Carbon tetrachloride Excellent solvent for grease and oil-based dirt. Fumes can be injurious

Chlorine A gas often produced in bleaching reactions. The fumes should be avoided

Engraving Engraving is usually performed on a metal plate. The inked impression of an engraved plate on paper is referred to as an engraving. Mezzotint and dry point are forms of engraving

Etching Similar process to engraving but the design is etched into a copper plate by means of acid

Fly spots These are due to deposits left by the common house fly

Gesso Ground chalk mixed with glue or gelatin as a binder. Used as a ground for painting on to bare canvas or wood

Gum Gum arabic in solution has adhesive properties and is sometimes used as a medium for watercolours

Megilp A mixture of oils, wax and varnish. Sometimes used in the eighteenth and nineteenth centuries as a painting medium

Oil paints These are composed not only of pigment but also a base, a medium such as linseed oil and other constituents to promote satisfactory drying and handling

Pastels A crayon made from pigment and fine chalk and bound with gum

Silver fish An insect that causes considerable damage due to its liking for sized paper. Fumigation with carbon disulphide is effective

Thymol An antiseptic of the phenol group. A valuable fungicide

Vellum Finely prepared skin of sheep, goat or calf. Used for miniature painting or illuminated texts

Silver, Pewter and Brass

Hamish Bowie

Illustrated by Roger Day

Introduction

Collecting and restoring old objects is becoming more interesting to many people, and this book covers some of the techniques of renovating items made in silver, pewter and brass. Although many repair jobs require major skills and specialist equipment, with guidance, knowledge, and some skill, the novice can renovate the battered pot or broken spoon so that it becomes once again a desirable, attractive object. Market stalls, sale-rooms and antique shops often have broken or damaged pieces lying in odd boxes which can often be bought quite cheaply. Even if beyond repair they are worth collecting to use as spares when renovating other things. Occasionally handles, knobs and legs are missing or broken, and a spare part from an irreparable object can sometimes be fitted, with perhaps some modification to make it harmonize with the piece being renovated. Worn out pieces of pewter and britannia metal are worth collecting, simply for the purpose of using them as solder to repair other pewter objects, or as raw material for casting new components. Similarly, silver objects which are worn out may be melted down to cast new parts.

Objects requiring renovation may range from large brass log boxes and pewter tankards to small pieces of

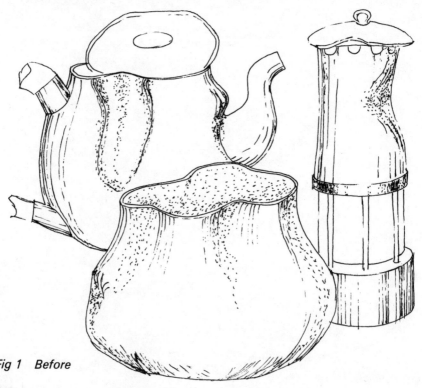

Fig 1   Before

248

silver jewellery. Whatever the size of the object the approach to renovation should have a well-planned sequence. Before any of the renovation techniques described in this book are used, it is important to be able to identify silver, pewter and brass. While it is easy to differentiate between them because of their distinctive colours, it is much more difficult to differentiate between silver, silver plate and Sheffield plate. The novice could easily confuse a fine piece of Sheffield plate with a piece of silver and try to solder it, with disastrous results. Sheffield plate was constructed with tin solder, and would fall to pieces if subjected to the high temperatures required for silver solder. For centuries, pewter has been made in varying proportions of tin and lead, culminating in britannia metal and modern pewter which contain no lead. Frequently britannia metal is silver-plated and could be accepted as silver if marks are not closely examined and underlying metal exposed by scraping. The term 'brass' embraces a large number of alloys containing copper and zinc, from bronze to common yellow brass. Occasionally these alloys are silver-plated and on rare occasions gold-plated, so careful scrutiny is required. Although some guidelines are given, familiarity through handling and study is essential, and further reading is suggested to increase your ability to identify the different metals.

Fig 2   After

The metals and the methods used to identify them

Silver

A fine, ductile and malleable metal, with a perfect metallic lustre which is one of its distinctive features. It is one of the best-known conductors of electricity and heat. This latter property soon reveals itself to the renovator when soldering, for the heat from the soldering torch is quickly transmitted through the object. Silver objects which have been made in the United Kingdom are usually hallmarked. The hallmark is stamped by an Assay Office whose job it is to take a sample scraping from the object and test its silver content. There are two recognised qualities, namely Sterling – 92.5 per cent and Britannia – 95.84 per cent. Figure 5 shows a hallmark which gives the following information: the

mark of the manufacturer, the quality of the silver alloy, the mark of the Assay Office, and the date letter. There are books available which give further information about hallmarks and date letter tables which are available from Assay Offices in Great Britain.

If the object is not hallmarked, identification of the metal is more difficult. A piece may be found with the mark 800, which is a continental mark for silver alloy of 80 per cent silver content. Sometimes only the name 'Sterling' or 'Silver' is stamped. These marks cannot be taken as proof of the identity of the metal, so careful examination and the following chemical test should be made.

Make the following solution:

10gms sodium dichromate
25ml concentrated nitric acid
100ml water

The sodium dichromate is dissolved in some of the water; it will not dissolve in the acid. Add the acid to

Fig 3   Testing metal by scraping

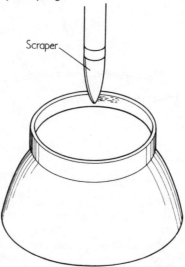

Scraper

Fig 5   A silver hallmark

Fig 6   EPNS mark

Fig 4   Features of Sheffield plate

the remainder of the water and then add the dissolved sodium dichromate. BUT *never add the water to the acid, always add the acid to the water*. Adding water to acid causes a violent reaction which is dangerous. Rubber gloves should be worn when handling the acid. This, and a range of solutions to test other metals, can be purchased from suppliers. Scrape a part of the object which is not visible as in Figure 3, such as the bottom of a foot or the inside of a base rim. The scraping must be sufficiently deep to prove that the object is not silver-plated base metal. When a drop of the solution is placed on a piece of silver, the spot will turn red immediately. The purer the alloy, the quicker the colour change and the deeper the red. If there is no colour change then the metal is not silver.

Silver plate and Sheffield plate

Objects which are electro-plated are usually so marked. The letters EPNS on an object mean electro-plated nickel silver, but beware, occasionally the letters are done in Old English lettering which can make the mark appear to be a Sterling silver hallmark. Sheffield plate was produced until about 1840 when electro-plating was invented. The principle of the method was to fuse silver on to copper using intense heat. The proportion of silver to copper was about one-tenth of the total thickness. The laminated billet produced was then rolled into a sheet. Early Sheffield plate had silver on one side only, so is easily identified, because the unplated side was simply tinned, but pieces made later, with silver coatings on both sides, are sometimes very difficult to identify. The secret is to examine edges and decorative applied parts with a magnifying glass, because they are attached with tin solder which makes a greyish line round the join. The edges of the open laminate always have a capping strip to conceal the copper core. There are touch marks peculiar to Sheffield plate, and specialist books are available on the subject.

251

The metals and the methods used to identify them

Pewter

This word is probably derived from the old English word 'spelter' and is applied as a general name for a number of alloys, all of which contain tin in diverse proportions. This is best illustrated by explaining a little of its historical development.

Roman pewter, the oldest known, was composed of tin and lead, but occasionally with some traces of iron which are believed to have been accidentally introduced. There seem to have been two alloys in use: (a) 71·5 parts tin to 28·5 parts lead; (b) 78·2 parts tin to 21·8 parts lead. Continental pewter has a considerable history. 1437 Montpelier pewter was 96 parts tin to 4 parts lead for dishes and porringers, and 90 parts tin to 10 parts lead for salt cellars and ewers. Limoges used 100 parts tin to 4 parts lead. In 1576 Nuremburg pewter was 10 parts tin to 1 part lead. In France in the eighteenth century, the legal limit for lead content was 15 per cent, later 16·5 per cent with a 1·5 per cent margin for error, and this alloy was considered safe for the storage of wines.

English pewter, like silver, was controlled by legislation from very early times, no doubt because of the strength of the Pewterers' Guilds which were established in various towns. A brief history of the development of English pewter may be of interest. The first ordinances known are those of the London Guild dated 1348 which state that the alloy for rounded vessels should be 26lb of

Fig 7   Pewter touch mark

lead to every 1cwt of tin. A formula apparently exclusive to English ware which may have given it the reputation of superiority was called 'Fyne peauter'. The recorded formula states, 'as much brass as tin as it wol receive of this nature'. This was clarified in 1474–5 and the law then required that 26lb of brass be mixed with 1cwt of tin. Infringements of the law were treated severely. Bismuth was added in 1561 and in 1653 it was ordered that 3lb of bismuth (tin glass) should be mixed with every 1000lb of tin. Subsequently antimony was added to make an alloy of 100 parts tin, 8 parts antimony, 4 parts copper, and 4 parts bismuth.

Pewter items can not only be dated from their style, but also from the maker's mark known as the 'touch mark'. Reference to the appropriate textbooks will give guidance to dating.

Britannia metal

A lead-free alloy of the pewter variety which consists of 5 per cent antimony, 3 per cent copper, and 92 per cent tin. It is frequently silver-plated but will, in its own right, polish up with a fine silvery lustre.

Identification of alloys

It is not possible with simple tests to identify all of the alloys of pewter, but it can be determined whether or not the object has a high lead content by rubbing one of its edges on a piece of white paper. The higher the lead content, the more the deposit of metal on the paper will resemble a pencil line. Conversely, the smaller the lead content, the fainter will be the line.

Brass

This is a yellow alloy of copper and zinc; the ingredients are used in varying proportions to produce alloys to suit particular applications. Common yellow brass is 50 per cent zinc and 50 per cent copper, is generally hard, and in the case of Delta metal, has almost the tensile strength of steel. Most of the alloys remain malleable and ductile, particularly Muntz metal which is 60 per cent copper and 40 per cent zinc.

Pinchbeck

A type of brass named after Christopher Pinchbeck (d. 1732), a London clockmaker who is said to have discovered it. It was extensively used in the last century to make inexpensive jewellery and watch cases, which are now collectors' items. The best pinchbeck consists of 89 per cent copper, 11 per cent zinc, to 93 per cent copper, 7 per cent zinc.

Gilding metal

An alloy of copper and zinc in the proportions of 80 to 20 is very suitable for the production of hollow-ware and jewellery which has to be plated. It is golden yellow in colour, ductile and malleable, but not as hard as common brass and has a melting point lower than copper.

Testing

A tiny drop of nitric acid applied to brass will cause a violent reaction giving a green froth. This is often useful for establishing whether a piece of jewellery is made of pinchbeck or gold, for the reaction on gold is negligible or, at most, very slow.

Fig 8   Testing with acid

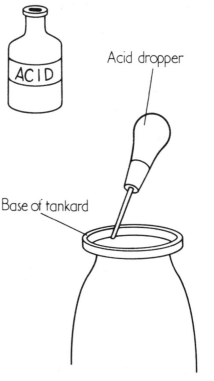

Acid dropper

ACID

Base of tankard

How far should renovation go?

The first thing to do is to assess the amount and type of damage to be tackled, how much of the damage is to be removed, and how much should be left as an acceptable sign of the age of the object. A piece should be restored to a condition where it has that pleasing quality peculiar to well-maintained, well-used metal. The odd blemish, a little oxide around the joint between a handle and the main body, or in an embossed area, are all things that give an old piece that muted appearance which develops with age. Dirt, crustations of old polish, oxides, sulphides and corrosion should be removed, not only to improve the appearance, but to prevent further attack on and deterioration of the metal's surface. Dents which are ugly and spoil the form of an object should be removed. Parts that are missing or badly broken should be replaced with new ones of the correct design. This is where the renovator turns researcher when he has to establish the shape of a missing part.

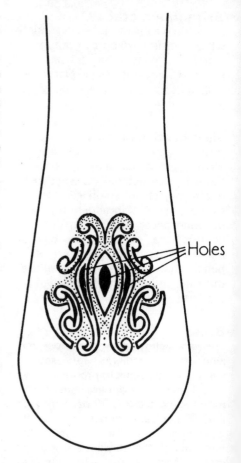

Fig 9   Wear on embossing

What cannot be repaired

Serious damage brought about by heavy use is generally irreversible, and damaged, heavily-worn objects should be left alone. When metal becomes worn and thin it is difficult to work, it invariably cracks, and may fall to pieces when manipulated. Examine objects carefully, in particular where there are raised parts such as an area of embossed design, where it is not uncommon to see the high spots worn off leaving tiny holes. A jeweller's magnifying glass of the

254

Fig 10   Jeweller's eyeglass

power 2X is useful for examining objects. If there is a dent, check to see if it has a smooth contour or if it has sharp creases with cracks which will open when a repair is attempted, for in such cases the metal is thin. Do not attempt to repair objects in such a condition. On knives or similar objects, examine the join between the handle and the blade

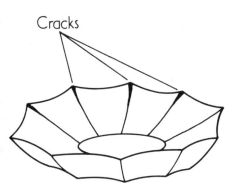

Cracks

Fig 11
Fluted brass dish displaying cracks down the fluting

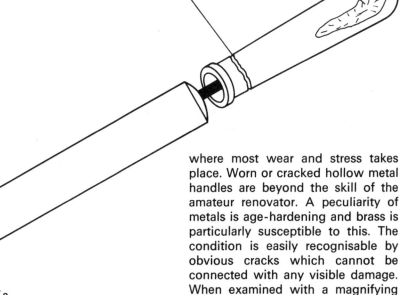

Dent

Break

Fig 11a
Repair of metal handles should be left to an expert

where most wear and stress takes place. Worn or cracked hollow metal handles are beyond the skill of the amateur renovator. A peculiarity of metals is age-hardening and brass is particularly susceptible to this. The condition is easily recognisable by obvious cracks which cannot be connected with any visible damage. When examined with a magnifying glass, a jagged crystalline feature may be seen in the crack. This condition is irreversible and renovation is impossible,

Removal of dents

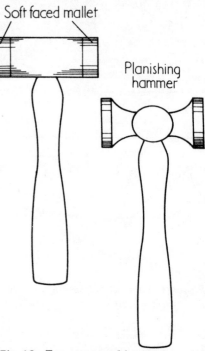

Soft faced mallet

Planishing hammer

Fig 12 Two types of hammer

When a dent occurs the metal is stretched, so in order to achieve a satisfactory repair further stretching of the metal must be avoided. Many would-be renovators pick up an old nailing hammer and merrily bash away. Not only do they transfer marks from the hammer face to the object, but they stretch the metal irrevocably. The object is usually beyond repair as a result of their efforts. This demonstrates the importance of two rules: (a) the force applied should be the minimum required and should only be applied for the minimum length of time. It should be well-thought out and applied in the correct place; (b) all tools should be impeccably clean and free from marks. Hammer faces should be polished and sharp edges rounded off.

First you must consider the type of metal from which the object is made, for that will influence the way in which the job should be tackled. A process of identification must be carried out (see metals identification, pages 250-3). Having identified the metal, the following characteristics will help to indicate the problems which may arise.

Silver
Presents few problems as it is a fine, ductile, malleable metal, providing it has not worn too thin.

Silver plate
The base metal can be brass, copper, nickel, or nickel silver (see page 251). Whichever it is, it may not be possible to remove the dent without damaging the plated surface. Use the

256

minimum of force, and in the event of the plate being damaged, it will have to be repolished and replated. There are firms who specialize in this type of highly skilled work. It is advisable to send items for replating to them, because it is beyond the scope of the average repair workshop.

Silver plate on britannia metal
Britannia metal has often been used as a base metal for silver-plating. It is a soft, pewter-like alloy. If it is treated with care it will respond to gentle operations involving pressure and burnishing.

Brass
Brass should present few problems, but look out for cracks caused by age hardening.

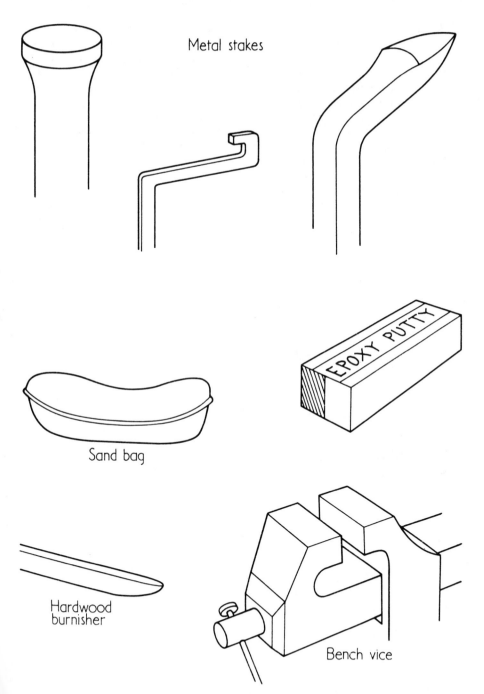

Metal stakes

Sand bag

EPOXY PUTTY

Hardwood
burnisher

Bench vice

Fig 13   Some useful equipment

257

Removal of dents

Principles of dent removal

One method is to support the dent against a surface which conforms as nearly as possible to the original form. Then apply a force which pushes the dent against that contoured surface. The tool with the contoured surface is known as a 'stake', and the force which pushes out the dent is applied either with hand pressure or with a soft-faced mallet.

Another method is to place the dented object on a soft surface such as a sandbag or folded blanket, and apply pressure with a contoured surface made either of steel or hardwood, using a moving action. This is known as 'burnishing' the dent. Never use a ball-ended hammer to remove a dent because the effect will be to stretch the metal and produce a series of small dents in the opposite direction to the original one, which will be difficult and in some cases impossible, to remove. Always make a careful appraisal of the problems likely to be encountered before starting to remove a dent, and never begrudge the time spent in making a stake or burnisher of the correct shape to tackle the job.

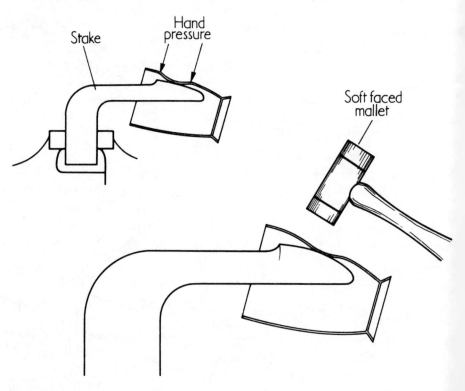

Fig 14   Removing a dent on a stake

Tools required

1 Nylon or hard rubber-faced mallet.
2 Flat-faced planishing hammer.
3 Stakes.
4 Epoxy resin putty.
5 Sand bag.
6 Hardwood for burnishers.
7 Strong bench and engineer's vice.

Preparation of tools

The soft-faced mallet requires no preparation except to clean the faces with a cloth if it is in good condition. Should the faces have foreign matter embedded in them or otherwise be uneven, they should be rubbed down with fine sandpaper, and then cleaned with a cloth. The flat-faced planishing hammer has to have its faces carefully prepared and polished. The edges of these faces must be rounded off because a sharp edge can cause a great deal of damage. Steel stakes must have their working surfaces clean and polished. Hardwood burnishers should be rubbed with progressively finer grades of glass paper until not only the contour is correct, but the surface is perfectly smooth.

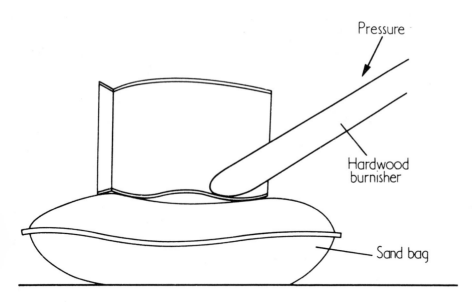

Fig 15   Removing a dent by burnishing

259

Removal of dents

Method

The object shown in Figure 16 illustrates a typical dent, in this case in the side of a teapot. A stake is selected which conforms to the internal shape of the teapot before it was dented. Steel stakes can be obtained from jewellers' suppliers but they are expensive, and one needs a whole range of shapes to cope with the variety of curvatures one is liable to encounter in renovation work. An alternative is to shape a piece of hardwood with rasps and glass paper. With the development of modern epoxy putty, a substance has come to the hand of the renovator which simplifies the work. It is purchased in a pack containing two different coloured putty-like substances which are coloured so as to assist even mixing. It is inexpensive and available from tool suppliers and some garages. Equal amounts of the substances are taken and kneaded together until a consistent colour is obtained. Plastic or rubber gloves must be worn. The putty is then pressed on to an undented surface of the teapot which has previously been smeared with grease to act as a release agent. A bolt of iron rod is then pressed into the putty which will be used as a handle later on. After the putty has solidified, it will be seen to have formed the exact contour of the undented part of the teapot, thus making an excellent stake.

The next step is to grip the stake in a vice and position the dent over it. Hand pressure may be enough to push out the dent; if not, a few well-placed blows with the nylon or rubber-faced mallet will do the trick. Creasing or stretch marks may then be removed by light planishing with the planishing hammer while the object is held against the stake.

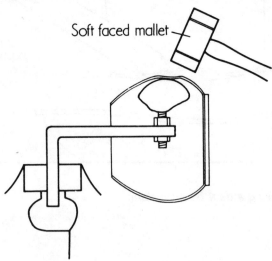

Soft faced mallet

Fig 16   Removing a dent from a teapot

260

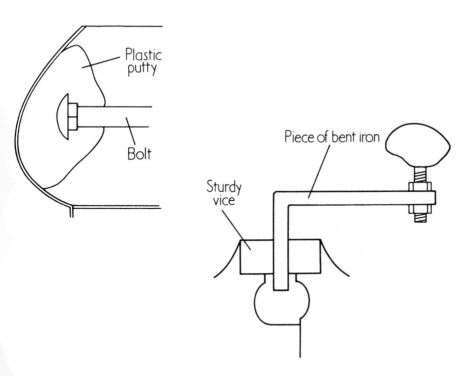

Fig 17   Making a plastic putty stake

261

Removal of dents

For dents in awkward places, like a narrow-necked vase where there is insufficient room to admit the normal stake, a tool called a 'snarling iron' can be made. This is a cranked length of steel rod; one end has a head which conforms to the contour of the internal shape of the object, the other end is held firmly in a vice. The dent in the vase is firmly held on to the contoured head of the tool. The shaft of the snarling iron is then struck with a hammer. Use an old household hammer because the steel may damage the surface of a good one. The shock from the hammer blow will be transmitted through the flexible shaft of the tool and push out the dent.

When a dent is in a hollow form, eg, a hollow bracelet, there are no means of working on one side of the dent. It is possible to silver solder a wire to the centre of the dent and pull it out. The dent may have to be pulled in more than one place to remove it, and then the solder has to be filed off. This method cannot be used on pewter, because soft solder is not strong enough to withstand the tension required to pull out a dent.

Planishing

When a dent has been removed by one of the methods previously described, it may be necessary to carry out further work to remove kinks or creases. This can be done with a planishing hammer prepared in the manner described. The job is placed on the stake and is struck very lightly with the planishing hammer to ensure

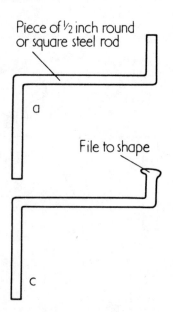

Piece of ½ inch round or square steel rod

a

File to shape

c

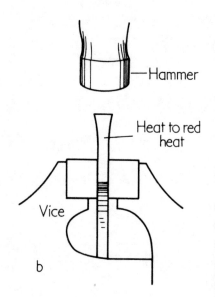

Hammer

Heat to red heat

Vice

b

Fig 18 Making a snarling iron

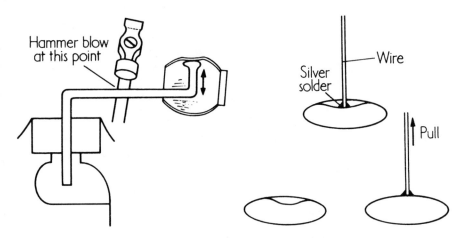

Fig 19   Removing a dent by using a snarling iron

Fig 20   Pulling out a dent

that it is supported on the stake at the correct point. A dull sound is emitted if the job is correctly supported on the stake, but if incorrectly supported a hollow ringing sound is produced. The sound is important because the object must be impinged between the planishing hammer and the stake, otherwise a dent will be created. Do not hammer heavily or the metal will be stretched, but tap sufficiently to achieve the desired effect and then cease. Planishing requires a great deal of skill, and should be used with discretion by the amateur for it is an operation that can cause serious damage if wrongly applied. It is well worth practising on some object of little value before working on a prized piece.

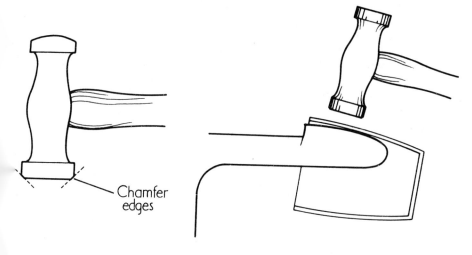

Fig 21   Planishing

Soldering

One of the best ways to join two pieces of metal is to apply a molten alloy to the join. When set the alloy makes a strong rigid bond. Briefly this explains the technique known as soldering.

There are two types of soldering, namely, hard and soft. In principle the difference is that the former is carried out at high temperatures (over 600°C) using solders which are often alloys containing silver, and the latter is burned out at low temperatures (300°C) using tin alloys as solder. In practice the two types are not compatible on the same object and one should adhere to the following rules.

1 Identify, through examination with a magnifying glass, which type of solder has been previously used on the object. Soft solder has a dull grey surface, whereas silver solder has a lustrous hard surface. A good repairer tries to conceal his work and previous repairs using soft solder may be difficult to perceive, especially if the object has been electro-plated after repair or assembly. Use the point of a penknife to scrape joints and then examine with the magnifying glass.

2 Never attempt to hard solder an object which has been previously soft soldered unless the latter is thoroughly cleaned from the surface, using the techniques described later.

3 Never soft solder silver objects.

4 Try to avoid the temptation to soft solder objects that have been assembled using hard solders.

5 Never attempt to hard solder pewter because the melting point of this alloy is very low and it is only possible to soft solder it.

6 In all soldering operations, cleanliness is of paramount importance. All solders, surfaces to be soldered, soldering hearths, irons and other equipment must be scrupulously clean.

7 Never soft solder on the same hearth as used for silver soldering.

8 Keep separate soldering areas, perferably at either end of the workshop, one for hard and one for soft soldering.

Hard soldering

What can be soldered by the amateur?

Certain hard soldering operations are within the scope of the amateur, but some are not. A successful renovator should know the limits of his skills and work within them. Silver is relatively easy to solder when one is dealing with small, simple repairs such as soldering a spoon handle. Large hollow-ware objects such as teapots or candlesticks are more difficult, and the problems are such that it is not feasible to attempt the work without some professional tuition. It is recommended that experience be gained on trial pieces of little value before attempting the real thing. Figure 22 shows the sort of work that is feasible.

Fig 22
Some examples of items that can be soldered

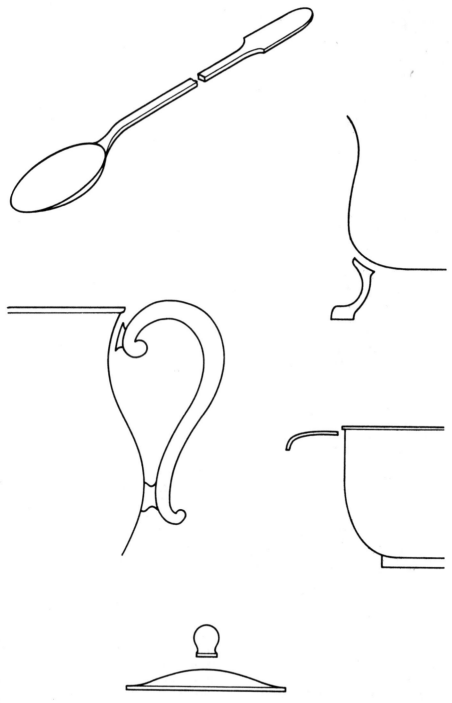

265

Soldering

Equipment

1 A brazing torch will be required like the propane type shown in Figure 24. It is portable, easy to use, and has a wide range of flame sizes. For large objects something more powerful will be required, but there are many propane gas appliances on the market which are very suitable for the purpose.

2 A soldering hearth made in the manner illustrated and supported on a strong bench.

3 A pair of strong tweezers and a pointer made from a large darning needle pushed into a cork for a handle. The pointer is used to clear debris and adjust the position of the solder during soldering.

4 A small cheap paint brush for applying flux to the solder and the metals to be joined.

5 Heated crock, pyrex, or lead container to warm 10 per cent sulphuric acid solution (battery acid or one of the proprietary non-acid pickles).

Fig 24
Propane soldering torch

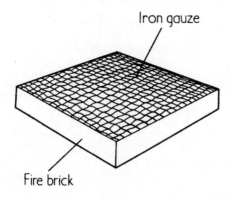

Iron gauze

Fire brick

Fig 23   A soldering hearth

WARNING   If concentrated acid has to be diluted to achieve the correct solution, always wear goggles and always add the acid to the water. NEVER add water to acid because it will react violently, and may cause serious injury.

Solders and fluxes

Soldering silver

It is important to use the correct hard solder for the metal concerned. For silver there are high grade soldering alloys which are available from

266

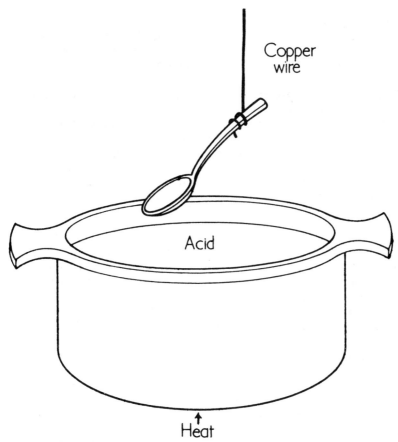

Fig 25   Acid pot

bullion dealers and other suppliers. These have several melting points commonly termed hard, medium and easy, but for repair work, medium and easy are the ones to use, as they have the lowest melting points.

The flux to use is called Borax, which is supplied in the form of a white cone. It is ground on the surface of a piece of slate with water to produce a milky solution. This is applied to the solder and to the area being soldered with a paint brush. Borax cones and slates are available from jewellers' suppliers.

Hard solders for brass and bronze

These are often called silver solders but in fact they have a very low silver content, if any, and should not be used on silver. There is a whole range of these solders, alloyed to suit the metals referred to. It is, therefore, necessary to ask suppliers for a solder suitable for the metal concerned. Special fluxes are supplied with these solders which are available from welding and brazing suppliers. The soldering procedure is exactly the same as that described for silver.

Soldering

Removing soft solder

Should the piece being renovated be contaminated with soft solder, it is essential to remove the solder before hard soldering is carried out. The procedure is to gently heat the object over a flame. Do not overheat or the soft solder will eat in and spoil the job. As soon as the solder melts, brush it off with a stiff bristle brush. This procedure may have to be carried out two or three times to remove the greater part of the soft solder. There should then be a thin film of solder remaining which can be dissolved by immersing the object for about half an hour in slightly diluted hydrochloric acid. It may require more than one immersion before the desired result is achieved, The surface is then cleaned to a bright finish with a file or emery paper, and examined for contamination with a magnifying glass.

Protecting other solder joints

Invariably the object being repaired will have many solder joints which were made when it was first constructed, and these will have to be protected from the effects of an additional soldering operation. Establish where the original ones are and paint them with a thick mixture of jeweller's rouge powder and water. This mixture should be applied carefully with a fine brush and should not be allowed to contaminate the new solder joint or the solder or flux being used. Select a solder with a low melting point (easy) for objects with more than one solder joint.

268

Soldering procedure

Figure 27 illustrates a spoon with a broken handle which will be used as an example.

1 Ensure that the two faces to be joined are clean by filing them square.
2 Set up the spoon so that it is well supported using pieces of steel which have been blued in a flame.
3 Select a solder alloy with a suitable melting point. In this instance, providing care is taken, the assembly join between bowl and stem is unlikely to be disturbed, so a medium melting point solder is used because it has a better colour. 'Easy' solders tend to be yellow in colour but are necessary when soldering close to an existing joint which may be disturbed by reheating.
4 Cut the solder into suitable sized pieces.
5 Paint the join with flux, together with the piece of solder, which is then placed on the join.
6 Heat the area gently at first so that the moisture in the flux evaporates slowly and does not boil, so displacing the solder.
7 The full heat of the flame can now be applied and the pointer used to

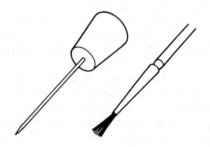

Fig 25a
A needle pointer and paint brush for flux

adjust the position of the solder which should contact the metal on each side of the join. Ensure that the two pieces being joined receive the same amount of heat because solder runs to the hottest point. The correct condition can only be achieved by closely watching the colour of the metal when it is being heated. Solders flow at just red heat, so that if each part reaches the correct temperature simultaneously, the solder will flow neatly into the space by capillary action.

8 Inspect the joint with a magnifying glass to ensure that the solder has flushed through to the other side. If it has not then apply more flux, and possibly more solder if the join looks short of it, and reheat. When cool, the spoon is placed in the hot acid (or non-acid pickle). This will remove the flux oxides from the surface of the metal. Never leave an object in the solution for more than a few minutes because both solder and metal may be attacked. The procedure is the same for brass and copper. After soldering silver, there is often the problem of 'fire stain'. This is dealt with under 'Refinishing', page 290.

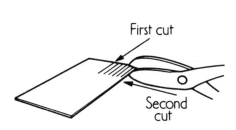

Fig 26   Cutting solder

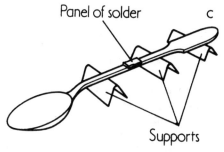

Fig 27   Repairing a spoon handle

269

Soldering

Soft soldering

Do not carry out soft soldering operations in the same area as that used for hard soldering. Have a separate hearth to minimize the risk of contaminating the hard soldering area.

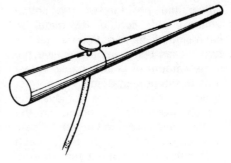

Fig 28
Soft soldering torch

Equipment for soft soldering

1 A soldering torch for heating soldering irons, and a gentle heating flame such as is produced by the lighting jet of a gas cooker, which has a flexible lead and gives a soft, pencil flame. Never use hard, hot flames for soft soldering. Propane torches, specially designed for the purpose, can be obtained from jewellers' suppliers.

2 A soldering hearth constructed in the manner described in Figure 23, page 266.

3 An electric or gas heated soldering iron.

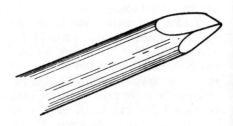

Fig 29
Soldering iron

4 A pointer made from a large darning needle pushed into a cork to form a handle (see Fig 25a, page 268). This is used to position solder and to clear debris during soldering.

5 A wooden stick like a cocktail stick for applying flux before and during soldering. Sometimes it is helpful to smear a little flux over solder to get it to flow smoothly.

Solders and fluxes

Most soft solders are alloys of tin and are available in stick form or as wire, often with the flux as a core. The most common is that used by plumbers which requires separate flux paste. Cored solders are very good for localized joins such as electrical connections or for small components. For

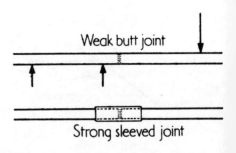

Weak butt joint

Strong sleeved joint

Fig 30
Strong and weak solder joints

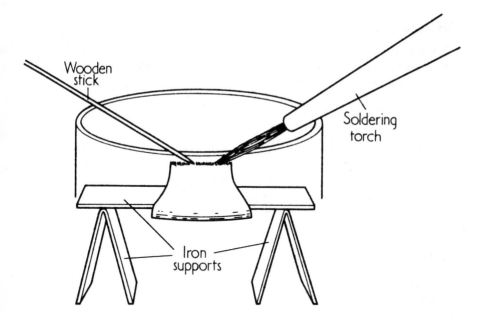

Fig 31   Soldering on a handle

large areas of solder, the separate flux is preferable because it can be spread to give a perfect covering of the area. Advice can be sought from DIY stores regarding the various soft solders which are available. Brass, copper and pewter (see 'Soldering pewter', page 274) may all be joined with soft solder, but never use it on silver because it will debase the metal and devalue the piece.

Where to use soft solder
Because soft solder will not tolerate much heat, stress or strain, the type of repairs for which it is used must be carefully considered. Figure 30 illustrates weak and strong joints. Techniques of riveting, dovetailing, or applying a patch may have to be used to achieve a joint of the required strength. Figure 30 shows that soft solder is at its weakest point when in a state of 'peel' and would be unsuitable for repairing the spoon handle which has been successfully repaired with hard solder. Figure 30 shows a sleeved joint which makes an obviously strong repair in conjunction with soft solder.

As previously mentioned, brass and copper may easily be soft soldered, and after a little practice both large and small objects may be soldered by the amateur. Pewter may also be soft soldered but it is particularly difficult to do so because it has a melting point which is close to that of soft solder. Pewter is treated later as a special case. As in the case of hard soldering. practise on scrap metal or on objects that have little value before attempting to work on the piece being renovated.

271

Soldering

The soldering iron

There are two types of soldering iron : (a) the simple copper ended one which is heated in a flame, and (b) the electric type. Both are available in a variety of sizes and a good weighty one should be selected for repair work. As they get dirty with use they must be cleaned with an old file or emery paper and then 'tinned' with solder. This is done in the following way for the non-electric type. Heat the copper bit of the iron in the flame, rotating it slowly. When it has reached the correct temperature a moving pattern of colours will be seen on the copper. Do not get the bit red-hot. At this point it should be dipped in flux and quickly coated with solder. The iron is then ready for use. The electric iron should be treated in the same way but it is not heated over a flame. Such irons have pre-set temperature regulators.

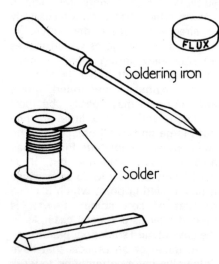

FLUX

Soldering iron

Solder

Fig 32   Some equipment for soft soldering

272

Soft soldering procedure

A typical soft soldering joint is shown in Figure 33, in this case a bracket from an old bulb horn.

1   Clean the surfaces to be joined using emery paper and files to remove old solder and to obtain bright clean surfaces.

2   Offer up the two components to each other to ensure that they fit together accurately.

3   Smear both surfaces with flux.

4   Cut off a piece of solder and place it on one of the soldering faces, in this case that of the bracket. Then heat the component until the solder melts. It should be evenly spread over the surface using the 'tinned' soldering iron. The other face is then 'tinned' with solder using the soldering iron.

5   Clean and flux the tinned surface and bring the two parts together. They can be bound in position with iron binding wire (0·5mm diameter). Once in position, gently heat both components with the gas lighting jet until the solder melts. The wooden stick smeared with flux can be run round the edge of the soldering to clean it and improve its finish. Do not overheat and do not move the components until the solder has solidified.

6   Flux and dirt may be washed off with hot water, and the oxides polished off using one of the finishing techniques described under 'Cleaning and polishing', pages 288-91.

Small components and thin metal may be joined to other parts by fluxing, then tinning with the soldering iron loaded with solder. Place in position and heat by conduction, by applying the hot soldering iron firmly to them. This is commonly called a 'sweated joint'.

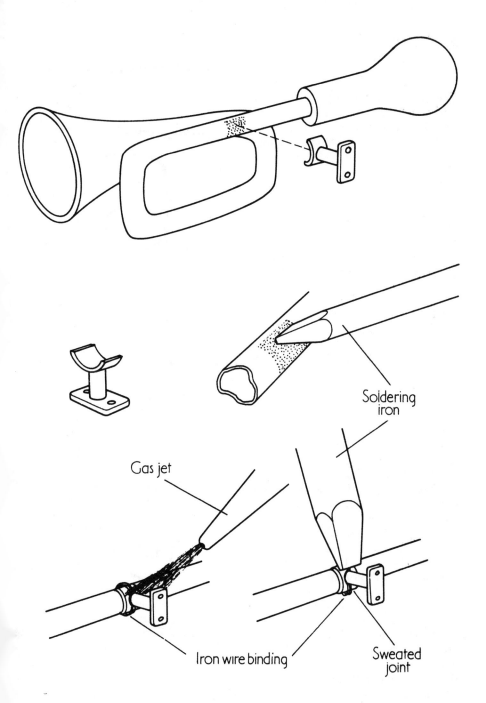

Gas jet

Soldering
iron

Iron wire binding

Sweated
joint

Fig 33   Soldering a bracket to a brass horn

Soldering

Soldering pewter

Small soldering repairs can be carried out using the soldering iron and soft solder, or preferably a specially formulated solder and flux as follows.

Solder

Proportions by weight, 2 parts tin, 2 parts lead, 1 part bismuth. Melt these together and pour the melt into grooves in a piece of wood to produce handy strips. Alternatively, pieces of old pewter or britannia metal may be used for solder.

Flux

Proportions by volume, 5 parts glycerine, 12 parts distilled water, 5 parts zinc chloride. The latter can be made by putting zinc into hydrochloric acid until the bubbling stops. Alternatively, one of the soft soldering paste fluxes may be used.

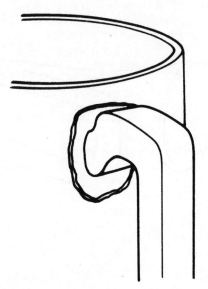

Fig 34
Scrape edge of break until clean and bright

Figure 34 depicts a pewter tankard whose handle has pulled off taking with it a piece out of the main body. This will be used as an example.

1   Clean the area to be soldered with detergent, hot water, and a stiff brush (a toothbrush is ideal). Then scrape the edges of the joint with the point of a sharp knife to remove oxides.
2   Push the handle back into position and bind it with iron binding wire.
3   Flux the area.
4   Load the previously tinned soldering iron with solder.
5   Apply it to the join and hold it there until the pewter has been heated sufficiently to fuse with the solder.
6   Apply solder to the point of the iron as necessary and gradually work round until the joint is complete.

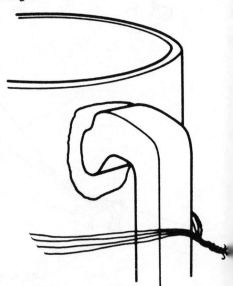

Fig 35
Bind handle in position with iron wire

274

Great care should be taken; it is easy to melt the pewter and make a hole in it. Unless you are very experienced, do not touch pewter with a flame.

If you wish to try soldering with a flame use a soft flame. The lighting jet of a gas cooker is good for pewter, if, as previously stated, the renovator is very experienced.

Method
Clean the join to be soldered, flux it, position the solder, and heat with the flame until the solder runs. Use a gentle flame to heat up the whole area, but take care not to overheat. A hard flame should be avoided. The application of the soldering iron at this stage may give a little localized heat to assist the solder to run.

Eruptions, holes and cracks in pewter
This type of damage is common in pewter. Eruptions and holes require radical treatment. They should be cleaned by drilling out until bright fresh metal is exposed. This is then plugged with pewter, fluxed and soldered in the manner described. Cracks should be cleaned by cutting through them with a fret-saw blade (page 278) to expose bright metal. A piece of pewter should then be fashioned to fit and soldered in place. If the surface is uneven this can be rectified by carving it with a sharp knife because pewter is soft. Finishing can then be done as described under 'Refinishing', page 290.

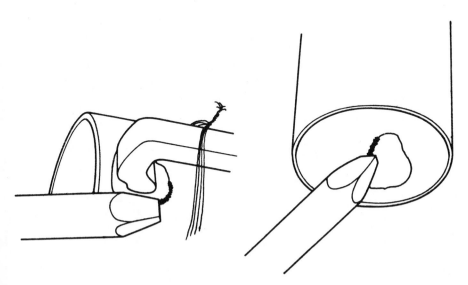

Fig 36
Flux joint and melt pewter solder with tinned soldering iron

Fig 37
Treat the inside in the same way

Making handles and knobs

Handles and knobs, such as those on teapots, are very often made in ebony, rosewood or ebonite. The latter is a black compressed composition of paper. A good handyman can make new ones. The following simple tools are required:
1 Stout bench.
2 Sawing peg and clamp for clamping objects to the bench.
3 Coping or fret-saw and suitable blades.
4 Thin brass for templates.
5 Suitable materials – ebony, rosewood or ebonite.
6 Piece of softwood for model.
7 Craft knife and chisels.

If the handle or knob is simply broken, it may be possible to repair it by the following method. You not only glue it using a good waterproof glue, but also drill and pin it. Ensure that the pieces are clamped together in the appropriate position, and then drill as shown, ensuring that the drill penetrates deep into the other part of the handle or knob. The pin should be a tight fit in the hole and must be pushed in with plenty of glue. If possible the ends of the pins should be peened over.

If the handle is beyond repair, then a new one will have to be made. Select a piece of wood of the appropriate type and thickness. If a fibre handle is required, use a piece of ebonite. If enough of the old handle

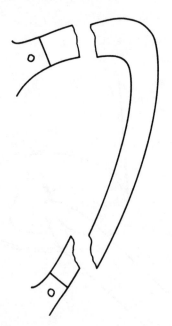

Fig 38
Repairing a wooden or fibre handle

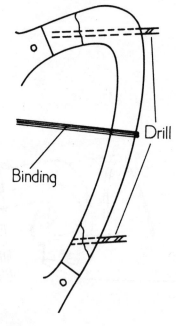

Fig 39
Bind the broken edges together and drill as shown

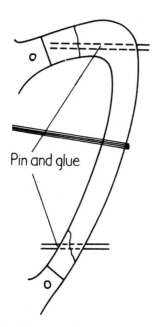

Pin and glue

Fig 40   Pin and glue

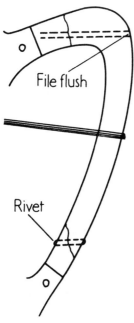

File flush

Rivet

Fig 41
File the pins flush with the handle

remains, a pencil can be run round it transferring the outline on to new material, which can then be cut out using the fret-saw (see Sawpiercing page 278).

If there is insufficient of the old handle to copy, then choose a suitable pattern for the new handle. Valuable information can be obtained from reference books from which you can make a drawing and then a model. The thin brass sheet can be cut out to the outline with the fret-saw. Try this profile in position on the object being repaired and check how it will fit and look. Use a pencil to mark round the brass profile on to a piece of soft wood and cut it out with the fret-saw. The model handle is then fettled and carved until it looks and feels right. A new handle can be made in the appropriate material, using the model as a pattern, and can then be fitted to the object (see riveting, page 282).

Knobs are made in much the same way as handles. It is possible to buy ebony, rosewood and ebonite in round sections, which can be drilled, filed and carved into shape. Knobs which are made in metal can be cast, using the methods described for casting on page 284.

Finishing the wood or ebonite
The handle or knob must be carefully rubbed down with successively finer grades of glass paper until a very smooth surface is achieved. No further finishing process is required with these woods, but they may be rubbed with teak oil or wax. Ebonite should be treated in the same way with successively finer grades of glass paper and finally polished with chrome cleaning polish as described on page 288.

Sawpiercing and replacing inlay

The renovator will find that a fret-saw is a very useful tool for a number of jobs which involve cutting out wood or metal. There are several sizes from which suitable saws should be selected. It is desirable to have two saws, a shallow one for small work, and a deep one for large work. It is important to select a blade which is suitable to cut the material being handled. Thinner finer-toothed blades are required for metal than for wood. The following chart of blade thicknesses may assist in deciding the appropriate blade to be used.

Thick blades
Numbers 4 and 3, suitable for wood.
Number 2, suitable for wood or metal.

Thin blades
Number 1, suitable for wood or metal.
Numbers 0, 2/0 and 3/0, suitable for thin wood or metal.

Equipment required
1 A rigid support for the object being worked on.
2 Fret-saw and suitable blades.
3 Gambouge powder and methylated spirits, or white water-colour paint.
4 Scriber.
5 Tracing paper.
6 Pencils.

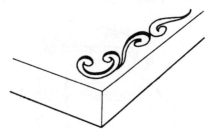

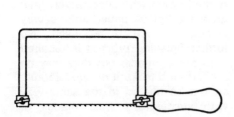

Fig 42   Fret-saw frames

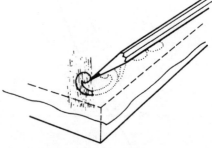

Fig 43   Replacing brass inlay

Figure 43 shows a piece of brass inlay which is missing from the lid of a rosewood box, and will be used to illustrate the sawpiercing technique. It applies equally to both wood and metal.

Establish the required material thickness first by carefully lifting some of the existing inlay and measuring it with a micrometer. If there is no means of ascertaining the thickness of the inlay, then take a sample to the metal supplier who will be able to advise.

Having obtained the correct material for the inlay, clean out the recess, remove old glue by scraping with a craft knife, and then make an accurate tracing of the shape of the

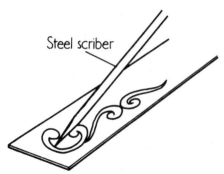

Steel scriber

Fig 44   Using a steel scriber

inlay. Lay tracing paper over the shape to be filled and rub over it with a soft pencil until the outline appears, as in Figure 43. Remove the paper and turn it over so that the reverse side is uppermost. Then place it on a piece of white paper so that the outline is more easily visible. Using the soft pencil go round the outline so that it is distinct on the reverse side. Gamboge powder (which can be obtained from tool suppliers) mixed with methylated spirits is then used to coat the surface of the metal. Alternatively, a thick coat of artist's white water-colour paint can be used for this purpose. After the coating has dried, place the tracing paper over the metal and rub over the paper with a hard pencil. This will transfer the pencil line from the back of the tracing paper on to the coating on the metal.

It is then necessary to scribe through the pencil line on the coated metal with a steel scriber which may be obtained from a tool supplier. Alternatively, a scriber may be made from a piece of tool steel or silver steel. Make sure the tool scratches into the metal. The coating can then be washed off leaving a fine accurate line which can easily be followed by the fret-saw.

Sawpiercing and replacing inlay

Preparing the fret-saw and supporting the work piece

Select a blade of suitable thickness for the material being cut, in this case number 1. Unfasten the clamping screws on the saw frame, and after ensuring that the teeth of the blade are facing backwards, fasten the blade firmly into the front clamp. Press the front of the saw frame against the work-bench so as to compress it slightly and clamp the saw blade in the rearmost clamp. On releasing the pressure, the saw blade should be rigid under the tension of the saw frame. A fret-sawing support can either be made in wood or purchased from a tool supplier. The support should be firmly attached to the work-bench with a clamp. Position the workpiece over the 'V' in the support and start to saw. Keep the saw blade moving vertically, and lubricate the blade from time to time with beeswax or spittle. The blade should be kept to the outside of the scribed line, never down the middle or the inside, otherwise the metal cut out will be too small.

The new inlay is then offered up to the space in the box lid. It may have to be adjusted by filing to get it to fit accurately. Once this has been achieved, roughen the underside of the metal with coarse emery paper and coat it with epoxy glue, afterwards placing it in position. Place a polythene sheet over it, then a flat piece of wood, and clamp in position. The polythene prevents the excess glue adhering to the piece of wood used as the clamp support.

280

Compress saw frame when fitting blade

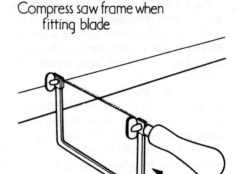

Fig 45   Fitting a fret-saw blade

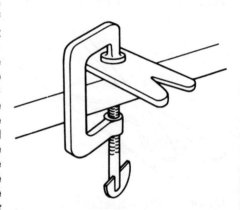

Fig 46   Fret-saw support

Finally, fasten a piece of emery paper to a block of wood and use it to carefully rub the piece of new inlay down to the same level as the surrounding wood. Finish this procedure by polishing with fine emery paper. Then clean the surface with methylated spirits and coat with a suitable lacquer.

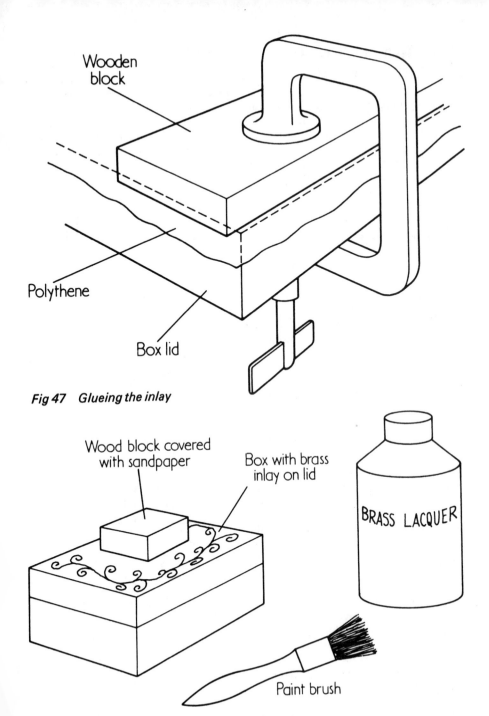

Wooden
block

Polythene

Box lid

Fig 47 Glueing the inlay

Wood block covered
with sandpaper

Box with brass
inlay on lid

BRASS LACQUER

Paint brush

Fig 48 Rub down the inlay prior to lacquering

Pinning, riveting and cheniering

Handles, hinges, legs, and even the main body of an object, are frequently riveted. The rivet may become loose or break and needs to be replaced. It also may be necessary to use rivets in addition to solder to strengthen an otherwise weak joint.

There are two types of rivet: dome headed and countersunk flat headed. Whichever type is used the rivet must fit the hole accurately through which it passes. After removing the old rivet, the first job is to true the hole which may have become oval or enlarged. To do this, use either a twist drill which is a fraction larger than the existing hole, or a jeweller's broach, available in a range of sizes from jewellers' suppliers. The rivet can be made from wire which accurately fits the hole. Figure 50 shows the tools for making the rivet heads and those that can be made for the riveting operation.

Hinge pins and the pins that pass through handle sockets to hold wooden or ebonite handles in place, simply have their ends peened over. Hinge pins are best made in nickel silver wire for it is durable and will take the wear of continual opening and closing. Use a wire that is an accurate fit in the hinge, push it through, trim off with a pair of wire cutters and leave just enough wire protruding to peen over. This peening expands the end of the wire which can be filed off flush with the hinge. Pins for holding handles in place should be made of the same metal as the body of the object. Like the hinge pin, the wire should be a tight fit in the hole and peened in exactly

282

the same way. It may be necessary to run a drill or broach through the holes because the hole in the handle very often wears larger than the one in the metal socket. If this is the case, the handle will be unstable, so it is important to ensure that the pin should be a tight fit in the wood.

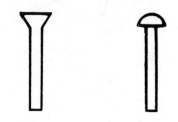

Fig 49   Types of rivet

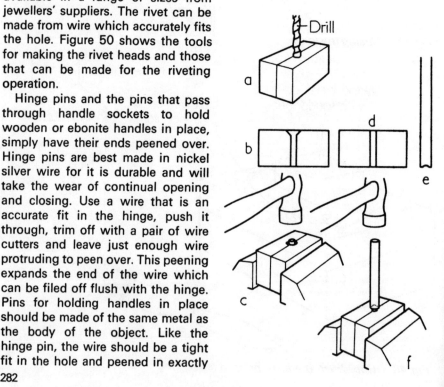

Cheniering

This technique is sometimes used by manufacturers to secure components of an object where parts are fragile, such as enamel decoration, and are not likely to withstand the pressures and percussive forces which have to be employed in riveting. A tube of similar metal to the object is attached to one component and then passed through a hole in the other component. The free end of the tube is then expanded with a special tool. Occasionally the tube becomes loose through wear, and this can be rectified by the method described. It should be emphasised that this technique is not one which the novice should use when riveting is possible.

Fig 51 A broach reamer and pin vice

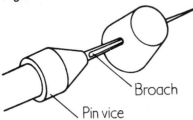

Broach

Pin vice

Fig 50 (left) *Making a rivet: a. Clamp two pieces of steel in a vice and drill between them, using a drill slightly smaller than the rivet wire; b. For a countersunk head, file the end of the hole to a funnel shape in each piece of steel; c. Clamp rivet wire between pieces of steel. Hammer protruding end which expands to fill funnel shape; d. For dome-headed rivets, do not file into funnel shape; e. Take a round steel rod, slightly larger than the rivet head, and drill an indentation in one end; f. Clamp rivet wire between the pieces of steel. Place indented end of steel rod on protruding end of wire and tap with hammer. The wire will take the form of the indent to produce a domed head*

Fig 53 (right) *Cheniering: a. Steel rod; b. File two tapering flats; c. File end to shape; centre pip should be wider at its thickest point than bore of tube; d. Place cheniering tool in drill, place pip in bore of tube and rotate using light pressure.*

Fig 52 Riveting

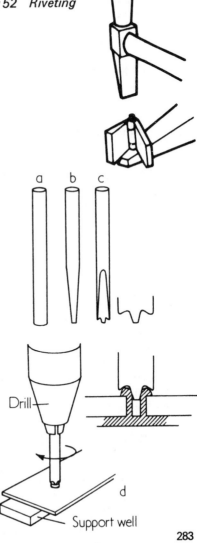

a   b   c

Drill

d

Support well

Casting new parts

Very often an object is minus a leg, knob or finial. It is possible for even a novice to cast a new part using simple methods. Pewter has a low melting point (320°C). It can be melted in a simple metal container, and then poured into plaster of Paris or papier mâché moulds. Silver and brass melt at a higher temperature (900–960°C) and must be melted in a fireclay crucible. Both metals may be poured into moulds made from cuttlefish bone, obtainable from pet shops which supply it for budgerigars.

Tools and equipment
1   Suitable melting pot made of iron for melting pewter. Flat fireclay crucible for melting silver and brass with simple sheet metal holder.
2   Pair of iron tongs.
3   Gas ring for melting the pewter. Powerful propane gas torch for silver and brass.
4   Large pieces of cuttlefish bone for casting brass and silver. Plaster of Paris or papier mâché for casting pewter.
5   Boric acid crystals or Borax as flux for brass and silver.
6   Materials for making patterns, that is, wood, pieces of wire, and epoxy putty or polyester resin filler.
7   Old pieces of silver, brass or pewter for melting down.

Making the casting pattern
It is important to identify the age and style of the object, and base the shape and form of the new part on an appropriate design. This will require research in reference books dealing with the historical aspect of design.
284

Having established what the replacement part should look like, a model should be made in wood, epoxy putty or filler. Make the model a little thicker than the part required, to allow for shrinkage during casting, and also to leave extra metal for fettling when casting is complete.

Figure 55 shows the technique for making a mould to cast pewter. Use a pewter alloy which matches the object being repaired. Modern hard lead-free pewter is bright in colour, so it is unsuitable for casting parts for old pewter. It is worth collecting a few old pewter objects which have no value or which are beyond repair as a source of metal for such castings. Melt the pewter in an iron pot on a gas ring and take care not to overheat. It may be easier to use an iron ladle to take the molten metal from the pot and pour it into the mould.

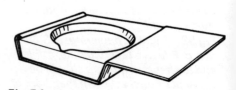

Fig 54

Melting pot for pewter and crucible for silver and brass

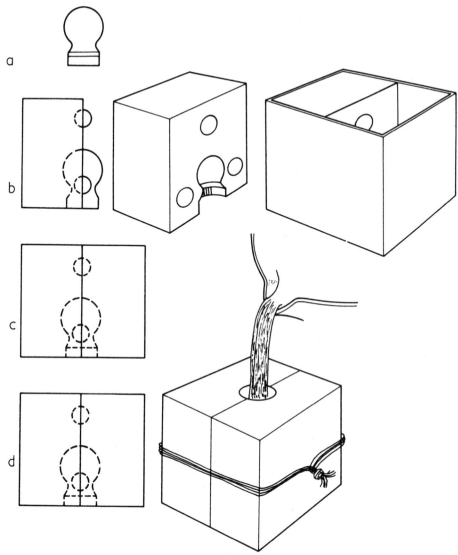

Fig 55

Casting pewter: a. Make a model of the knob, from wood or epoxy resin putty; b. Press the model and three ball bearings halfway into plasticine. Smear exposed half with grease; c. Make a cardboard frame for the mould; fill the other side with plaster of Paris; d. Remove the plasticine half, leaving the model embedded in the plaster, and grease exposed plaster face. Pour plaster in to replace plasticine. Split the mould, remove the model, bind the two halves with iron wire. The molten pewter is poured into the mould and allowed to solidify

Casting new parts

Figure 56 shows the method for making the mould to cast brass and silver. These metals should be melted in a shallow fireclay crucible which can be obtained from a jewellers' supplier. Use a powerful propane gas flame to melt the metal; a small piece of borax or a pinch of boric acid crystals applied at red-hot heat will help to clear oxides. A black iron rod may be used to scrape away oxides prior to pouring the metal into the mould. Pouring should be speedy but smooth. The metal should enter and fill the mould in a continuous stream. If there is a break in pouring this may cause a fault line in the casting. It should be remembered that because of the high melting point of brass and silver, they solidify more quickly than pewter.

Brass and silver castings should be cleaned in hot acid pickle. Fettling should then be done with files and emery paper as described in 'Re-finishing', page 290.

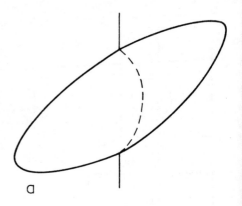

a

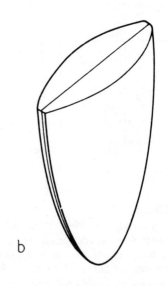

b

Fig 56

Fig 56
Casting silver and brass: a. Cut a large piece of cuttle bone in half; b. Smooth the two soft faces flat using emery paper; c. Press the model of the knob into one half; d. Cut a funnel for the molten metal and scratch two air holes with the point of a nail; e. Press other half of cuttle bone on to first half; push two skewers through both pieces so they can easily be found; f. Remove model, bind both pieces of cuttle together with wire then pour in molten silver or brass

286

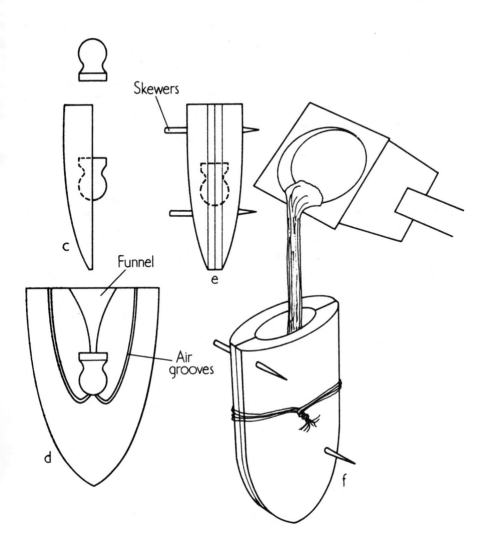

Skewers

Funnel

Air grooves

c

d

e

f

Cleaning and polishing

This is a very important operation in the renovation cycle. For the three metals in question, methods should usually be gentle, and strong chemicals and coarse abrasives should be avoided. However, in certain circumstances radical methods have to be applied, such as in the case of heavy corrosion. The way to treat each of the metals will be dealt with first, followed by the methods of stripping the surface and repolishing which are necessary following a soldering operation or when corrosion is very severe.

In all cases, the first thing to do is to wash off all dirt and old polish deposits with warm water and detergent, applied with a bristle brush.

Silver

This should be treated as gently as possible because it is a soft metal which can easily be rubbed away. Special care should be taken where there is an embossed or raised pattern so as not to rub off the high spots. If there is a black sulphide layer present (often incorrectly called the oxide) this can be removed from the surface by using one of the dipping solutions which are available. If the object is too large to dip, place it in a plastic bowl and, wearing plastic gloves, douse the surface with the solution applied with cotton wool. This should be continued until the surface of the metal is white. Then polish with silver polish on a soft cloth to create a bright finish. On intricate surfaces such as engraving or embossing, use a fairly stiff bristle brush with silver polish, or alternatively, a paste com-

posed of either jewellers' rouge and water, or whitening (chalk) and water. Once a good polish has been achieved it is important to carry out regular light cleaning so reducing the amount of wear. After treatment with the dipping solution, persistent corrosion can be rubbed with a fine brass wire brush (known as a scratch brush) used with copious quantities of a solution of warm water, liquid detergent and a splash of ammonia. If the corrosion still persists, it can be treated with a fibre-glass brush (known as a glass brush) which can be obtained from jewellers' suppliers. This brush is very abrasive so it must be used with great care. If the surfaces are so badly attacked that they do not respond to any of these treatments, then refinishing may be necessary.

Silver plate

This should be treated in the same way as silver, but even more care is necessary because of the additional risk of rubbing through the plated surface and exposing the base metal. Beware of prolonged rubbing on raised surfaces, edges and corners. On embossed surfaces use the same brushing techniques as described for silver.

Pewter

With age, pewter develops a patina (oxide) which, if the object has been regularly cleaned and polished, develops into a pleasant, muted, mature surface with a dull shine. However, if the patina has been allowed to develop unchecked, it becomes a thick brittle layer with an unpleasant black colour. It is possible to remove the patina by immersing the object in a caustic soda solution, or in a solution of hydrochloric acid. This is a radical step because the removal of the thick oxide will often leave a pitted surface, and worse still, trigger off a reaction which causes small bubbles of pewter to quake up months after the chemical treatment. The reason for this is that old pewter (100–300 years) has oxidised, not only on the surface, but into the grain structure of the metal alloy. Some of the metals in the alloy are more prone to this attack than others. Together, the metal and oxide have a consistent appearance; dissolve the oxide and one is left with pits, cracks and fissures which the metal oxides have vacated. Worse still, this chemical attack on the oxide permeates the grain structure of the metal and continues reacting with the oxide remaining, so causing the eruptions described. Chemicals are, therefore, to be used with the utmost care, and should not be used on very old and valuable pieces, especially if they have intricate marks or engraving. Just polish with furniture polish and leave well alone.

If the pewter is reasonably clean then regular cleaning with a good metal polish will maintain and improve the appearance. This may be preserved to some extent by spraying the object with one of the silicone spraying fluids used to insulate car ignition systems from moisture.

If there is an ugly scale present, remove it gradually, working on a small area at a time using the following methods. Apply a solution of household cleaning detergent powder to a section, scatter a little of the detergent powder on the dampened area and rub with a pumice block or coarse wet-or-dry paper. This should be carried on until areas of bright metal are revealed. Change to a medium grit wet-or-dry paper (400–600) and work it with the detergent solution as a lubricant. To keep the surface contour even, change the direction of the rubbing frequently. Do not use wire wool. Continue until the finest wet-or-dry paper has been used, and then work across the object with metal polish applied with a piece of leather stretched and fastened to a piece of wood (see Figure 57). A lot of hard rubbing will be necessary before the required finish is obtained.

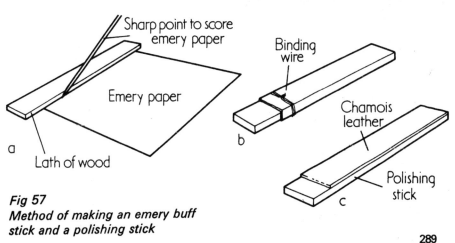

Fig 57
Method of making an emery buff stick and a polishing stick

Cleaning and polishing

Brass

If brass has been kept in a damp atmosphere without regular cleaning, it will probably have a thick, greenish-black deposit on the surface. This is very difficult to remove by simple rubbing techniques. It is much easier to start by using the following methods. Make up a strong solution of washing-up liquid, warm water and ammonia. Allow the object to soak for some time, giving it an occasional rub with a fine brass wire brush. When this treatment is complete, a dull brass-coloured surface should appear. Normal polishing will usually prove effective, using the method outlined for silver with appropriate brass polishes. Some chrome cleaning pastes sold in tubes are also very effective. Certain brands have white aluminium oxide as a constituent which has excellent polishing qualities. Once the object is clean, regular light cleaning is preferable to infrequent heavy applications of the polishing abrasive.

Refinishing

When the surface of a metal requires resurfacing, either as a result of corrosion, scratching, dents or removal of excess solder following a soldering operation, the procedure outlined in this section should be followed.

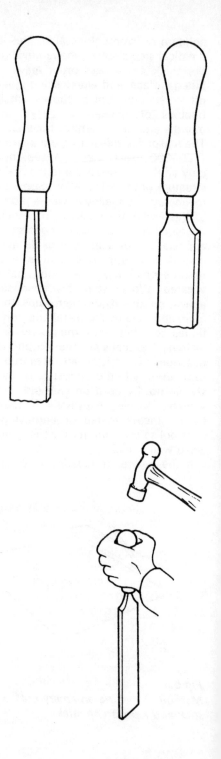

Fig 58   Fitting a file handle

Tools required

1   A 1 × 8in smooth cut flat file and handle; two $\frac{1}{2}$ × 6in half round files with handles, one smooth cut, the other medium.

2   Four laths of wood 1 × 12 × $\frac{1}{4}$in; twelve inches of $\frac{3}{8}$in diameter dowel; sheets of emery paper grades 1, 0, 00; wet-or-dry paper, 400, 600 and 800.

3   A piece of 'Water of Ayre' stone.

4   Soft leather (chamois) polishing cloths, and the polishing medium which suits the metal being treated.

Preparation of tools

New files should be treated in the following way. Dip them in turpentine and holding the tip downwards, light the turpentine. Allow it to burn freely along the whole length of the file until all of the turpentine has burned away. This tempers the file, making it less brittle and more suitable for soft metals. The handle must then be fitted. The best method of doing this is to heat the tang to a red heat and push the handle on to it. Final tightening is achieved by holding the handle firmly in one hand, and hitting it with a hammer or mallet. Do not allow the file to rest against any hard surface while doing so or it may break. Finally rub chalk thoroughly into the teeth of the file to prevent them becoming clogged with metal.

Buffing and polishing sticks should be prepared as shown in Figure 57.

Removing scratches, marks, unwanted engraving and excess solder

An object may be scratched, have superfluous engraved inscriptions, or have excess solder on the surface following a soldering operation. These blemishes have to be removed by filing the metal away. In the case of

pewter which is very soft, a scraping tool such as a craft knife may be used.

First you must support the object against a firm surface such as a bench top. Never try to file an unsupported object because it will be impossible to do so accurately. Use as large a file as is reasonably possible. Small files are only suitable for small intricate areas. A large file will spread its effect over a larger area and give a more even surface. All traces of the blemish must be removed before the next stage. In the case of an engraved inscription, watch the lettering carefully during the filing operation. The deep parts of the inscription will be the last to go, and if they disappear in unison, this will indicate that an even amount of metal has been removed.

Having removed the blemish, the next stage is to remove the file marks with the emery buff stick. Start with the coarsest grade and work across the direction of the file marks until they have been eradicated. Then using the medium emery, work across the direction of the previous operation and so on, working across the direction of the previous stage until a fine, slightly matt finish is obtained. The metal is then ready to polish.

Fire stain

Fire stain affects silver when it has been heated to a dull red heat. Its appearance is slightly greyer than the unaffected silver, often in patches. One solution is to grind the surface with the 'Water of Ayre' stone and water, or with buff sticks, thus removing the surface layer containing the fire stain. This is followed by polishing. Or, heat the object once or twice to induce an even fire stain over the entire surface. Clean the object in acid pickle (see page 286) and repolish.

291

Index